ENTERTAINING
LIGHT

Also by Martha Rose Shulman

Light Basics Cookbook
Provençal Light
Mexican Light
Mediterranean Light
Fast Vegetarian Feasts
The Vegetarian Feast
Little Vegetarian Feasts
Feasts and Fêtes
The Classic Party Fare Cookbook
Great Breads
Gourmet Vegetarian Feasts
The Spice of Vegetarian Cooking

ENTERTAINING
LIGHT

Healthy Company Menus
with Great Style

—

MARTHA ROSE SHULMAN

Foreword by Patricia Wells

WILLIAM MORROW
An Imprint of HarperCollinsPublishers

HarperCollins books may be purchased for educational, business, or sales promotional use. For information please write: Special Markets Department, HarperCollins Publishers Inc., 10 East 53rd Street, New York, NY 10022.

A hardcover edition of this book was published in 1991 by Bantam Books.

FIRST PAPERBACK EDITION PUBLISHED 2000.

Designed by Joel Avirom

Library of Congress Cataloging-in-Publication Data

Shulman, Martha Rose.
Entertaining light/ by Martha Rose Shulman
p.   cm.
Includes index.
ISBN 0-688-17468-X
1. Entertaining.   2. Quantity cookery.   3. Low-fat diet—Recipes.
I. Title.
TX731.S47   1991
641.5′7—dc20   91-14581
CIP

00 01 02 03 04 QW 10 9 8 7 6 5 4 3 2 1

In memory of my father, Max Shulman

He threw a great party

———

Men have always feasted, in huts and palaces and temples. . . . It is their way of admitting, subconsciously or not, that hunger is more than a problem of belly and guts, and that the satisfying of it can and must and does nourish the spirit as well as the body.

M. F. K. Fisher, *Here Let Us Feast*

C O N T E N T S

CHAPTER ONE

CHAPTER TWO

CHAPTER THREE

CHAPTER FOUR

FOREWORD

The French have a marvelous expression for someone who is doing exactly what she wants to be doing and should be doing with her life. They would say about Martha Rose Shulman that she's *bien dans sa peau*, meaning relaxed with herself, who she is, and how she has taken charge of her life.

Martha usually defines herself as one who "writes and gives parties," but that does not say it all. Better yet, she's a model for the life she presents to us: a person devoted to food and sane living, attentive to health but by no means obsessed by it. She truly loves to eat, and her healthy glow speaks for itself. She practices what she believes in, but never preaches.

Entertaining Light is more than a simple collection of recipes; it's a way of life. If this book can offer one lesson, it can teach us to be relaxed about food, to realize that low-fat need not be boring, and that good eating offers great pleasure.

Full of ideas for everyday, healthful fare as well as menus for special occasions, *Entertaining Light* reflects Martha Shulman's real life. She's remarkably spontaneous, comfortable calling friends in the late afternoon to come over for a salad, or just to drop by on a moment's notice to share a fresh loaf of bread.

What's best, Martha has style, her very own style. Some time ago, I realized that one of the secrets to making guests happy is to perfect a couple of signature items, foods that people link with you, making sure they'll be eager to return to your table. Martha's signatures are many, but when I think of the food she serves at her table I think of her great homemade breads, a new wine to discover, and at least one appealing signature dish like Asparagus and Herb Lasagne, Warm Black-Eyed Peas Vinaigrette, Cornmeal Blinis, and Rhubarb and Strawberry Crumble with Crème Anglaise.

In this book, Martha also solves one of the biggest trouble-spots we all need to consider when entertaining—appetizers. How do we escape those calorie-laden, rich, overwhelming starters full of nuts, cheese, crackers, or chips? Martha has the answer: tons of fresh vegetables and light but flavorful dips, brilliant ideas like Giant White Beans with Sage, Lemon, and Olive Oil, served on a toothpick (so we eat them one by one, not by the handful), tortellini on skewers, or a flavorful relish of diced eggplant.

So often we decide to "cook light" then abandon the whole idea because the satisfaction just isn't there. Martha solves this problem with her sane approach that extracts the maximum amount of flavor from food using a minimum of fat. This book isn't filled with false this or mock that, but dishes that are intelligently skimmed of excess fat, leaving all the flavor on your plate. Try her low-fat vinaigrette, grated carrots with lemon yogurt vinaigrette, marinated fish with pickled ginger, and her fat-reduced pastry shells for a soul-satisfying taste.

Here are recipes that make you want to rush right into the kitchen and start cooking, recipes such as Fresh Tarragon Biscuits, Pureed Red Pepper and Potato Soup, Sorrel Flan, Christine's Baked New Potatoes, and Spoon Bread. Likewise there's an intelligent use of pungently flavored fresh greens—arugula, spinach, and sorrel—to boost the flavors of a dish and help us not miss the fat. But Martha doesn't take it all away, because she realizes that fat fixes flavor, and a dish without a gram of fat is likely to leave us unfulfilled and heading straight for the refrigerator a few hours later.

So here you have it: food that is neither made up nor concocted, for each dish has authentic roots in Paris, the French countryside, Italy, and even Texas. Lucky for us, Martha Shulman has thought intelligently about the foods we do love to eat—breads and grains, pastas and pastries, salads and fish—and figured out how we can manage to have it all without the excess baggage.

Patricia Wells
Paris, 1991

ACKNOWLEDGMENTS

First of all I'd like to thank my loving husband, Bill Grantham, who shares my enthusiasm for entertaining and never complains when I transform his office into a dining room for a big dinner. It was Bill who, having co-hosted, set tables, and poured endless glasses of wine at countless parties over the last four years, urged me to write this book in the first place.

Thanks to Anne Trager for testing the recipes and lending me her unfailing palate, skill in the kitchen, and good judgment. She has contributed much to this book.

As always, thanks to my editors, Frances McCullough and Coleen O'Shea, and my agent, Molly Friedrich, for your never-ending support.

And finally, thanks to all of my guests. Without you there would be no party.

with little fat will burn whatever I'm sautéing. Often I use a combination of oil and water to sauté. My penchant, as always, is for southern flavors, from the Mediterranean and from Mexico, foods that are naturally vibrant and healthful, redolent of fresh herbs, garlic, tomatoes, and olive oil. I prefer fish to meat and avoid heavy, fat-laden red meat altogether, opting for lean meats like rabbit and poultry. Salads and vegetables are as important an aspect of my meals as the main dishes (which might be vegetarian in any case); they are never just "side dishes." My sauces are vegetable-based, or I use *fromage blanc* or plain low-fat yogurt. Yogurt often replaces oil in my salad dressings. And most desserts are fruit-sweetened, with a minimum of sugar or honey. There are a few that I consider extravagant (like the Bitter Chocolate Sorbet with Mint on page 104), but even these are light by more traditional standards, and in any case they will be balanced out by lighter dishes in the rest of the menu.

As for eggs, these wonderfully nutritious items are certainly high-cholesterol, which may be a concern for you or some of your guests. This collection of recipes is not without its omelets, flans, crème Anglaise, and quiches. There's even a cheese soufflé. But there are many other recipes to choose from if you cannot or don't wish to eat egg yolks. And even here there is moderation; many of the omelets are made with more egg whites than yolks. There is even a fresh pasta made with egg whites only.

The final word isn't in yet on which fats are "healthier," but there's plenty of support for olive oil, which is usually my preference, in quantities as small as taste will allow. There are also arguments for and against wine, but again, there's solid research to reassure us that a glass or two of wine with our dinner is actually a good thing, as well as being one of the greatest pleasures of the table. And pleasure is what this book is all about; it's useless to offer your guests food that's less than delicious, however "good for them" it may be. All the feasts in this book, however simple or elaborate, can be presented to your guests with a clear conscience and a glad heart.

ENTERTAINING WITHOUT FEAR

Hosting a party, be it a sit-down dinner, buffet, cocktail party, or brunch, can be like being the star on opening night, with all the accompanying stage fright. There is a curtain time, a set, and scene changes; your guests are your audience, and when the curtain goes down and they've all gone home, you heave a sigh of relief as you strike the set and load the dishwasher.

Is it possible to have a good time at these events?

It is. There are two keys to successful entertaining, insofar as the food is concerned: choosing the right menu and *organization*. If you're on top of these two things, you'll be able to come to your own party. You may be impossible to live with during the week before (as I can be), but on the night itself you'll have a good time.

Choosing the Menu

There are two main things to consider when you're planning your menu: your available time and the overall balance of the meal. Your menu should consist of some items that can be made ahead of time and will hold well, and there should be a balance of simple dishes and dishes that involve more chopping and supervision. If all of your menu has to be cooked at the last minute, you'll be a wreck; but if some dishes require only reheating, you can concentrate on those dishes that need to be served as soon as they're cooked, like certain fish dishes, pasta, or *risotto*. If you know that you'll have very little time for advance shopping and preparation, choose simple menus. In this collection I've put together many simple meals in addition to menus that require more planning, so you'll have a choice. Or you might want to create your own menus. All of the recipes have tips for advance preparation.

The layout of your house or apartment is also something to consider when planning your menu. If your kitchen is far away from the living room and small, think twice about preparing food that will keep you away from your guests the entire time they're having their cocktails. My kitchen is nowhere near the living room, so I try to plan meals that will allow me to be at the party for the first bit; once everyone is relaxed and talking to each other, I can leave them in order to do the last-minute cooking. If, on the other hand, you have an open kitchen, you can be busy preparing food without deserting your guests.

In addition to the advance preparation tips that follow the recipes, bear in mind that many vegetables can be cut up a day ahead of time and held in the refrigerator. These include onions and leeks, carrots, celery, zucchini, and tomatoes. Garlic cloves can be peeled. Fresh herbs can be plucked, washed, and dried (but not chopped, as they tend to discolor); wrap them in paper towels and seal in plastic bags. Lettuce can be washed, thoroughly dried, wrapped in clean towels, and sealed in plastic bags a day ahead of time.

OTHER TIPS FOR STORING FOOD

Knowing how to store food is important when it comes to entertaining, because the more you can store, the more you can get done in advance. The plastic bag is one of the most indispensable of items in a kitchen with a small refrigerator. Instead of storing prepped vegetables in bowls, bag them once they're prepped; this applies to blanched and steamed vegetables as well as raw. However, raw carrots, celery, and radishes should be kept in a bowl of cold water if you're going to serve them as *crudités*. To keep unplucked bunches of herbs fresh, cut the stem ends off about ¼ inch from the end. Dampen a double or triple thickness of paper towel and wrap around the bottom of the stems. Secure by wrapping the toweled stem ends tightly in aluminum foil. Seal tightly in a plastic bag.

STORING MADE-UP PLATTERS OF FOOD IN THE REFRIGERATOR

If you've made up a plate of something and you don't want to ruin the arrangement by covering it with plastic wrap, place some corks on the plate (cut the corks into thirds, halves, or whatever size is necessary so they are higher than the surface of the food) and cover with plastic wrap. The corks will hold the plastic above the food, like a tent.

BALANCING THE MENU

Consider the overall composition of the meal. If there is one rich dish (nothing is *too* rich here, but some dishes are lusty and filling), make sure the other dishes are light. If one of your dishes has spicy or complex flavors, the rest of the dishes should be simpler. It's important not to confuse the palate during the course of a meal, and you will do so if you serve too many contrasting dishes. There should be a synchronization of textures, flavors, and colors: bright green herbs and vegetables alongside pale fish, grains, pasta, or meat; crisp salads after full-bodied, gutsy main courses. There should also be a thematic harmony: Obviously you wouldn't follow borscht with a Mediterranean pasta dish. Also, consider the weather: Many menus that work in December aren't as appetizing in August. If you follow the menus in this book, you will see that these considerations have already been taken into account.

Organization

You can't be too organized. Checklists are the key. Once you've decided on your menu, make lists. I keep an entertaining notebook; on one page I write my menu, on the next pages I write shopping lists, and finally I make up a "Work Schedule," which I copy onto a piece of typing paper and tack up on my kitchen wall so that I can refer to it and check things off as I get them done. There's something very reassuring about those lines through the accomplished tasks.

The shopping list includes all of the ingredients I'll need for the recipes as well as other items I might need, like napkins, toothpicks, aluminum foil, candles, etc. It's always a good idea to double-check to make sure you have these things on hand, as well as herbs and spices, salt, and pepper.

The "Work Schedule" is actually a calendar. I write the menu at the top, and the days leading up to the day of my dinner underneath, with the tasks I plan to get done on each day. I always leave myself a bit of leeway, enough time on each day (especially the day of the party) for things I might not have gotten to on the days before. Here's an example:

A WHOLE BAKED FISH AT AN

INFORMAL DINNER FOR SIX

———

CHAMPAGNE
▪
RADISHES
HUMMUS *on* CRACKERS *or* PITA TRIANGLES
▪
FRISÉE *with* GARLIC CROUTONS *and* WALNUTS
FRENCH SOURDOUGH COUNTRY BREAD
▪
BAKED WHOLE SALMON *or* TROUT
with SLIVERED VEGETABLES
SAUTÉED OYSTER MUSHROOMS
▪
PRUNE SOUFFLÉ
▪
TOKAY PINOT GRIS D'ALSACE *or*
VOUVRAY *or* CHARDONNAY

A NOTE ON THE NUTRITIONAL DATA

Nutritional values have been supplied by Hill Nutrition Associates for calories, fat, sodium, protein, carbohydrates, and cholesterol. The numbers have been rounded off to the nearest whole number. Optional ingredients have not been included, nor have variations on a dish. Oil for the baking pan, where not listed in the ingredients, has not been factored in; however, the additional fat will be negligible, since you won't need more than a teaspoon in most cases and some of it stays in the pan. Because I have left the amount of salt up to your taste in most recipes, sodium counts in the data are low. Garnishes have not been included except when they contain significant nutrients. In recipes where the number of servings varies, the estimates are for the larger number of servings—e.g., if a dish serves two to four, the data were prepared for four servings.

The menus in the book are carefully balanced to stay under 1,000 calories, with no more than 31 grams of fat per menu, and under 30 percent total calories from fat. Wine and bread have not been included. All the recipes are relatively low in calories, fat, sodium, and cholesterol, but if you start combining recipes without regard for the data, it's possible to end up with a menu that's over the limits I've set for this book. I encourage you to develop your own menus, but if cholesterol, fat, and sodium are a serious concern for you, do pay attention to the bottom line.

Some of the recipes, particularly hors d'oeuvres that call for a choice of fillings or toppings, have not been analyzed. To get an idea of the nutritional values for these dishes, refer to the recipes for the fillings or toppings called for.

CHAPTER ONE

APERITIFS

The first half hour of any dinner party can be the tensest time, both for you and your guests. One of the ways to set everyone at ease is to offer a glass of something very nice to drink. Except for Mexican meals, when I almost always serve Margaritas for the aperitif, I usually choose one kind of wine and serve that throughout the cocktail hour before dinner. Although I do have other liquor available for those who are habitual about their scotch or vodka, I consider the aperitif to be an important part of the menu. The wine chosen will be the first thing tasted that evening, and there is a world of wines to choose from.

For those who don't drink, there is always mineral water, both with and without bubbles, with thin slices of lemon or lime to go into the glasses. Another good drink for people who don't drink alcohol, both before and with the meal, is iced peppermint tea. I also keep apple juice and orange or grapefruit juice on hand for those who prefer juice. And I have beer in the refrigerator for certain friends who prefer it to wine.

Bubbly Wine

It's *always* nice to serve something with bubbles in it. Right away you're celebrating. Champagne is ideal, but it's also expensive, and this is one wine it isn't worth cutting corners on. That's not to say that you should buy luxury champagnes, which are always overpriced. But avoid cheap Spanish champagne and inexpensive California sparkling wines, which don't come anywhere near the quality of French champagnes. Good buys are still to be found from smaller French producers, and certain larger estates produce good values for the money (see Robert Parker's excellent book, *Wine Buyer's Guide*).

But champagne is not the only good bubbly. Some very good sparkling wines are made in Saumur and other parts of the Loire Valley, Burgundy, and Alsace (called, respectively, Crémant de la Loire, Crémant de Bourgogne, and Crémant d'Alsace). Some great sparkling wine is made in Vouvray, Vouvray pétillant; some is dry, some semidry, and it can be delicious. Another bubbly that can be very good, given the right producer, is Blanquette de Limoux, from the Languedoc-Roussillon. These can all be dry and delicious and are worth looking for, especially if you are buying for a large party. But it's important to become familiar with the good producers, because there are many bad producers making harsh industrial versions.

Another sparkling wine that I love is Italian Prosecco. This pale yellow, dry bubbly wine comes from the Veneto. The quality can be variable, but if you have a reliable source, Prosecco can be a most pleasant aperitif wine.

White Wine

I often serve chilled white wine before dinner. There are many ways you can go. You could serve something crisp and dry, like a Sauvignon de Touraine, Sancerre, or Pouilly Fumé (all of which are made from the Sauvignon grape) or a Fumé Blanc from California; or you could serve something a bit rounder and fruitier, like a Vouvray or a Chardonnay. In fact, I think big Chardonnays from California and Australia have such prepossessing flavors that I would rather drink one nice glass before dinner than try to match the wine with a whole meal. A very good, much lighter, and more delicate Chardonnay is imported from the Loire Valley, from the Caves Cooperatives du Haut Poitou; this makes a lovely aperitif wine. The aperitif could also be one of the less expensive white Burgundies, such as a Mâcon or a Rully.

The cocktail hour is the perfect time to taste marvelous, fruity, less dry white wines. Alsace produces a delicious wine called Muscat d'Alsace, which has a bouquet full of the sweet, unmistakable aroma of Muscat grapes but a dry flavor. It's a beguiling wine that I love to serve before a meal. Gewürztraminer is spicy, heady, and full of tropical fruit flavors; it makes a terrific aperitif. A good Vouvray demi-sec would be another suitable choice. German Spätleses, Ausleses, and Kabinetts are also slightly sweet and make good aperitifs.

Rosé

Rosé got a well-deserved bad reputation years ago, when industrial, cloying wines were shipped to the United States. But now people know otherwise. The good, fruity, dry rosés from the south of France are some of the most drinkable wines in France. The best ones, from Bandol and Tavel, are rich and complex. So is the rosé from appellation Palette's Château Simone. Charles Joguet in Chinon (Loire) also makes a good rosé. Less complex but very-high-quality rosés are made in the Côtes de Provence, the Côtes du Luberon, and in the Languedoc-Roussillon. These wines not only make good aperitifs but also go very well with fish and heady Provençal vegetable dishes.

Red Wine

A light-bodied, fruity red wine can make a delicious aperitif. Beaujolais and Gamay de Touraine are the two wines that come to mind immediately. Serve them slightly chilled. Be careful, though, when you choose these wines, because many producers, especially in the Beaujolais, are making industrial sulfured wines (sulfur is usually added to wines just before bottling, to act as a stabilizing agent and bactericide; too much of it can cause a headache). Beaujolais producers are also notorious for adding lots of sugar to the wine to increase its alcohol content. The *négociant* Georges Duboeuf ships reliable Beaujolais to the United States.

Sweet Wines

Some sweet wines make excellent appetite whetters. There is an enormous range to choose from. Some make equally good desserts. And while we're on the subject of sweet wine, what about Kirs? A Kir is a drink made by adding a drop of a liqueur made from black currants, Crème de Cassis, to a glass of dry white wine. Let me emphasize the word *drop*. Most people murder their Kirs by filling a wineglass about one-third full of cloying Crème de Cassis, then adding white wine. Cafés do it to mask the fact that they are using industrial white wines (so you end up with a sweet aftertaste in your mouth and a headache). A Kir can be a delicious drink, but you should add only a very small amount of Crème de Cassis to the white wine, which should not be too complicated—a Mâcon, a Muscadet, or a Sauvignon Blanc. Kirs can also be made with raspberry liqueur (Crème de Framboises) or blackberry liqueur (Crème de Mûres). Champagne Kirs, or Kirs Royales, can also be delicious; but choose a less expensive sparkling wine than champagne, a Crémant de Bourgogne or Crémant de la Loire.

APERITIFS AT A GLANCE

Sparkling Wines
Champagne
Crémant de la Loire
Crémant de Bourgogne
Crémant d'Alsace
Vouvray Pétillant (Loire)
Blanquette de Limoux (Languedoc-Roussillon)
Prosecco (Italy)

Dry White Wines
Sauvignon de Touraine (Loire)
Sancerre (Loire)
Pouilly Fumé (Loire)
Muscadet de Sèvre-et-Maine (Loire)
Fumé Blanc from California
Sauvignon Blanc from New Zealand
Côtes de Provence
Coteaux d'Aix-en-Provence
Côtes du Luberon (Provence)
Sylvaner (Alsace)
Pinot d'Alsace
Chardonnay (from France or the New World)
Kabinett (Germany)

less expensive Burgundies from Rully, St.-Véran, St.-Aubin,
Mâcon-Villages, Mercurey, Auxey-Duresses, St. Romain,
Santenay, Mâcon-Pierreclos, and Montagny

Less Dry White Wines
Vouvray (Loire)
Muscat d'Alsace
Gewürztraminer (Alsace)
Spätlese (Germany)
Auslese (Germany)

Rosé
Rosés from Provence, especially Bandol, Tavel, or the
Languedoc-Roussillon

Light, Fruity Red Wines
Beaujolais
Beaujolais-Villages
Gamay de Touraine (Loire)

Sweet Wines
Sauternes (Bordeaux)
Barzac (Bordeaux)
Coteaux du Layon (Loire)
Bonnezeaux (Loire)
Quarts de Chaume (Loire)
Vouvray Moelleux (Loire)
Rivesaltes Vin Doux Naturel (Languedoc-Roussillon)
Muscat de Beaumes de Venise (Rhône)
Muscat de Rivesaltes (Languedoc-Roussillon)
Muscat de Frontignan (Languedoc-Roussillon)
Muscat from California or Australia
Moscato d'Alba (Italy)
Banyuls (Languedoc-Roussillon)

Nonalcoholic Aperitifs
Bubbly mineral water
Flat mineral water
Iced mint tea
Fruit juice

FOOD TO NIBBLE WITH DRINKS

It isn't essential to have hors d'oeuvres that require preparation and/or cooking with drinks, but of course there must be something to eat. I particularly like to serve radishes. If they are large and I've bought them in time to make radish roses, that's what I'll do (see the instructions on page 18). If I don't have the time or inclination, or the radishes are small, I'll simply wash them well and trim the ends off. They're prettiest when the leaves are left on, but if there are a lot of people and not many ashtrays, I find that the leaves can be an inconvenience.

Another very easy tidbit is wafer-thin slices of good Parmesan cheese. It's the only kind of cheese I ever serve before dinner, and it must be sliced very thin; I use a potato peeler or a cheese slicer to cut the slivers.

I always have good crackers on hand. All the better if there's a jar of tapenade in the refrigerator; but a good cracker, like Dar Vida, or a yeasted Olive Oil Pastry like the one on page 395, can stand alone. So can Toasted Pita Triangles (page 71), which keep very well in a plastic bag.

Provençal olives are another favorite. But these do have a high fat content, so consider the overall fat content of the meal.

MARGARITAS

I have learned over the years to cut my margaritas with a lot of ice when I'm making them for a big group. For one thing, they go further, and everyone doesn't get so sloshed. The drink is still the most congenial cocktail you can serve, and my margaritas always contribute to a very animated table.

Freshly squeezed lime juice is the key to a good margarita. It can be squeezed a couple of hours ahead of time, but then the taste begins to sour. Obviously, the more salt you add, the higher the sodium count.

FOR EACH DRINK

- 1½ ounces tequila
- 1 ounce fresh lime juice
- ⅔ to ¾ ounce Triple Sec or Cointreau to taste (I use ¾ ounce, as people seem to prefer the slightly sweeter version)
- 5 ice cubes, approximately
  coarse salt for the glass

Mix together the tequila, lime juice, and Triple Sec. Blend the mixture with the ice in a blender. For a stronger drink, shake the margaritas with ice and pour them off or serve them on the rocks.

FOR A LARGE BATCH, JUST REMEMBER

1 part lime juice

1½ parts tequila

⅔ to ¾ part Triple Sec or Cointreau, depending on how sweet you like it

For a crowd of 24 I usually use two fifths of tequila, one fifth of Triple Sec, and a quart of lime juice (about 32 limes).

SALTING THE GLASSES: The salt for a margarita should be coarser than table salt but finer than coarse salt. Blend coarse salt in a blender, spice mill, or a food processor fitted with the steel blade. Rub the rims of all the glasses with a wedge of lime. Since some people like the salt and others don't, salt only one-half of the rim of each glass. Put the salt in a saucer and dip the rim of the glasses in the salt, tilting them to one side so that only half will be salted.

ADVANCE PREPARATION: These are best made close to serving time, but if you mix up the lime juice with the tequila and Triple Sec or Cointreau the mixture can hold for a few hours. For a big party, I always mix them up a few hours ahead of time and blend the ice in just before serving.

PER PORTION

Calories	171	Protein	0
Fat	.03 G	Carbohydrate	9 G
Sodium	1 MG	Cholesterol	0

RADISH ROSES

I serve radishes with drinks at almost all of my dinner parties. If I can get little ones, I just trim the tips and tails, but if they are large, I make radish roses. To make radish roses, wash the radishes, then trim away the tops and the tails if you wish. Using a small sharp knife, cut lengthwise "petals" by cutting slits just inside the red outer skin on three or four sides of the radish (if it's a long, thin radish you might have room for only 3 "petals"), cutting from the root end almost down to the stem. Put the radishes in a bowl of cold water and refrigerate. They will open up in a few hours. If you're doing this a day or two in advance, change the water daily.

ADVANCE PREPARATION: Radish roses can be prepared 2 days before serving and kept in water in the refrigerator.

PER RADISH			
Calories	2	Protein	0
Fat	.06 G	Carbohydrate	0
Sodium	3 MG	Cholesterol	0

CHAPTER TWO

HORS D'OEUVRES YOU CAN EAT WITH ONE HAND:

Balancing Drinks, Food, and Conversation

There are two main criteria to meet when planning hors d'oeuvres for a buffet or cocktail party. The hors d'oeuvres have to be nourishing, and they have to be easy to eat. Nourishing because your guests will be drinking while they are nibbling, and they should be getting some protein here and there, especially since there is always a chance that the cocktail party will turn into dinner. For this reason you will find recipes for quiches, vegetable tarts, and flat omelets, variations on deviled eggs, and fish and bean pâtés and mousses in this chapter. Many of the recipes are also suitable for main dishes, but here they're served in bite-size portions. There are also lots of vegetable hors d'oeuvres (some of which could also be served as salads), food that makes you feel wholesome and not like you've just been eating peanuts or petits fours all night (in France these are, amazingly, the two main elements of cocktail-party food).

It's annoying to have to put your drink down to eat whatever tidbit is being served. Your guests need to be able to eat, drink, and talk while standing up, and the answer is to serve hors d'oeuvres they can eat with one hand in one or two bites. That doesn't mean you have to spend hours in the kitchen stuffing tiny vegetables and making little pastries. Many of the recipes here are cooked in one big portion and then cut up, or they are spreads or pâtés that can easily be piped or spread onto vegetables or *crostini*. A pizza, omelet, or quiche cut into small squares or diamonds is suddenly a nourishing hors d'oeuvre.

If you're planning hors d'oeuvres for a dinner party, serve only a few different kinds, even as few as one, with radishes or *crudités,* and no more than three. If you're throwing a cocktail or nighttime party, you should have a selection of five or more, with a balance of protein-rich, vegetable, and high-carbohydrate items—for instance, one or two kinds of vegetable tart or omelet, cut up, a fish or bean pâté, and two or three vegetable dishes like the Escalivada Hors d'Oeuvre, the Diced Eggplant Relish, or *crudités* with Chipotle Mayonnaise or Herbed Goat Cheese. Have some grainy things—*Crostini* or Toasted Pita Triangles with toppings, or Potato Slices with Toppings, or Grilled or Baked Polenta Squares with Green Tomatillo Mole.

When I give a party, I always like to have some food within reach of guests, on tables, end tables, coffee tables; and I pass other dishes. I'll put one platter of *crudités* with a dip on a long table I use as the bar and another one on the coffee table. I'll distribute bowls of olives and radishes everywhere and plates with *crostini* or cucumbers piped with *hummus,* or stuffed cherry tomatoes, here and there. Then I'll pass platters of hot hors d'oeuvres. That way people can eat whether they're sitting or standing. It's important, though, if you're putting platters out on tables, to have pretty backup platters in the kitchen so that the food always looks fresh. When you see plates half-full, whisk them away and replace them with full plates, then replenish the half-full plates for the next round. Also, have lots of colorful napkins distributed around the room.

Beyond the recipes in this chapter, you should always have certain items on hand to serve with aperitifs. Some of these are listed in Chapter 5, Impromptu Entertaining, and include good olives, crackers, anchovies, sun-dried tomatoes, Parmesan, tuna, eggs, and capers. I also like to keep radishes, carrots, cucumbers, and *fromage blanc* on hand.

Hors d'oeuvres, whether they precede the meal or *are* the meal, are the first things your guests will eat; they are one of the ways you as the host or hostess will make your guests feel welcome. Some of the recipes that follow are extremely simple. But no matter how simple or elaborate the food you serve before a meal is, it's one of the most important aspects of entertaining.

NOTE: The following recipes, which you will find in Chapter 5, also make fine hors d'oeuvres: Bruschette with Veracruzana Sauce (page 310), Hard-Boiled Eggs with Aillade (page 319).

ASPARAGUS TART

SERVES 12 AS AN HORS D'OEUVRE, 6 AS A MAIN DISH

Of course this luscious tart would make a great main dish for lunch or dinner, but it's also a marvelous hors d'oeuvre when cut into small squares. It's a beautiful spring and summer dish.

$\frac{1}{2}$ recipe Yeasted Olive Oil Pastry (page 395)

1 pound asparagus, trimmed

2 ounces Gruyère cheese, grated (about $\frac{1}{2}$ cup)

1 ounce Parmesan cheese, grated (about $\frac{1}{4}$ cup)

2 or 3 tablespoons chopped fresh parsley

5 medium or large eggs at room temperature

$\frac{1}{2}$ to $\frac{3}{4}$ cup skim milk

$\frac{1}{2}$ teaspoon salt

freshly ground pepper to taste

pinch of freshly grated nutmeg

Prepare the pastry according to the directions and let it rise. Preheat the oven to 375 degrees.

Steam the asparagus for 5 to 10 minutes, until tender. Refresh under cold water, drain, and cut into 1-inch lengths. Place in a bowl and toss with the cheeses and parsley.

(continued)

Roll out the pastry and line a 10- or 12-inch tart pan or line just the bottom of an oblong pan.

Beat the eggs, brush the pastry with a little beaten egg, then beat the eggs together with the milk. Add the salt, pepper, and nutmeg.

Bake the crust for 7 minutes. Remove from the oven and spread the asparagus mixture over the bottom. Pour on the egg mixture. Smooth out the top and bake for 40 minutes or until set and just beginning to brown.

Remove from the oven, allow to cool for 5 or 10 minutes, and serve. Or allow to cool completely, cut into small squares (about 2 inches) or triangles, and serve as an hors d'oeuvre.

ADVANCE PREPARATION: The crust can be prepared days in advance and frozen; transfer it directly from the freezer to the oven for prebaking and prebake 10 minutes. The asparagus can be cooked and prepped and the cheese grated hours ahead of making the tart and held in or out of the refrigerator. The finished tart will hold for several hours.

PER PORTION

Calories	122	Protein	7 G
Fat	7 G	Carbohydrate	9 G
Sodium	236 MG	Cholesterol	93 MG

MIXED MUSHROOM TART

SERVES 15 AS AN HORS D'OEUVRE, 6 TO 8 AS A MAIN DISH

A combination of wild and cultivated mushrooms gives this tart a meaty consistency and a marvelous savory flavor. The slightly sweet browned shallots make a nice contrast with the earthy mushrooms. This is quite a thick tart if you make it in a 12-inch tart pan. That's fine if you're serving it as a main dish, but if you're going to cut it into pieces for hors d'oeuvres, make it in a 14-inch tart pan or a rectangular baking dish. The pieces will be easier to eat if they're a bit thinner.

1 recipe Yeasted Olive Oil Pastry (page 395)

2 ounces dried *porcini* (*cèpes*)

   boiling water to cover

3 tablespoons olive oil

2 medium shallots, chopped

1 pound fresh wild mushrooms, such as oyster mushrooms, cèpes, girolles, or a combination, trimmed, rinsed and dried, and cut into pieces if very large

1 pound fresh cultivated mushrooms, trimmed, rinsed and dried, and quartered

3 to 4 garlic cloves to taste, minced or put through a press

¼ cup dry white wine

1 to 2 tablespoons soy sauce to taste

1 teaspoon crumbled dried thyme *or* 2 teaspoons fresh leaves

1 teaspoon crumbled dried rosemary *or* 1 to 2 teaspoons chopped fresh

   salt and freshly ground pepper to taste

¼ cup chopped fresh parsley

4 medium eggs

½ cup skim milk

3 ounces Gruyère cheese, grated (about ¾ cup)

1 ounce Parmesan cheese, grated (about ¼ cup)

Prepare the pastry according to the directions and let it rise.

   Place the dried mushrooms in a bowl and pour on boiling water. Let sit for 15 to 30 minutes, until the mushrooms are tender. Drain off the water through a cheesecloth- or paper-towel-lined strainer and squeeze the mushrooms to obtain all of the soaking liquid. Rinse the mushrooms thoroughly, squeeze dry, and chop. Set aside.

Heat 2 tablespoons of the olive oil over medium-low heat in a heavy-bottomed well-seasoned or nonstick frying pan. Add the shallots and cook, stirring often, until they begin to caramelize, about 10 to 15 minutes or a little longer. If the shallots begin to brown and stick, add a couple of tablespoons of water and continue to stir over medium-low heat.

Add the remaining tablespoon of oil, turn up the heat to medium, and add the dried and fresh mushrooms. Cook, stirring, for about 5 minutes, until they begin to release their liquid. Add the garlic and cook for a few minutes more; then add the wine, 3 tablespoons of the mushroom soaking liquid, and the soy sauce. Stir, then reduce the heat to medium-low, and cook, stirring from time to time, for 10 minutes. Add the thyme, rosemary, salt, and freshly ground pepper to taste and continue to cook for another 10 minutes or until the liquid in the pan has been reduced to a glaze. Remove from the heat and adjust the seasonings. Stir in the parsley.

Preheat the oven to 375 degrees. Roll out the dough to fit a 12- to 14-inch rectangular pan. You don't need to bring the edges up to the rim of the pan if the tart is to be cut into squares for hors d'oeuvres. You may not need all of the pastry. The crust should be thin.

Beat the eggs in a large bowl. Brush the piecrust with a little of the beaten egg, then add the milk, cheeses, and salt and freshly ground pepper to taste to the eggs. Stir in the mushroom mixture and combine thoroughly.

Bake the piecrust for 7 minutes and remove from the oven. Turn the mushroom mixture into the crust and bake for 30 to 40 minutes, until the tart is firm and beginning to brown on the top. Remove from the oven, allow to cool slightly, and cut into 2-inch squares. Serve warm or at room temperature.

ADVANCE PREPARATION: The crust can be made a day ahead of time and refrigerated before being rolled out, or it can be rolled out and frozen. Transfer frozen dough directly to the oven for prebaking. Prebake 10 minutes. The mushroom filling, without the eggs, can be made a day ahead of time and held in the refrigerator. Allow it to come to room temperature before mixing it with the eggs and baking it. The tart can be baked a few hours before serving and reheated at the last minute or served at room temperature.

PER PORTION

Calories	149	Protein	7 G
Fat	9 G	Carbohydrate	12 G
Sodium	224 MG	Cholesterol	64 MG

SPINACH AND GRUYÈRE TART IN OLIVE OIL PASTRY

SERVES 12 AS AN HORS D'OEUVRE, 6 AS A MAIN DISH OR ENTRÉE

This savory quichelike tart could also be made as a *flan*, without the crust. Accompany this with a dry white wine.

    ½ recipe Yeasted Olive Oil Pastry (page 395)
   1½ pounds fresh spinach, washed and stemmed, *or* 2
         10-ounce packages frozen spinach, thawed
    1 tablespoon olive oil
    1 medium onion, finely chopped
    2 large garlic cloves, minced or put through a press (optional)
   ⅔ cup grated Gruyère cheese
   ¼ cup freshly grated Parmesan cheese
    4 medium eggs
   ¾ cup skim milk
   ½ teaspoon crumbled dried rosemary *or* 1 teaspoon chopped fresh
         or 1 heaped tablespoon chopped fresh basil (about 12 large
         leaves)
   ½ teaspoon crumbled dried thyme
         pinch of freshly grated nutmeg
   ¼ to ½ teaspoon salt to taste
         freshly ground pepper to taste

Prepare the pastry according to the directions and roll it out to fit an oiled or buttered 12- or 14-inch tart pan. If you are going to be cutting the tart into squares for hors d'oeuvres, just line the bottom and halfway up the sides of the pan and don't worry about a lip around the edge. Preheat the oven to 350 degrees.

In a dry frying pan, wilt the fresh spinach in the water left on its leaves. Remove from the heat and squeeze dry in a towel. If you're using thawed frozen spinach, squeeze it dry in a towel. Chop the spinach fairly fine and set aside.

Heat the oil in a frying pan and add the onion. Cook over medium-low heat, stirring, until the onion is tender and beginning to brown. Add the garlic if you're using it, cook for a minute or two longer, and remove from the heat. Toss the spinach, onion and garlic, and cheeses in a bowl.

(continued)

Beat the eggs and brush the bottom of the pastry with a little of the beaten egg. Bake the piecrust for 7 minutes. Remove from the oven and spread the spinach mixture over it in an even layer.

Combine the remaining beaten eggs with the milk, rosemary, thyme, nutmeg, salt, and pepper. Mix together well and pour over the spinach mixture. If the spinach isn't spread evenly over the pan but is in little bunches, use the back of a spoon or your hand to distribute the spinach through the egg mixture.

Bake for 35 minutes or until set. Remove from the heat and allow to cool for a few minutes before serving or serve at room temperature.

ADVANCE PREPARATION: The crust can be prepared hours ahead of time and refrigerated after being rolled out or days ahead of time and frozen. Transfer frozen dough directly to the oven for prebaking. The spinach filling will hold for several hours, in or out of the refrigerator (but allow it to come to room temperature before assembling and baking the tart).

PER PORTION

Calories	140	Protein	8 G
Fat	8 G	Carbohydrate	10 G
Sodium	248 MG	Cholesterol	79 MG

OLIVE OIL PASTRY CANAPÉS

MAKES 60 CRACKERS

The Yeasted Olive Oil Pastry on page 395 is marvelous on its own and can be topped with any number of good things. One of my favorite aperitifs is rounds or triangles of this pastry, brushed with a little olive oil, sprinkled with thyme or rosemary, and baked until crisp and beginning to brown.

Make the dough according to the recipe on page 395. Once you roll it out, you needn't let it rest. Preheat the oven to 375 degrees. Roll out the dough and cut it into rounds, triangles, or squares. Use a cookie cutter for rounds; for triangles or squares, roll out the pastry into long strips and cut the desired shapes. For herb pastries, brush with olive oil and sprinkle with crumbled dried or chopped fresh thyme or rosemary, or add the herbs to the dough.

Bake the pastry for 8 to 10 minutes, until it's beginning to brown on the top and is crunchy. Allow to cool on a rack. Serve plain or with toppings.

ADVANCE PREPARATION: These canapés will keep for a couple of weeks in a cookie tin.

PER PORTION

Calories	92	Protein	2 G
Fat	6 G	Carbohydrate	9 G
Sodium	72 MG	Cholesterol	9 MG

27

FISH FLAN

SERVES 12 AS AN HORS D'OEUVRE

You can use either leftovers or fresh fish for this dish. White-fleshed fish such as cod or whiting works well, but so do more substantial types like salmon, tuna, and swordfish. Cooled and cut into squares, this flan makes a terrific hors d'oeuvre. Or bake it in a crust; try the Yeasted Olive Oil Pastry on page 395.

    2 cups flaked cooked fish
  3/4 cup Fresh Tomato *Concassée* (page 423) or any leftover tomato-
       based sauce
    6 ounces new potatoes, steamed and cut into cubes
    3 medium eggs
  1/2 cup skim milk
  1/2 teaspoon crumbled dried thyme
    2 tablespoons chopped fresh parsley
    1 ounce Parmesan cheese, grated (about 1/4 cup)
       salt and freshly ground pepper to taste

Preheat the oven to 375 degrees. Butter or oil a 10-inch tart pan or baking dish. Combine the cooked fish and tomato *concassée* or sauce in a bowl. Toss with the potatoes.

Beat the eggs in another bowl and beat in the milk, thyme, and parsley. Add to the fish mixture along with the cheese; combine well. Add salt and pepper.

Turn the mixture into the prepared baking dish. Bake for 40 minutes or until the *flan* is set and beginning to brown on the top. Remove from the oven and allow to cool for about 5 minutes before serving. This hors d'oeuvre can also be served cold or at room temperature.

ADVANCE PREPARATION: The fish can be cooked a day ahead of time. The tomato sauce or *concassée* and the new potatoes can be cooked up to 2 days ahead. The parsley can be washed, dried, and chopped and the Parmesan grated several hours ahead of time.

PER PORTION

Calories	77	Protein	9 G
Fat	3 G	Carbohydrate	5 G
Sodium	80 MG	Cholesterol	62 MG

PIZZA WITH SWEET PEPPERS

MAKES ONE 15-INCH PIZZA, SERVING 12 AS AN HORS D'OEUVRE

This is a very pretty, easy pizza. The peppers are sweetened with a little balsamic vinegar and go beautifully with the tomato sauce.

1 regular or Sourdough Pizza Crust (page 390)

2 tablespoons olive oil

3 to 4 garlic cloves, to taste, minced or put through a press

2 pounds tomatoes (10 medium), peeled, seeded, and chopped

  pinch of sugar

  salt and freshly ground pepper to taste

1 pound (2 large) red bell peppers, seeded and finely diced

1 pound (2 large) yellow bell peppers, seeded and finely diced

2 teaspoons balsamic vinegar

2 tablespoons water

1 tablespoon fresh thyme leaves *or* 1 teaspoon crumbled dried

Prepare the pizza crust according to the directions and let rise.

In a heavy-bottomed saucepan or frying pan, heat 1 tablespoon of the olive oil and add 2 of the garlic cloves. Sauté over medium heat until the garlic begins to color; then add the tomatoes, a pinch of sugar, and salt. Cook, uncovered, over medium-high heat, stirring often, until the mixture is thick and fragrant, about 20 to 30 minutes. Remove from the heat, adjust seasonings, and set aside.

Heat the remaining tablespoon of oil in a heavy-bottomed or nonstick frying pan and add the peppers and remaining 1 or 2 garlic cloves. Sauté for about a minute over medium heat and add the balsamic vinegar and the water. Continue to sauté for about 15 minutes, until the peppers are tender but still have some texture. Stir in the thyme and add salt and pepper.

Preheat the oven to 500 degrees. Roll out the pizza dough and line a 15-inch round pizza pan or a rectangular baking sheet. Spread the pizza dough with the tomato sauce. Top with the sautéed peppers. Bake for 15 to 20 minutes, until the crust is browned. Remove from the heat, cut into 2-inch squares, and serve.

(continued)

ADVANCE PREPARATION: The tomato sauce can be made a day ahead of time. The peppers can be sautéed hours in advance and kept at room temperature or in the refrigerator, then reheated gently just before baking. The pizza dough can be made days or weeks in advance and frozen.

PER PORTION

Calories	141	Protein	4 G
Fat	4 G	Carbohydrate	25 G
Sodium	189 MG	Cholesterol	0

FLAT OMELET WITH POTATOES, RED PEPPERS, AND PEAS

SERVES 10 TO 12 AS AN HORS D'OEUVRE, 4 TO 6 AS A MAIN COURSE

Flat omelets cut into small diamond-shaped pieces make beautiful hors d'oeuvres, especially when they're as colorful as this one. This is very close to a traditional *tortilla española,* with a fraction of the oil.

1 pound new potatoes, scrubbed, peeled if desired, and diced

1 cup shelled fresh or frozen peas

2 tablespoons olive oil

1 medium onion, chopped

1 to 2 garlic cloves to taste, minced or put through a press

1 large red bell pepper, seeded and diced

3 tablespoons water

6 medium eggs

6 medium egg whites

salt and freshly ground pepper to taste

1/2 teaspoon fresh thyme leaves *or* 1/4 teaspoon crumbled dried or more to taste

3 tablespoons skim milk

Steam the potatoes until tender, about 10 minutes. Set aside.

Steam the peas until tender, about 5 minutes, or thaw frozen peas. Set aside.

Heat 1 teaspoon of the olive oil in a nonstick frying pan and add the onion, garlic, and red pepper. Sauté for a minute, then add the water. Sauté, stirring, over medium heat until the onions have softened and are beginning to brown, about 5 minutes. Remove from the heat.

Beat the eggs and egg whites together in a large bowl. Stir in all the vegetables, the salt and pepper, and the thyme. Stir in the milk.

Heat the remaining olive oil over medium heat in a well-seasoned or nonstick 10- or 12-inch frying pan. Pour in the egg mixture and swirl the pan to distribute the vegetables and eggs evenly over the surface. Cook over medium-low heat for a minute or two, shaking the pan gently and lifting up the edges of the omelet to let the eggs run underneath. Turn down the heat to low, cover, and cook 10 to 15 minutes, until the eggs are just about set.

Uncover the pan and finish for 2 to 3 minutes under the broiler if you want the omelet to have a browned surface. Remove from the heat, allow to cool to room temperature, and serve, cut into thin wedges or squares. Or refrigerate overnight and serve the next day. You can also serve this hot as a main dish.

NOTE: You can halve the ingredients in this recipe and cook the omelet in the same-size pan. You'll have a thinner omelet but just as many servings.

ADVANCE PREPARATION: The vegetables can be prepped and cooked hours in advance of making the omelet. The omelet can be cooked up to a day ahead of serving. Allow to come to room temperature before serving.

PER PORTION

Calories	107	Protein	6 G
Fat	5 G	Carbohydrate	10 G
Sodium	58 MG	Cholesterol	94 MG

FLAT OMELET WITH SMOKED TROUT
AND ASPARAGUS

SERVES 12 AS AN HORS D'OEUVRE, 4 TO 6 AS A MAIN DISH

This beautiful pink (if you use salmon trout), green, and yellow combination is very quick to prepare. You can use smoked salmon instead of trout, but I like the rich, meaty flavor of the trout.

1 pound asparagus, trimmed
6 medium eggs
6 medium egg whites
1/2 pound smoked trout, diced
   salt and freshly ground pepper to taste
3 tablespoons chopped fresh parsley or dill
3 tablespoons skim milk
2 tablespoons olive oil

Steam the asparagus until tender, about 8 minutes. Drain and refresh under cold water. Cut into 1/2-inch pieces.

Beat the eggs and egg whites together in a large bowl. Stir in the smoked trout, asparagus, salt and pepper, and parsley or dill. Stir in the milk.

Heat the olive oil in a 10- or 12-inch well-seasoned or nonstick frying pan over medium heat. Pour in the egg mixture and swirl the pan to distribute everything evenly over the surface of the pan. Cook over medium-low heat for a minute or 2, shaking the pan gently and lifting up the edges of the omelet to let the eggs run underneath. Turn down the heat to low, cover, and cook for 10 to 15 minutes, until the eggs are just about set. Meanwhile, preheat the broiler.

Uncover the pan and finish for 2 to 3 minutes under the broiler if the omelet is still runny on top. Remove from the heat, allow to cool to room temperature, and serve, cut into thin wedges or squares. Or refrigerate overnight and serve the next day.

NOTE: You can halve the ingredients in this recipe and cook the omelet in the same-size pan. You'll have a thinner omelet but just as many servings.

GOAT CHEESE SPREAD

MAKES JUST UNDER 2 CUPS, SERVING 20 AS AN HORS D'OEUVRE

This is one of the most convenient items in my refrigerator. I keep it there to use for hors d'oeuvres like Crackers with Goat Cheese Spread and Sun-dried Tomatoes (page 73), or as a dip, or simply as a spread, on bread for a quick lunch, on crackers for an aperitif. Add it to salads; stir it into pastas and soups. This recipe stretches a long way.

1 **cup low-fat cottage cheese**

½ **pound goat cheese**

Beat the cottage cheese and goat cheese together in a food processor fitted with the steel blade or in an electric mixer. Transfer to a jar. Cover with a thin film of olive oil if you're not going to use it right away. Cover the jar and refrigerate.

ADVANCE PREPARATION: This spread will keep for a week if you pour a thin film of olive oil over the top.

PER PORTION			
Calories	49	Protein	4 G
Fat	3 G	Carbohydrate	I G
Sodium	116 MG	Cholesterol	11 MG

HERBED GOAT CHEESE

MAKES JUST UNDER 2 CUPS, SERVING 20 AS AN HORS D'OEUVRE

This recipe—a flavored version of the preceding recipe—makes a terrific dip, a spread for vegetables or crackers, or a delicious addition to salads (add a few spoonfuls to the salad and toss).

1 cup low-fat cottage cheese

1/2 pound goat cheese

1 to 2 garlic cloves, minced or put through a press (optional)

1/2 cup chopped fresh herbs such as tarragon, basil, parsley, dill, chives

freshly ground pepper to taste

Beat the cottage cheese and goat cheese together in a food processor fitted with the steel blade or in an electric mixer. Combine well and stir in the garlic if you're using it, the herbs, and pepper. Transfer to a bowl, cover, and refrigerate until ready to use.

ADVANCE PREPARATION: This will hold for a day in the refrigerator.

PER PORTION

Calories	50	Protein	4 G
Fat	3 G	Carbohydrate	I G
Sodium	116 MG	Cholesterol	11 MG

CHIPOTLE MAYONNAISE

MAKES 1 CUP, SERVING 16

This isn't a real mayonnaise; it's more than half low-fat *fromage blanc*. The chipotle peppers, which come in jars, are smoke-flavored and quite hot. The picante mixture is very versatile: It can be served as a sauce with fish, as a dip with vegetables, or as a spread for *crostini*, crackers, or cooked potato slices (see page 55). It can also be spread on bread for sandwiches.

$\frac{1}{3}$ cup Olive Oil Mayonnaise (page 418)

$1\frac{1}{2}$ tablespoons chopped drained chipotle chilies

$\frac{2}{3}$ cup *fromage blanc* (page 417)

salt and freshly ground pepper to taste

Combine the mayonnaise and chilies in a food processor fitted with the steel blade and blend together. Stir in the *fromage blanc* and add salt and pepper to taste. Transfer to a jar and refrigerate.

ADVANCE PREPARATION: This spread will keep for 5 days in the refrigerator.

		PER PORTION	
Calories	37	Protein	1 G
Fat	3 G	Carbohydrate	1 G
Sodium	69 MG	Cholesterol	3 MG

TAPENADE

MAKES ABOUT 2 CUPS, SERVING 32 AS AN HORS D'OEUVRE

If you have tapenade, the Provençal olive paste, in your refrigerator, you have the makings for fabulous hors d'oeuvres anytime. Tapenade is not exactly low-fat, but a little goes a long way. You can buy it in gourmet stores, but it never tastes as good as this recipe. Spread it on crackers or *crostini*, stuff vegetables with it, toss it with pasta; you may become addicted.

$^1/_2$ pound imported black Provençal olives (use Greek if these cannot be found)

2 garlic cloves, minced or put through a press

$1^1/_2$ tablespoons drained capers

4 to 6 anchovy fillets to taste

$^1/_4$ to $^1/_2$ teaspoon crumbled dried thyme to taste

$^1/_4$ to $^1/_2$ teaspoon crumbled dried rosemary to taste

2 tablespoons fresh lemon juice

1 teaspoon Dijon mustard

2 tablespoons olive oil

  lots of freshly ground black pepper

1 to 2 tablespoons cognac to taste (optional)

Pit the olives and puree, along with the garlic, capers, anchovies, thyme, and rosemary, with a mortar and pestle or in a food processor fitted with the steel blade. Add the remaining ingredients and continue to process until you have a smooth paste. Place in a bowl, cover, and refrigerate until ready to use.

Spread thinly on croutons or raw vegetables and serve as an hors d'oeuvre with a Provençal rosé, a dry white wine, or champagne.

ADVANCE PREPARATION: Tapenade will hold for weeks in the refrigerator. Keep it in a jar or covered container and pour a thin film of olive oil over the surface to keep it from drying out.

PER PORTION

Calories	16	Protein	0
Fat	2 G	Carbohydrate	1 G
Sodium	91 MG	Cholesterol	0

Peel the skin away from the flesh of the eggplant when it is cool enough to handle. Cut the eggplant into small dice.

Heat the olive oil in a heavy-bottomed frying pan or a wide saucepan and add the garlic. Cook over medium-low heat just until it begins to color, then add the eggplant. Cook, stirring over medium heat, for 5 minutes, until the eggplant is cooked through and fragrant. Add the tomatoes, the vinegar, salt, and pepper and cook for another couple of minutes. Remove from the heat, stir in the lime juice and basil, and correct the seasonings. Allow to cool and refrigerate overnight. Serve as an hors d'oeuvre in a pretty bowl with Toasted Pita Triangles (page 71) or *crostini* (page 392) or on wedges of sweet red pepper.

ADVANCE PREPARATION: This relish will keep for a week in the refrigerator.

PER PORTION			
Calories	32	Protein	I G
Fat	I G	Carbohydrate	5 G
Sodium	5 MG	Cholesterol	0

ESCALIVADA HORS D'OEUVRE
(Catalan Roasted Vegetables)

SERVES 12 AS AN HORS D'OEUVRE

Escalivada is a Catalan dish of vegetables roasted in hot embers. Most versions I have seen combine eggplant, onion, garlic, and sweet peppers, and some have potatoes and tomatoes. It's something like a *ratatouille* in which the vegetables are roasted instead of stewed, so the vegetables acquire a grilled flavor. It's best, of course, to grill the vegetables until they are charred and take on that wonderful smoky flavor. If that isn't possible, char the vegetables over a flame or under a broiler, then bake them in the oven. *Escalivada* is sometimes doused with vinaigrette or just sprinkled with olive oil and chopped fresh garlic. I like both versions. Here I chop the cooked vegetables very small to make an hors d'oeuvre that can be served on pastries or toasted pita. If you wish, leave them in larger pieces and serve as a first course or a side dish or toss them with pasta. The cooking instructions here come in part from Colman Andrew's excellent *Catalan Cuisine*.

    Be forewarned that this dish is very garlicky. You can reduce the amount of garlic if you wish.

2 pounds (4 to 6) small eggplant (preferably small Japanese)

4 red bell peppers

2 onions

6 garlic cloves, unpeeled

1 pound (5 medium) ripe tomatoes

1 tablespoon olive oil

   coarse salt and freshly ground pepper to taste

2 large garlic cloves or less to taste, minced or put through a press

   a handful of chopped fresh basil (optional)

FOR THE VINAIGRETTE (optional)

2 tablespoons sherry vinegar

5 tablespoons olive oil

2 tablespoons finely minced fresh parsley

   salt and freshly ground pepper to taste

TO GRILL THE VEGETABLES: Grill the vegetables directly on hot coals or wood embers or on a gas grill or barbecue over a hot fire, turning them regularly until blackened on all sides. Watch the tomatoes closely, as they will cook quickly and begin to fall apart. Remove from the heat and place each type of vegetable except the tomatoes in a separate paper or plastic bag or covered bowl. Close and allow the vegetables to cool and steam for 10 to 15 minutes.

TO COOK THE VEGETABLES IN THE OVEN: Place the vegetables over burner flames or under a broiler and cook, turning, until they're just beginning to char. Then transfer all but the tomatoes to a large earthenware baking dish and toss with the tablespoon of olive oil (the tomatoes, once charred, can be allowed to cool and then chopped). Preheat the oven to 400 degrees and bake the vegetables for about 30 to 40 minutes, tossing the mixture from time to time, until softened but not mushy. Allow to cool in paper or plastic bags or covered bowls.

Peel the vegetables. For the minced hors d'oeuvre, chop (except the garlic, which will be quite soft and can be crushed and mixed with the others) and toss together. For a starter dish or side dish, leave the garlic whole and chop the tomatoes and eggplant (they will be mushy). Slice the onions and seed and slice the peppers.

Toss the vegetables in a bowl with coarse salt and 2 cloves minced or pressed garlic. If you have grilled the vegetables, add the olive oil at this point. Add freshly ground pepper to taste. Allow to cool. Toss with chopped fresh basil if desired.

If you're topping the vegetables with a vinaigrette, mix together the vinegar, oil, and salt and pepper. Stir in the parsley. Place the vegetable mixture in an attractive bowl and douse with the vinaigrette. Spoon onto Toasted Pita Triangles (page 71), crackers, or Olive Oil Pastries (page 27), or serve on red pepper wedges.

ADVANCE PREPARATION: *Escalivada* can be made a day or two ahead of time and tossed with the garlic and basil just before serving.

LEFTOVERS: Toss with pasta, spread on pizzas, use for omelets, or keep serving the *escalivada* as an hors d'oeuvre.

PER PORTION

Calories	100	Protein	2 G
Fat	7 G	Carbohydrate	9 G
Sodium	8 MG	Cholesterol	0

SPICY ZUCCHINI PUREE
ON RED PEPPER PIECES

SERVES 20 AS AN HORS D'OEUVRE

This zucchini puree is called *ajlouke* in North Africa, where the recipe originates. It's a spicy, very easy puree that looks beautiful on red pepper pieces.

- 6 medium zucchini, thinly sliced
- 3/4 teaspoon *harissa* or other chili paste (can be found in gourmet shops) *or* about 6 pinches of cayenne pepper

  juice of 1 1/2 to 3 lemons to taste
- 6 garlic cloves, minced or put through a press
- 1 1/2 teaspoons ground caraway
- 1 1/2 teaspoons ground coriander

  salt and freshly ground pepper to taste
- 6 to 8 brightly colored red bell peppers

Steam the zucchini for 10 to 15 minutes, until quite tender. Drain and refresh under cold water. Press out as much water as possible and transfer to a bowl.

Using a fork, crush the zucchini and add the remaining ingredients except the bell peppers. Correct the seasonings. Cover and chill until you're ready to top the peppers.

Cut the peppers in half lengthwise and remove the seeds and membranes. Cut into wide strips, about 6 per pepper, and cut the strips in half lengthwise. Place on a platter and top with generous dollops of the zucchini puree.

ADVANCE PREPARATION: The puree can be held in the refrigerator for a couple of hours before topping the peppers.

PER PORTION

Calories	16	Protein	1 G
Fat	.20 G	Carbohydrate	3 G
Sodium	3 MG	Cholesterol	0

SAUTÉED MINCED MUSHROOM STEMS

MAKES ABOUT ½ CUP, SERVING 8

Here's what to do with the mushroom stems you trim off when you're making stuffed or marinated mushroom caps. The stems are minced and sautéed in olive oil with garlic and white wine, then stored, covered with olive oil, in a jar in the refrigerator. Whenever you need a quick topping for *crostini,* voilà, you drain off the olive oil and spread the mushroom stems on toasted bread. Or add them to pasta or salads.

stems from 1 pound mushrooms

1 tablespoon olive oil for sautéing plus olive oil to cover the cooked mushroom stems

1 or 2 large garlic cloves to taste, minced or put through a press

2 tablespoons dry white wine

salt and freshly ground pepper to taste

Trim off the sandy ends of the mushroom stems, wash, shake dry, and mince. Heat the tablespoon of olive oil over medium-high heat in a well-seasoned or nonstick frying pan and add the mushroom stems. Sauté for a couple of minutes and add the garlic. Sauté, stirring, until the mushroom stems begin to release some of their liquid. Add the white wine and salt and pepper. Continue to sauté for about 5 or 10 minutes, stirring often, until the mushrooms are cooked through and fragrant and most of the liquid has evaporated. Remove from the heat and allow to cool. Adjust seasonings and transfer to a jar. Pour on olive oil to cover, cover the jar, and refrigerate.

ADVANCE PREPARATION: The stems will keep for a week in the refrigerator.

PER PORTION

Calories	39	Protein	I G
Fat	3 G	Carbohydrate	I G
Sodium	I MG	Cholesterol	0

SMOKED HADDOCK FLAN

SERVES 6

This recipe was inspired by a superb haddock flan I ate at David Wilson's restaurant, The Peat Inn, in Scotland. His is particularly luscious because of the type of fish he uses, a local smoked haddock called an "Arbroath Smoky." Arbroath Smokys are rich and moist, and his flan is ethereal. This flan is made with ordinary smoked haddock, moistened further with olive oil. Instead of the 6 tablespoons of crème fraîche in the original recipe, I've used part crème fraîche and part *fromage blanc*. The flan is very easy to make, sets in a *bain marie* in about 12 minutes, and is good hot or cold. If you serve it hot, cook it in individual molds and serve as a first course. I usually serve it as a cold hors d'oeuvre, either sliced, on little plates, or spread on bread or on small Olive Oil Pastries (page 27).

> 1/2 **pound smoked haddock**
> 1 **tablespoon olive oil**
> 2 **medium eggs**
> 1 **medium egg white**
> 2 **tablespoons crème fraîche**
> 3 **tablespoons** *fromage blanc* **(page 417)**
> 2 **tablespoons fresh lemon juice**
> **plenty of freshly ground black pepper**

IF THE FLAN WILL BE SERVED HOT

> **lettuce leaves or blanched large spinach or cabbage leaves for the plates**
> **lemon wedges**
> **chopped fresh parsley or chervil**
> **tomato wedges and/or thinly sliced cucumber (optional)**

Butter 6 1-cup molds or an 8- by 4-inch nonstick loaf pan and line with buttered parchment.

Flake the fish in a food processor fitted with the steel blade and add the olive oil, eggs, and egg white. Puree together, then press through a medium sieve (this will take a bit of work). Stir in the crème fraîche, *fromage blanc*, and lemon juice. Add freshly ground pepper and mix thoroughly.

Transfer to the molds or pan and place in a pan of simmering water over medium heat. Cover and cook in the *bain marie* for 7 to 8 minutes for small molds, 12 to 15 for a large one, or until set. If you're serving the flan hot, allow it to cool for a minute or two, then unmold onto plates lined with lettuce or blanched large spinach or cabbage leaves, garnished with lemon wedges and sprinkled with chopped fresh parsley or chervil. If you're serving it cold, allow it to cool a little longer in the mold, then unmold onto a plate. Water will probably run out from the flan after you unmold it. That's fine for hot flans (the liquid will season the leaves nicely), but for cold flans you will probably want to drain off the liquid. If you're serving the flan cold, chill it and spread generous amounts on croutons or bread.

NOTE: This flan is equally good made with other smoked fish, such as herring, which has a stronger, saltier flavor, or trout, which has a milder flavor.

ADVANCE PREPARATION: This dish can be prepared a day ahead of time if you're serving it cold. It keeps nicely, and the flavors mature overnight. The pureed mixture will hold for several hours before cooking.

PER PORTION

Calories	111	Protein	13 G
Fat	6 G	Carbohydrate	1 G
Sodium	340 MG	Cholesterol	98 MG

TUNA OR SALMON
AND HORSERADISH TARTARE

SERVES 8 AS AN HORS D'OEUVRE, 3 OR 4 AS A FIRST COURSE

Either tuna or salmon will work well here, as long as it's very fresh. The sauce is almost exactly like the sauce for Tuna Carpaccio on page 350, with a little more Worcestershire added. Here the fish is very finely chopped and tossed with the horseradish sauce, capers, shallots, and diced avocado. Served on pita triangles, *crostini,* or cucumber slices, it makes a marvelous hors d'oeuvre with a glass of not-too-dry white wine, such as Gewürztraminer. The dish could also be served as a first course or light supper.

FOR THE FISH

- ½ pound center-cut tuna fillet, dark meat and connective tissue trimmed away, or salmon fillet, skin and small bones removed
- ½ small avocado, pitted and finely diced
- 1 or 2 shallots to taste, finely minced
- 1 tablespoon drained capers or more to taste, rinsed
  salt and freshly ground pepper to taste
- ½ teaspoon Worcestershire sauce
- 2 tablespoons fresh lemon juice

FOR THE HORSERADISH SAUCE

- 4 teaspoons finely grated fresh horseradish
- 1 tablespoon sherry vinegar or red wine vinegar
- ½ teaspoon tamari soy sauce
- 4 teaspoons *fromage blanc* (page 417) or cream
- 1 tablespoon olive oil
- 1 tablespoon water
  salt and freshly ground pepper to taste

TO SERVE

> Toasted Pita Triangles (page 71), crackers, very small lettuce
> cups, cucumber slices, or *crostini* (page 392) if serving as hors
> d'oeuvres
>
> Sprigs of fresh herbs, such as thyme, chervil, or parsley, or
> chopped fresh herbs for garnish
>
> Lettuce leaves for lining plates if serving as a first course

Mince the fish in a food processor (do not puree) or with a knife and mix with
the avocado, shallots, capers, salt and pepper, Worcestershire sauce, and lemon
juice.

Combine the ingredients for the horseradish sauce and toss with the fish
mixture. Cover and refrigerate until shortly before serving.

Spoon onto toasted pita triangles, crackers, lettuce cups, cucumbers cut
into thin slices on the diagonal, or *crostini* and arrange on a platter. Sprinkle
with chopped fresh herbs or decorate with sprigs of herbs and serve. Or serve on
small plates lined with lettuce leaves.

ADVANCE PREPARATION: This recipe can be made several hours before
serving and held in the refrigerator in a covered container.

PER PORTION

Calories	76	Protein	7 G
Fat	5 G	Carbohydrate	2 G
Sodium	72 MG	Cholesterol	11 MG

GIANT WHITE BEANS
ON TOOTHPICKS

SERVES 12 TO 20 AS AN HORS D'OEUVRE

Giant white beans (fava beans) are so big that they qualify, in my book, as a snack. You can eat them one at a time and feel that you're munching on something substantial (I feel the same way about chick-peas, although they're not so big; but they're tasty enough to be eaten like nuts). This hors d'oeuvre may seem strange, but everyone will steal your idea.

Make the chilled version of Giant White Beans with Sage, Lemon, and Olive Oil (page 346). Transfer to an attractive bowl. Stick toothpicks in some of the beans and have more toothpicks next to the salad. Or divide the salad among small plates, spear the beans with toothpicks, and distribute the plates throughout the room.

ADVANCE PREPARATION: The beans can be cooked and marinated a day ahead of time, but don't add fresh herbs until shortly before serving.

PER PORTION

Calories	89	Protein	5 G
Fat	2 G	Carbohydrate	13 G
Sodium	168 MG	Cholesterol	0

JICAMA WITH LIME JUICE AND CHILI POWDER

SERVES AT LEAST 12 AS AN HORS D'OEUVRE

Anyone who's ever been to Mexico has probably sampled this delightful combination. Peeled, sliced jicama is sprinkled with lime juice and mild chili powder—a great combination.

1 medium or large jicama, peeled
  juice of 1 large lime
  chili powder

Peel the jicama and cut into ¼-inch slices. Cut the slices into small pieces if they are very large. They should be about the size of cucumber rounds (but they can be square or half-moon-shaped). Sprinkle with lime juice and chili powder just before serving and serve on a platter.

ADVANCE PREPARATION: You can slice the jicama hours ahead of serving and refrigerate in a covered bowl. Be careful to cover it well or it will dry out. You could also keep the jicama in a bowl of water in the refrigerator.

PER PORTION

Calories	11	Protein	0
Fat	.05 G	Carbohydrate	3 G
Sodium	2 G	Cholesterol	0

STUFFED CHERRY TOMATOES

SERVES 20 AS AN HORS D'OEUVRE

Cherry tomatoes make a good vehicle for various fillings. Here I've selected *hummus*, tapenade, Smoked Trout Spread, and Herbed Goat Cheese. A mix of red and yellow tomatoes makes a particularly pretty platter. You can vary the selection of fillings or serve just one or two. This goes fastest if you use a melon baller to remove the seeds and pulp and a pastry bag to fill the tomatoes.

1½ pounds cherry tomatoes (red and/or yellow)
2 cups *pesto* (page 64),
   tapenade (page 38),
   Smoked Trout Spread (page 61),
   Herbed Goat Cheese (page 36),
   or *hummus* (page 39)
   finely chopped fresh parsley or dill (optional)

Wash the cherry tomatoes and remove the stems. Slice off the tops with a sharp knife and, using a small spoon or melon baller, remove the seeds and pulp. Fill the tomatoes using a pastry bag or a zip-close bag with the corner snipped off, with a teaspoon or so of the various fillings or the filling of your choice. Arrange on a platter, sprinkle with chopped fresh parsley or dill if you wish, and serve.

ADVANCE PREPARATION: The filled tomatoes will hold for a few hours in the refrigerator but should be covered tightly with plastic wrap so that the surface of the filling doesn't dry out. Place corks on the plate so that the plastic doesn't squash the filling.

BABY VEGETABLES
STUFFED WITH TAPENADE

SERVES 6 AS AN HORS D'OEUVRE

Cherry tomatoes and baby zucchini are delicious filled with heady Provençal tapenade. These look beautiful as part of a big buffet or as the main hors d'oeuvre attraction.

    24 cherry tomatoes, approximately
    12 baby zucchini
    ½ recipe tapenade (page 38)
        chopped fresh parsley
        radishes and lemon wedges for garnish

Using a small sharp knife, slice off the top ¼ inch of the cherry tomatoes. Using a small spoon or a melon baller, carefully scoop out the seeds and pulp.

Bring a pot of water to a boil, add a little salt, and add the baby zucchini. Boil for 4 minutes, drain, and refresh under cold water. Cut in half lengthwise and, using a teaspoon, carefully scoop out the seeds.

Fill the tomatoes and zucchini with tapenade and place on an attractive platter. Sprinkle with parsley and garnish with radishes and lemon wedges. Serve or chill until ready to serve.

NOTE: If baby vegetables aren't available, spread on wide slices of red pepper and thick slices of zucchini, blanched and seeds removed.

ADVANCE PREPARATION: These hors d'oeuvres will hold for a few hours in the refrigerator.

PER PORTION

Calories	67	Protein	2 G
Fat	4 G	Carbohydrate	6 G
Sodium	250 MG	Cholesterol	I MG

POTATOES FILLED WITH CORN AND SAGE SALAD

SERVES 10 AS AN HORS D'OEUVRE

I discovered what a wonderful combination corn and fresh sage are by chance one night when I added both of them to a salad. I already knew how well the fresh herb goes with potatoes. The salad is nice on its own but also makes a very pretty hors d'oeuvre in little hollowed-out new potatoes. It's important to find small waxy new potatoes that will hold their shape and not to slice them too thick. Otherwise it will be difficult to eat these little hors d'oeuvres in one mouthful, and the corn will fall all over the place.

FOR THE SALAD

2 ears of sweet corn

1 small *or* ½ large red bell pepper, finely minced

2 heaped tablespoons slivered fresh sage leaves

¼ cup low-fat vinaigrette (pages 433–35)

salt and freshly ground pepper to taste

FOR THE POTATOES

2 pounds small new potatoes

salt and freshly ground pepper to taste

small fresh sage leaves for garnish

Steam the corn until tender, about 5 to 7 minutes. Run under cold water and, when cool enough to handle, cut the kernels from the cobs. Chop coarsely with a large knife or in a food processor fitted with the steel blade (just pulse a couple of times; you don't want a mush).

Toss together the corn, minced red pepper, sage, and dressing. Add salt and pepper and set aside.

Boil the potatoes, in their skins, in salted water until tender but not mushy. Drain and run under cold water. When cool enough to handle, cut the potatoes in half crosswise or into ¾-inch slices. Peel off the skins if you wish and cut a small sliver across the bottom end so that they will sit upright on a plate. Using a small melon baller or knife, make a little crater in the cut side of the potatoes. Salt and pepper lightly.

Spoon the corn filling into the hollowed-out potatoes, pressing down firmly to lodge the corn in the crater, and arrange on an attractive platter. Garnish with small fresh sage leaves. Serve at once or cover with plastic wrap and refrigerate until ready to serve.

NOTE: The corn and sage salad can also be served in small lettuce cups, as an hors d'oeuvre or a first course. For 4 to 6 people, double the quantities.

ADVANCE PREPARATION: The salad will hold for a day in the refrigerator without the sage and for a few hours with the sage. The assembled potatoes will hold in the refrigerator for a few hours.

PER PORTION

Calories	107	Protein	3 G
Fat	.92 G	Carbohydrate	23 G
Sodium	22 MG	Cholesterol	0

POTATO SLICES WITH TOPPINGS

SERVES 12 AS AN HORS D'OEUVRE

I'm not sure where I first got the idea of serving garnished potato slices as an hors d'oeuvre. Perhaps I was inspired by the potatoes topped with caviar served at Pile ou Face, one of my favorite Paris restaurants. That's the luxury version of this dish, but there are plenty of less expensive items that go nicely on top of a sweet slice of new potato. Some toppings are browned under the broiler; others are served cold.

1 pound new potatoes, scrubbed and sliced a little less than ½ inch thick

Caviar Topping

a little freshly ground pepper

3 tablespoons *fromage blanc* (page 417) for spreading on the potatoes, approximately

4 to 6 tablespoons caviar (Beluga is the best, but red salmon roe or golden caviar is a less expensive and quite good choice)

Steam the potato slices or bake them in a 350-degree oven on a nonstick baking sheet until just tender. Pepper lightly and spread with a thin layer of *fromage blanc*. Top with a small spoonful of caviar. Serve cold or at room temperature.

(continued)

PER PORTION

Calories	49	Protein	3 G
Fat	1 G	Carbohydrate	7 G
Sodium	114 MG	Cholesterol	39 MG

Chipotle Mayonnaise

1/3 cup Olive Oil Mayonnaise (page 418)

1½ tablespoons chopped drained chipotle chilies

2/3 cup *fromage blanc* (page 417)

salt and freshly ground pepper to taste

Cook the potatoes. Spread a thin film of the mayonnaise on each potato slice.

PER PORTION

Calories	39	Protein	1 G
Fat	.86 G	Carbohydrate	7 G
Sodium	20 MG	Cholesterol	1 MG

Gruyère Topping

a little salt and freshly ground pepper

2 ounces good-quality Gruyère and/or Parmesan cheese, or a combination, grated (about ½ cup)

Cook the potatoes. Salt and pepper lightly. Preheat the broiler. Sprinkle each slice with about 1 teaspoon grated Gruyère or Parmesan cheese or a combination. Run under the broiler until the cheese melts and begins to bubble; serve.

PER PORTION

Calories	49	Protein	2 G
Fat	2 G	Carbohydrate	7 G
Sodium	18 MG	Cholesterol	5 MG

Cantal or Cheddar and Garlic Topping

2 ounces Cantal or sharp Cheddar cheese, grated (about ½ cup)

1 large garlic clove, minced or put through a press

   a little salt and freshly ground pepper

Mix together the cheese and the garlic. Cook the potatoes and salt and pepper lightly. Preheat the broiler. Top each slice with the cheese and garlic. Run under the broiler until the cheese melts and begins to bubble; serve.

PER PORTION

Calories	49	Protein	2 G
Fat	2 G	Carbohydrate	7 G
Sodium	32 MG	Cholesterol	5 MG

Dill Topping

1 lemon

   salt and freshly ground pepper to taste

2 tablespoons *fromage blanc* (page 417), approximately

3 heaped tablespoons chopped fresh dill

Cook the potatoes and salt and pepper lightly. Squeeze lemon juice over the slices. Stir salt and freshly ground pepper into the *fromage blanc*. Spread a thin layer of *fromage blanc* on each slice and sprinkle generously with dill. Serve cold or at room temperature.

ADVANCE PREPARATION: For these recipes, the cooked potatoes will hold for a day in the refrigerator. Grated cheese and mayonnaise can be held for a couple of days in the refrigerator, and herbs can be chopped a few hours ahead.

PER PORTION

Calories	33	Protein	I G
Fat	.06 G	Carbohydrate	7 G
Sodium	I0 MG	Cholesterol	0

VARIATIONS ON DEVILED EGGS

MAKES 12 DEVILED EGGS

Deviled eggs may seem pedestrian, but there are so many intriguing ways to fill them. The high-fat filling I grew up with was a mixture of egg yolks, mayonnaise, and mustard. You can reduce the quantity of egg yolks and mix them with *fromage blanc* or yogurt mixed with tuna, pureed sorrel or other herbs, tofu, or smoked salmon. You could also fill the eggs with a mixture of tapenade and the egg yolks (not a low-fat mixture, but you don't need much of the powerfully flavored filling). Make sure the eggs you use are at least 4 days old, or they will be difficult to peel.

TUNA FILLING

> 6 medium eggs
>
> 3 tablespoons plain nonfat yogurt or *fromage blanc* (page 417)
>
> $1/2$ $6^1/2$-ounce can water-packed tuna, drained
>
> 1 garlic clove, minced or put through a press
>
> 2 teaspoons Dijon mustard
>
> 1 to 2 tablespoons fresh lemon juice to taste
>
> 2 tablespoons minced fresh chives
>
> $1/4$ cup finely minced fresh parsley
>
> freshly ground pepper to taste
>
> chopped fresh parsley or parsley sprigs for garnish

Bring the eggs slowly to a boil in a saucepan. As soon as they reach a boil, cover tightly, and remove from the heat. Allow to sit for 15 minutes. Drain and immerse the eggs in cold water. Allow to cool, then peel, and cut in half lengthwise. Remove the yolks and set aside 3 of them for another use. Put the other 3 through a sieve or mash in a food processor fitted with a steel blade. Stir in the yogurt or *fromage blanc*.

Finely chop the tuna in a food processor fitted with the steel blade. Mix with the egg yolk mixture and stir in the remaining ingredients except the parsley. Adjust the seasonings.

Pipe the filling into the halved egg whites through a pastry bag or mound it into the whites using a spoon. Decorate the tops with parsley sprigs or chopped parsley and serve on an attractive platter.

PER PORTION

Calories	47	Protein	7 G
Fat	2 G	Carbohydrate	I G
Sodium	117 MG	Cholesterol	55 MG

EGG YOLK AND ARUGULA FILLING

6 medium eggs

$^1/_4$ cup plain nonfat yogurt or *fromage blanc* (page 417)

1 teaspoon sherry vinegar or balsamic vinegar

1 to 2 tablespoons fresh lemon juice to taste

1 teaspoon Dijon mustard

$^1/_4$ pound arugula, stemmed, washed, dried, and chopped

salt and freshly ground pepper to taste

Boil and peel the eggs. Cut in half lengthwise and set aside 2 of the egg yolks. Put the remaining 4 yolks through a sieve or chop fine in a food processor fitted with the steel blade. Mix with the yogurt or *fromage blanc,* the vinegar, lemon juice, and mustard. Stir in the arugula. Season to taste with salt and freshly ground pepper. Fill the eggs (you'll have to spoon this filling in as it's a bit too runny for piping) and serve.

PER PORTION

Calories	30	Protein	3 G
Fat	2 G	Carbohydrate	I G
Sodium	46 MG	Cholesterol	64 MG

EGG YOLK, POTATO, AND SORREL FILLING

6 medium eggs

5 tablespoons plain nonfat yogurt or *fromage blanc* (page 417)

1 medium-size new or boiling potato, boiled or steamed until tender and peeled

¼ pound sorrel, stemmed and washed

salt and freshly ground pepper to taste

1 to 2 tablespoons fresh lemon juice to taste

1 teaspoon Dijon mustard

chopped fresh parsley or parsley sprigs for garnish

Boil and peel the eggs. Cut in half lengthwise and set aside 3 of the egg yolks. Put the remaining 3 yolks through a sieve or chop fine in a food processor fitted with the steel blade. Mix with the yogurt or *fromage blanc*. Mash the potato and put through a sieve. Stir into the egg yolks.

In a nonaluminum frying pan, heat the sorrel in the water remaining on its leaves. Stir for just a minute, until it collapses (it will change color as well). Remove from the heat and press out all excess water with the back of a spoon. Puree or put through a sieve. Mix in with the eggs and potatoes. Season with salt and pepper and add the lemon juice and Dijon mustard. Fill the eggs, garnish with parsley, and serve.

PER PORTION

Calories	38	Protein	3 G
Fat	I G	Carbohydrate	4 G
Sodium	44 MG	Cholesterol	48 MG

SMOKED TROUT OR SALMON AND EGG YOLK FILLING

This makes more filling than you'll need to fill the eggs, but the combination is terrific and makes a marvelous spread or stuffing for cherry tomatoes.

    6 medium eggs
  1/4 pound smoked trout or salmon, chopped
    3 tablespoons plain nonfat yogurt or *fromage blanc* (page 417)
    1 teaspoon Dijon mustard
    1 to 2 tablespoons fresh lemon juice to taste
       salt and freshly ground pepper to taste
    2 tablespoons red salmon caviar or finely minced fresh parsley or
       dill

Cook the eggs. Cut in half lengthwise and set aside 3 of the egg yolks for another use. Finely chop the smoked trout or salmon or puree it in a food processor fitted with the steel blade. Add the remaining 3 egg yolks and blend with the smoked trout or salmon. Blend in the yogurt or *fromage blanc*, mustard, lemon juice, and salt and pepper. Fill the eggs. Decorate with the salmon caviar or chopped fresh parsley or dill and serve.

ADVANCE PREPARATION: All of the fillings except the arugula filling will hold for a day in the refrigerator (the arugula filling will hold for a few hours). The filled eggs will hold for a few hours in the refrigerator. Store them on plates, with corks on the plates to keep the plastic wrap from touching the filling.

PER PORTION

Calories	41	Protein	5 G
Fat	2 G	Carbohydrate	1 G
Sodium	155 MG	Cholesterol	66 MG

RED PEPPER SQUARES TOPPED
WITH HERBED GOAT CHEESE

SERVES 12 AS AN HORS D'OEUVRE

Red peppers, cut into small squares, make very attractive vehicles for the Herbed Goat Cheese on page 36.

> 1 pound (2 large) red bell peppers, seeds and membranes removed, cut into 1-inch squares
>
> 3/4 cup Herbed Goat Cheese (page 36)

Top each square with about a heaped teaspoon of the cheese. Refrigerate until ready to serve. For a prettier version, pipe the goat cheese onto the squares through a star-shaped tip.

ADVANCE PREPARATION: The peppers can be cut and the herbed goat cheese prepared hours before serving. The assembled squares will hold for a couple of hours in the refrigerator.

PER PORTION

Calories	115	Protein	8 G
Fat	7 G	Carbohydrate	6 G
Sodium	235 MG	Cholesterol	22 MG

MUSHROOM CAPS FILLED
WITH PIPERADE

SERVES 16 AS AN HORS D'OEUVRE

Piperade, the savory mixture of sweet peppers, tomato, onion, and scrambled eggs, is just one of many good fillings for mushroom caps. This is a particularly pretty one. You will need to serve these with napkins.

50 medium (about 2$\frac{1}{2}$ pounds) very fresh mushrooms

2 tablespoons olive oil

1 large garlic clove, minced or put through a press

    salt and freshly ground pepper to taste

1 recipe *Piperade au Basilic* (page 275)

Preheat the oven to 350 degrees. Brush a baking sheet or dish with olive oil.

Pull the entire stem out from each mushroom cap. Rinse the caps and wipe them dry. Save the stems and use for sautéed mushroom stems, page 45.

Heat the olive oil in a frying pan over medium heat. Add the garlic and sauté for about 30 seconds, stirring; then add the mushrooms, rounded side down. Sauté, shaking the pan, for about 3 minutes or until the mushrooms just begin to brown and soften. Add salt and pepper and remove from the heat.

Fill the mushrooms with the *piperade* mixture. Place on the baking sheet or dish, filled side up. Heat through in the oven for 10 minutes, drain for a few seconds on paper towels if the mushrooms are quite moist, and serve warm.

ADVANCE PREPARATION: The mushrooms and *piperade* can each be prepared several hours before serving. The filled mushrooms will also hold for a couple of hours before being heated through.

PER PORTION

Calories	95	Protein	5 G
Fat	6 G	Carbohydrate	6 G
Sodium	37 MG	Cholesterol	107 MG

MUSHROOM CAPS
FILLED WITH PESTO

SERVES 12 AS AN HORS D'OEUVRE

Pesto makes a great filling for mushrooms. The savory flavors of the 2 are very complementary—just one more reason to make as much *pesto* as you can during summer months, to hoard in the freezer and use through the winter. The *pesto* here, unlike authentic Genovese *pesto*, doesn't contain pine nuts or pecorino Romano cheese. It more closely resembles the Provençal *pistou*.

FOR THE PESTO

1½ cups tightly packed fresh basil leaves, washed and dried

2 large garlic cloves

¼ teaspoon salt or more to taste

¼ cup fruity olive oil

⅓ cup freshly grated Parmesan cheese (about 1½ ounces)

freshly ground pepper to taste

FOR THE MUSHROOMS

20 to 25 (about 1 pound) medium-size very fresh mushrooms

salt and freshly ground pepper to taste

First make the *pesto*. Place the basil, garlic, and salt in the bowl of a food processor, a blender jar, or a mortar and pestle. Process or pound until finely chopped or pureed. Slowly add the olive oil and continue to process until the mixture is smooth and uniform. Stir in the cheese and freshly ground pepper.

Preheat the oven to 400 degrees. Brush a baking sheet or dish with olive oil.

Stem the mushrooms, pulling the entire stem out from the cap, rinse, and wipe dry. Put the stems aside for another use (see page 45). Toss the caps with salt and freshly ground pepper.

LITTLE SPRING ROLLS WITH VEGETABLES, SHRIMP, HERBS, AND GINGER

MAKES 20 SMALL SPRING ROLLS, SERVING 10

I love the idea of spring rolls—very fresh, uncooked egg-roll-like rolls that are commonly served as starters in Vietnamese restaurants. The wrapper is a rice flour pastry that needs only a few seconds' soaking in warm water to become pliable and easy to work with. Spring rolls are usually filled with fresh, crunchy vegetables like bean sprouts, lettuce, and herbs and shrimp and rice vermicelli. But I find most restaurant spring rolls pretty dull, because they don't have enough herbs in them, and they're underseasoned. Mine are pretty perky, with pickled ginger and a lot of cilantro and mint. You can make a vegetarian version of spring rolls by omitting the shrimp and substituting 1/4 pound of bean sprouts, slivered cucumber, or carrots. These spring rolls are very small and are easy to handle at cocktail parties. Because they're seasoned on the inside, in my opinion they need no dipping sauce. However, you could use one. These go particularly well with Gewürztraminer, Muscat d'Alsace, Chardonnay, and beer.

   2 ounces rice vermicelli*

 2/3 cup coarsely snipped cilantro leaves

 2/3 cup coarsely snipped mint leaves

   3 ounces carrots, peeled and grated (about 1/2 cup tightly packed)

 1/2 pound shrimp, cooked, peeled, deveined, and cut in half crosswise

   2 heaped tablespoons pickled ginger, chopped or cut into fine slivers*

   8 large romaine lettuce leaves, washed, dried, and cut into thin *chiffonnade*

 1/4 cup fresh lime juice

   1 tablespoon Chinese or dark sesame oil

     lots of freshly ground pepper

     salt to taste

  20 small round dry rice flour wrappers, about 6 inches in diameter*

* Rice vermicelli, pickled ginger, and dry rice flour wrappers are available in Asian markets. You'll have to buy a lot more wrappers than you need, because they come in big packages. But they keep for months in the pantry.

MAKE THE FILLING: Soak the rice vermicelli in warm water for about 20 to 30 minutes, until tender. Drain and break them apart. Pat dry with paper towels and transfer to a bowl. Add all the remaining ingredients except the wrappers and toss together. Taste and adjust seasonings.

MAKE THE SPRING ROLLS: One at a time, place a wrapper in a bowl of hot water for about 30 seconds, until tender. Remove from the water, drain on a kitchen towel, and lay out on the towel. Place a heaped tablespoon, which I measure by taking up a small quantity of the filling between my thumb and two first fingers, slightly off center (closer to you) in the middle of the wrapper. Fold the sides of the wrapper over the filling and roll up tightly. The spring roll should be about 1½ to 2 inches long. Arrange the spring rolls on a plate and continue until you've used up all of the filling. Cover tightly with plastic wrap and refrigerate until shortly before serving.

ADVANCE PREPARATION: These spring rolls will hold well for several hours, or up to a day, in the refrigerator. They could be made a day ahead of time, but the color of the herbs will be less vivid.

PER PORTION

Calories	49	Protein	3 G
Fat	.90 G	Carbohydrate	7 G
Sodium	18 MG	Cholesterol	14 MG

PHYLLO PASTRIES WITH CABBAGE FILLING

MAKES 60 CIGAR-SHAPED OR 90 SMALL TRIANGULAR PASTRIES, SERVING 20 TO 30

I developed this filling originally for yeasted dumplings, but I liked the filling much better than the bready dumplings and decided to wrap it in delicate phyllo pastry instead. In the past I've avoided phyllo pastry when working with low-fat recipes, but this time I experimented with brushing the pastry sheets with olive oil and a small amount of butter instead of the usual lavish amount of butter alone. It works very well, and it's good to know that you don't really need that much fat when working with phyllo pastry. Phyllo always makes such a nice crisp wrapping for any filling. The cabbage is savory and subtle. If you feel like being very extravagant, stir in a finely chopped truffle. Otherwise, make the caraway version—or make both. You can also stir in about ½ cup of the minced mushroom stems on page 45.

FOR THE FILLING

1	tablespoon unsalted butter
1	medium onion *or* 3 shallots, finely chopped
1½	pounds green or Savoy cabbage, cored and shredded
1	teaspoon sugar
	salt and freshly ground pepper to taste
1	cup water
2	hard-cooked medium eggs
¼	cup finely chopped fresh parsley
2	medium eggs, beaten
1	to 2 teaspoons caraway seeds to taste, slightly crushed, *or* 2 small truffles, finely chopped (or divide the filling in half and mix half with 1 scant teaspoon caraway seeds and half with a finely chopped truffle), *or* ½ cup minced mushroom stems sautéed with garlic (optional)

FOR THE PASTRIES

½	pound phyllo dough
¼	cup olive oil
2	tablespoons unsalted butter

TO MAKE THE FILLING: Heat the butter over medium-low heat in a non-stick saucepan and add the onion or shallots. Cook, stirring, until they begin to brown, about 8 minutes. Add the cabbage, sugar, and salt and pepper and stir together. Add the water, bring to a boil, then reduce the heat and simmer for 15 minutes or until the cabbage is very tender. Remove from the heat.

Finely chop the hard-cooked eggs in a food processor fitted with the steel blade or put them through a sieve. Chop the cabbage mixture in a food processor fitted with the steel blade (do not puree) or with a large sharp knife and combine with the hard-cooked eggs. Transfer to a bowl. Stir in the parsley, correct the seasonings, and stir in the beaten eggs. Stir in the caraway or truffles if desired.

TO MAKE THE PASTRIES: Preheat the oven to 325 degrees. Keep the phyllo dough wrapped in a towel. Take 1 sheet at a time, each time returning the rest of the dough to a towel so it doesn't dry out. Lay the sheet of phyllo across a cutting board and cut down the shorter length into strips, about 2½ inches wide for small triangles, 3 inches wide for cigar shapes. Put the olive oil and butter in a small saucepan and heat over very low heat until the butter melts.

Cigar Shapes: Brush the strips of phyllo lightly with the olive oil and butter mixture. Place a heaped teaspoon of filling about ½ inch down from end of the strip of phyllo dough, spreading it to about ½ inch of the edges. Fold the edges over the filling so that it doesn't ooze out when you roll up the cigar. Fold the end over the filling and roll up into a cylinder. Place on a nonstick or lightly oiled baking sheet. Continue with the remaining strips of phyllo, working with 1 sheet at a time and keeping the remaining dough wrapped in the towel.

Triangles: Work with 1 sheet of dough at a time as above. Brush the strips of phyllo lightly with the olive oil and butter mixture. Place a teaspoon of the filling on the right side of 1 end of a strip of pastry, about ½ inch down from the end. Fold the left-hand corner of the pastry diagonally over the filling so that the filling is inside a triangle. Fold the triangle over at the bottom and continue folding the pastry over itself until you reach the end. Place on a nonstick or lightly oiled baking sheet. Continue with the remaining strips of phyllo, working with 1 sheet at a time and keeping the remaining dough wrapped in the towel.

Bake the pastries for 30 to 40 minutes or until golden brown. Serve hot.

ADVANCE PREPARATION: The cabbage filling can be made hours or even a day or two before filling the pastries. The pastries can be filled hours or even a day before serving. Refrigerate until shortly before baking and bake shortly before serving. The unbaked pastries can also be frozen and transferred directly from the freezer to the preheated oven.

LEFTOVERS: Leftovers can be reheated in a 325-degree oven. They won't be quite as crispy.

PER PORTION

Calories	22	Protein	1 G
Fat	1 G	Carbohydrate	2 G
Sodium	18 MG	Cholesterol	10 MG

TOASTED PITA TRIANGLES
WITH TOPPINGS

MAKES 48 LARGE OR 72 SMALL TRIANGLES

Pita bread, split into 2 thin rounds and cut into triangles, is the low-fat answer to tortilla chips. These triangles make a perfect vehicle for all kinds of toppings. The suggestions below are just a beginning.

6 pita breads, preferably whole wheat

FOR THE TOPPINGS

Tomatoes Vinaigrette (page 424)

Diced Eggplant Relish (page 40)

Tuna Ceviche (page 352)

Spicy Zucchini Puree (page 44)

Hummus (page 39)

Zucchini and Avocado Salsa Salad (page 142)

Céleri Rémoulade (page 371)

Roasted Red Bell Peppers (page 419), diced

Escalivada (page 42)

Tuna or Salmon and Horseradish Tartare (page 48)

Preheat the oven to 375 degrees.

Cut the pita breads in half, then divide the halves into 2 thin layers. Cut these into triangles. Each pita should yield 8 triangles. You can make smaller triangles if you aren't topping them with anything. The smaller ones (12 per pita) would be suitable for dips.

Place the pita triangles on a baking sheet and bake for 5 to 10 minutes. They should be crisp but not too brown. Remove from the oven and allow to cool.

ADVANCE PREPARATION: The toasted pita triangles will keep for weeks in a plastic bag.

GRILLED OR BAKED POLENTA SQUARES WITH GREEN TOMATILLO MOLE

MAKES 50 SMALL SQUARES

Just because *polenta* is an Italian creation doesn't mean it won't go wonderfully with a Mexican sauce. It is, after all, made from corn. Here the *polenta* is cut into small thin squares and crisped on the outside in the oven or on a grill; it should remain creamy in the middle. Then the squares are topped with Green Tomatillo *Mole*.

- 2 teaspoons unsalted butter
- 5 cups water
- 1¼ teaspoons salt
- ½ pound coarse stone-ground yellow cornmeal
  freshly ground black pepper to taste
- ½ recipe Green Tomatillo Mole (page 156)
- 3 tablespoons olive oil, as needed
  cilantro leaves for garnish

Line the sides and bottom of a loaf pan with wax paper and grease the paper with the butter.

Bring the water to a boil in a large pot and add the salt. Turn the heat down to medium-low so that the water is boiling gently, a little faster than a simmer. Very slowly add the cornmeal, taking it up in handfuls and letting it run between your fingers in a very thin stream. Whisk the water constantly as you add the cornmeal. This should take about 5 minutes.

Now change to a long-handled wooden spoon and turn the heat down to low. Stir the *polenta* constantly with the wooden spoon over low heat until it thickens and is difficult to stir. It is done when it comes away from the sides of the pot. This should take about 25 minutes. Stir in some freshly ground pepper and transfer the *polenta* to the prepared pan. Allow it to cool, then refrigerate for at least 2 hours.

Meanwhile, make the *mole* according to the directions.

Preheat the oven to 300 degrees or prepare a fire in your grill. When the fire has died down and the heat is low, or when your oven is preheated, slice the *polenta* ¼ to ⅓ inch thick. Cut the slices in half. Brush with olive oil and place on a baking sheet if you're baking them. Bake or grill for 30 minutes, until the edges are crisp but the inside is still creamy. Remove from the heat, top with the *mole,* and arrange on a platter. Garnish with cilantro leaves and serve.

ADVANCE PREPARATION: The *polenta* can be made up to 2 days ahead of time and refrigerated, tightly covered, in the pan before being grilled. The *mole* can be made a day ahead of time and refrigerated.

PER PORTION

Calories	34	Protein	I G
Fat	I G	Carbohydrate	5 G
Sodium	67 MG	Cholesterol	0

CRACKERS WITH GOAT CHEESE SPREAD AND SUN-DRIED TOMATOES

SERVES 4 TO 6

It's easy to keep everything on hand for this starter, so that if people drop by unexpectedly—or even if they don't—you can serve up the dish. It takes almost no time to put together, and it's one of those hors d'oeuvres that always surprises and pleases my guests.

- ¼ to ½ cup Goat Cheese Spread (page 35)
- 12 to 16 crackers, preferably Dar Vida whole wheat or sesame, or matzo or Toasted Pita Triangles (page 71)
- 4 to 6 sun-dried tomatoes, drained, patted dry with a paper towel, and cut into thin slivers

Spread the cheese on the crackers. Top with a couple of slivers of sun-dried tomatoes. Serve on a nice platter.

NOTE: You can also finely chop the sun-dried tomatoes and mix them right into the cheese.

ADVANCE PREPARATION: The tomatoes can be drained, blotted, and slivered hours ahead of time. The crackers should be assembled just before serving.

THICK LITTLE BLINIS
WITH TOPPINGS

MAKES 40 SMALL BLINIS, SERVING 15 AS AN HORS D'OEUVRE,
6 TO 8 AS A MAIN DISH

Little blinis make marvelous hors d'oeuvres. The obvious toppings are caviar, smoked salmon, and *fromage blanc*. But lots of other things go well with them. They are earthy-tasting and moist, with a rich buckwheat flavor, and they're very convenient because you can make them far ahead of time and they freeze well.

FOR THE BLINIS

1 teaspoon active dry yeast

2 tablespoons lukewarm water

1 cup plus 2 tablespoons lukewarm skim milk

4 ounces (about $7/8$ cup) buckwheat flour

4 ounces (about $7/8$ cup) unbleached white flour

$3/4$ to 1 teaspoon salt to taste

$1/2$ cup buttermilk or plain nonfat yogurt

2 large *or* 3 medium eggs, separated

FOR THE TOPPINGS

$1/2$ pound smoked salmon, approximately, and 1 to 2 teaspoons *fromage blanc* (page 417)

Egg Salad with Herbs (page 367)

caviar and *fromage blanc* (page 417)

Tuna or Salmon and Horseradish Tartare (page 48)

Diced Eggplant Relish (page 40)

Herbed Goat Cheese (page 36)

Dissolve the yeast in the lukewarm water in a large bowl, add the milk, and let sit for 5 minutes. Combine the flours and salt and stir into the milk. Stir in the buttermilk or yogurt. Beat in the egg yolks.

Cover the batter with plastic wrap and a towel and let rise in a warm place for about 1 hour or longer, until spongy and bubbly.

Beat the egg whites to soft peaks and fold them into the batter. Cover and let rise for another hour or more. The batter will be spongy and light.

Lightly grease special blini pans or a heavy cast-iron griddle or frying pan and heat over medium-low heat. Ladle on a few small ladlefuls of batter, about 2 tablespoons per blini. They should be 2½ to 3 inches in diameter. Cook for 1 minute or so, until holes break through. Turn and brown on the other side for about 30 seconds. Reverse onto a plate.

Stack the blinis in 2 overlapping piles, like shuffled cards. This keeps the blinis from becoming soggy. If you're not serving them right away, wrap in a towel or aluminum foil and keep warm in a medium oven. If you're serving them much later, wrap in foil and reheat for 30 minutes in a 325-degree oven.

Shortly before serving, top the blinis with 1 to 2 teaspoons of your choice of the toppings and arrange on plates.

NOTES: These blinis also freeze well. Stack them in between pieces of wax paper or parchment and wrap tightly in foil. Seal in a plastic bag. To thaw, remove them from the plastic bag and place in a 350-degree oven, still wrapped in foil, for 1 hour.

This batter will of course make good large blinis (about 12), which can be served as a first course or main dish with the topping of your choice.

ADVANCE PREPARATION: These blinis can be made a day ahead of time and refrigerated or weeks ahead of time and frozen.

PER PORTION

Calories	48	Protein	2 G
Fat	.79 G	Carbohydrate	8 G
Sodium	94 MG	Cholesterol	24 MG

CRÊPES HORS D'OEUVRES

MAKES 12 CRÊPES

Crêpes, on their own or spread with a small amount of *fromage blanc* (page 417), Herbed Goat Cheese (page 36), smoked salmon, or Smoked Haddock Flan (page 46), are a mouth-watering hors d'oeuvre. Fold them into triangles and serve them nice and warm. Herb crêpes are especially good. Follow the directions for crêpes on page 399. Spread with any of the suggestions above, fold in half, then fold in half again. You can fold them in half yet again if these seem unwieldy. Serve warm.

ADVANCE PREPARATION: Crêpes can be made a day or two ahead of time and refrigerated, stacked between pieces of wax paper. Or they can be frozen weeks in advance (see recipe). The filled and folded crêpes can be assembled hours ahead of time and refrigerated, covered with plastic wrap. Heat through for 20 minutes in a 350-degree oven.

HERB BRUSCHETTE

I first tasted toast topped with nothing more than olive oil and chopped fresh tarragon at a restaurant called Arpège in Paris. What a brilliant idea. I like tarragon and basil the best, but try other herbs if you wish. Serve these *bruschette* on the side with soups, fish, or chicken (the chef at Arpège served them alongside lobster topped with a peppery *rouille*) or as an hors d'oeuvre. They are particularly good with the Dried Porcini Soup on page 88.

For hors d'oeuvres, small pieces of bread sliced about ¼ inch thick are most manageable; for a side dish, larger slices cut ½ inch thick are appropriate. There are so many variables here that nutritional data have not been calculated.

Country Bread (such as the one on page 380), sliced about ½ inch thick

olive oil

garlic cloves, cut in half (optional)

2 to 3 teaspoons chopped fresh herbs, such as tarragon, basil, chervil, per *bruschetta*

Toast the bread. It should still be slightly soft in the middle. Brush with olive oil and rub with a cut clove of garlic if you wish. Sprinkle with the chopped fresh herbs and serve.

ADVANCE PREPARATION: The herbs can be chopped several hours ahead of time and held in the refrigerator.

FRESH TARRAGON BISCUITS

MAKES 12 BISCUITS OR 24 BITE-SIZE BISCUITS

Fresh tarragon has a vibrant flavor that makes these biscuits wonderfully fragrant. Good with soups and salads, they, like the Thyme Biscuits in the following recipe, make a great hors d'oeuvre, spread with a small amount of butter or *fromage blanc* (page 417); or make bite-size biscuits and eat them plain. These work only if you use fresh tarragon.

- ¼ pound (⅞ cup) unbleached white flour
- ¼ pound (⅞ cup) whole wheat flour or whole wheat pastry flour
- ¾ teaspoon salt
- 1 teaspoon sugar
- 2 teaspoons baking powder
- ½ teaspoon baking soda
- 2 tablespoons minced fresh tarragon
- 5 tablespoons unsalted butter
- ⅔ cup sour skim milk, buttermilk, or plain low-fat yogurt

Preheat the oven to 450 degrees. Butter a baking sheet.

Sift together the flours, salt, sugar, baking powder, and baking soda. Stir in the tarragon. Cut in the butter, then take up the flour and roll briskly between the palms of your hands so the mixture has the consistency of coarse cornmeal. This step can also be done in a food processor fitted with the steel blade, using the pulse action.

Stir the milk, buttermilk, or yogurt into the mixture. Gather up the dough and gently knead it, not working the dough like bread but just pressing it together so that it comes together in a cohesive lump. It will be slightly sticky, so lightly flour your hands. The less you work the dough, the lighter your biscuits will be. Roll out to a thickness of about ¾ inch and cut into squares, triangles, or rounds. For bite-size biscuits, cut into squares, then cut the squares diagonally into small triangles.

Place on the prepared baking sheet and bake for 12 to 15 minutes, until they're beginning to brown. Serve warm.

ADVANCE PREPARATION: These biscuits can be made several hours before serving and reheated in a 325-degree oven.

PER PORTION (BITE-SIZE BISCUITS)

Calories	58	Protein	I G
Fat	3 G	Carbohydrate	8 G
Sodium	129 MG	Cholesterol	7 MG

THYME BISCUITS

MAKES 12 BISCUITS OR 24 BITE-SIZE BISCUITS

These biscuits are great with soups and salads, but they also make a very nice hors d'oeuvre, especially the bite-size version. Eat them plain or cut them in half, spread them with a small amount of butter or *fromage blanc* (page 417), and serve them warm.

$1/4$ pound (about $7/8$ cup) unbleached white flour

$1/4$ pound (about $7/8$ cup) whole wheat flour or whole wheat pastry flour

$3/4$ teaspoon salt

1 teaspoon sugar

2 teaspoons baking powder

$1/2$ teaspoon baking soda

1 tablespoon fresh thyme leaves *or* $1 1/2$ teaspoons crumbled dried

5 tablespoons unsalted butter

$2/3$ cup sour milk, buttermilk, or plain nonfat yogurt

Preheat the oven to 450 degrees. Butter a baking sheet.

Sift together the flours, salt, sugar, baking powder, and baking soda. Stir in the thyme. Cut in the butter, then take up the flour and roll briskly between the palms of your hands so the mixture has the consistency of coarse cornmeal. This step can also be done in a food processor fitted with the steel blade, using the pulse action.

Stir the milk, buttermilk, or yogurt into the mixture. Gather up the dough and gently knead it, not working the dough like bread but just pressing it together so that it comes together in a cohesive lump. It will be slightly sticky, so lightly flour your hands. The less you work the dough, the lighter your biscuits will be. Roll out to a thickness of about ¾ inch and cut into squares, triangles, or rounds. For bite-size biscuits, cut into squares, then cut the squares diagonally into small triangles.

Place on the prepared baking sheet and bake for 12 to 15 minutes, until they're beginning to brown. Serve warm.

ADVANCE PREPARATION: These biscuits can be made several hours before serving and reheated in a 325-degree oven.

PER PORTION (BITE-SIZE BISCUITS)

Calories	58	Protein	I G
Fat	3 G	Carbohydrate	8 G
Sodium	129 MG	Cholesterol	7 MG

Here is a repertoire of dinners, both vegetarian and nonvegetarian, to please a wide range of people. Many are menus that require a certain amount of planning. They don't all require long hours in the kitchen and days of work, but for those that do you can get several tasks out of the way during the week leading up to your party. Many, like the Informal Dinner for Six Featuring a Whole Baked Fish on page 106 or the Festive Dinner for Six Featuring *Lapin à la Moutarde,* on page 183, can be shopped for and put together all on the same day. What all of these menus have in common is that they're suitable for elegant dinner parties. That said, several can be dressed up or down, such as the New Year's Eve Buffet for 20 on page 219 or the Two Fall/Winter Menus with Roast Chicken and Fine Wines on page 174. And some of the simpler menus in Chapter 4 can be dressed up.

The menus range from dinner parties for four to buffets for 20. Most fall into the six-to-eight range, as that's a common dinner party number, but all of them can be altered to feed more people. Five of the menus are restricted to sit-down dinners: all of them are so indicated in the menu titles. Otherwise the menus work for buffets as well as sit-down dinners. They're arranged more or less by season, spring to fall.

I love giving a dinner party, whether it's for four, eight, or 20. I love composing the menu, thinking about the aperitifs, planning the wines. Often I'll begin with one idea, an entrée or a main dish, and take a long walk, thinking about what I'll serve around it. Sometimes the whole menu falls into place at once. When I put together the menu on page 86 featuring the Asparagus and Herb Lasagne, I knew right away that the Dried Porcini Soup would be a great way to kick off the meal. But I can't live without something saladly; I fulfilled that need by serving the Tarragon Bruschette along with the soup and a small arugula salad with the lasagne. Dessert was the one thing I mulled over for a while. Rhubarb was coming in, and I knew I wanted to do a rhubarb dessert, but I had to decide on a crumble, compote, or sorbet. In the end I decided on the sorbet, because it's so light and refreshing.

The menus do not include suggestions for hors d'oeuvres or breads. I always serve something to eat with drinks, but if it's a big dinner party, that something could be as simple as radishes or other *crudités.* Since I usually have tapenade on hand, I sometimes serve it on croutons, or I'll serve a vegetable puree on toasted pita triangles. With Mexican meals the Jicama with Lime Juice and Chili Powder on page 51 is very good and very low in calories; you could also have baskets of Toasted Pita Triangles (page 71) here and there, with salsa close by. Your choice should be based on the overall complexity of the meal, its calorie and fat content, and your available time.

TORTELLINI ON SKEWERS

SERVES 15 AS AN HORS D'OEUVRE

This is an ingenious hors d'oeuvre. All you have to do is cook the tortellini and spear them on toothpicks. It's easy to find ready-made tortellini in pasta shops and supermarkets.

- 1 **pound small tortellini, either cheese or meat-filled, preferably a combination of green and white (about 60 tortellini)**
- ¼ **cup olive oil**
- 3 **tablespoons chopped fresh parsley, basil, or tarragon**

Cook the tortellini in a large pot of salted boiling water until *al dente.* Drain and toss with the olive oil and the chopped fresh herbs. Place each tortellini on a toothpick. Serve warm or at room temperature with drinks.

ADVANCE PREPARATION: If you are serving them at room temperature, you can cook the tortellini a few hours before assembling the skewers. Toss with the oil right after cooking. I think these are best if reheated gently before serving in a nonstick pan.

PER PORTION			
Calories	122	Protein	5 G
Fat	5 G	Carbohydrate	14 G
Sodium	136 MG	Cholesterol	17 MG

RAW TUNA OR SALMON AND PICKLED GINGER SKEWERS

SERVES 10 AS AN HORS D'OEUVRE

These are marinated sashimilike hors d'oeuvres on toothpicks. They're very easy to put together. Either tuna or salmon would be suitable for this. Make sure the fish is impeccably fresh.

1 pound very fresh tuna, weighed after the bones, dark meat, and skin are removed, cut into 1/2-inch chunks, *or* salmon fillet, small bones and skin removed, cut into 1/2-inch chunks

salt and freshly ground pepper to taste

1 tablespoon tamari soy sauce

1 tablespoon rice wine vinegar, cider vinegar, or balsamic vinegar

2 tablespoons mirin *or* 2 teaspoons mild-flavored honey

a 1-inch piece of fresh ginger, peeled and grated or minced

2 tablespoons water

1 tablespoon chopped cilantro

3 ounces (about 1/2 cup tightly packed) drained pickled ginger

Place the fish chunks in a bowl and sprinkle with salt and pepper. Mix together the soy sauce, vinegar, mirin or honey, ginger, water, and cilantro and toss with the fish. Marinate in the refrigerator for at least 30 minutes.

Make small *brochettes* on toothpicks, alternating tuna or salmon pieces and rolled-up or folded strips of pickled ginger. There should be 2 pieces of fish and 2 pieces of ginger per toothpick. Arrange on a platter and serve.

ADVANCE PREPARATION: The marinade can be made a day ahead of time. The skewers can be assembled an hour or so before serving, but make sure you cover them tightly with plastic wrap and refrigerate until shortly before serving.

PER PORTION

Calories	84	Protein	11 G
Fat	2 G	Carbohydrate	3 G
Sodium	121 MG	Cholesterol	17 MG

CHAPTER THREE

SIT-DOWN DINNER PARTIES AND BUFFETS

As for breads, my most frequent choices are the Partially Whole Wheat Sourdough Country Bread on page 382 and the French Sourdough Country Bread on page 380. That's because these are the breads I make every week. When other breads go particularly well with a meal, I have listed them. Naturally, if you really want to keep calories down, bread can be omitted.

I urge you to prepare work schedules with all of these menus. You will often have a choice as to when you begin preparation; for example, you can make sorbets a week before your party if you wish, but also the day before. Work schedules will make entertaining as free of stress as possible for you. The menus are designed to make your guests look forward to coming to your house for dinner, knowing the meal will be not only delicious but also healthful.

AN ELEGANT APRIL SIT-DOWN DINNER
WITH ASPARAGUS AND HERB LASAGNE

———

PINOT D'ALSACE
•
DRIED PORCINI SOUP
TARRAGON BRUSCHETTE (PAGE 77)
•
ASPARAGUS and HERB LASAGNE
SAVORY BAKED TOMATOES, or PAN-FRIED RED
BELL PEPPERS
A SIMPLE SALAD OF ARUGULA and LAMB'S LETTUCE
•
RHUBARB, HONEY, and BLOOD ORANGE SORBET
•
TOKAY PINOT GRIS D'ALSACE or GAVI DI GAVI
CHÂTEAU SIMONE ROUGE (APPELLATION PALETTE)

In this menu, the Asparagus and Herb Lasagne is the essence of new spring produce, a perfect way to celebrate the new season.

The soup, which is really a bouillon, bursting with the flavor of dried mushrooms, is not necessarily a springtime dish; you can make it any time of year, but it happens to make a perfect starter for the lasagne. Intensely flavored but not at all filling, it excites the palate and opens the appetite for the next course. Toasted country bread that has been rubbed with garlic, brushed with olive oil, and sprinkled with fresh tarragon is passed on platters to accompany the soup. I have drunk both a round, not too acidic white wine (a Tokay Pinot Gris d'Alsace or a Gavi dei Gavi or a Chardonnay) and a full-bodied, fruity and not too tannic red wine with this soup (in this case a velvety Château Simone, from just outside Aix-en-Provence). Both go well with it.

The Asparagus and Herb Lasagne is not a tomato sauce lasagne (friends often look confused when I say "asparagus lasagne" until I explain that there is no tomato sauce) but a "white" or béchamel-sauced lasagne, composed of heavenly layers of homemade pasta, parboiled asparagus, fragrant béchamel packed with fresh herbs, and Parmesan. It is pale green and cream colored, so the plate needs a little color to set it off—thus the baked tomatoes. And because I can't serve a meal without a salad (although there are enough herbs in the lasagne to count as a salad), I serve a very lightly seasoned salad of arugula and lamb's lettuce at the same time. This can go right on the plate or on a side plate.

The lasagne, like the soup, could be accompanied by a white wine or a red. The white should be round and not too acidic, the red fruity and full-bodied but not with so big a taste as to overwhelm the lasagne, which is quite subtle. My choice is a Provençal red from the area around Aix, appellation Palette, from Château Simone.

Since rhubarb, strawberries, and asparagus all appear at around the same time, this meal can be an event announcing spring's arrival.

Making This Dinner for a Crowd

The soup will expand easily for a crowd. Just make sure you have 1½ cups per serving.

For the béchamel, as I state in the recipe, you will probably not need all the liquid. I would make the *roux* and stir in about three-quarters of the liquid called for and see how thick a sauce you get. If it is very thick, then continue to add more liquid until you have a creamy consistency. It shouldn't be too thick.

The sorbet is easy to expand for a crowd.

DRIED PORCINI SOUP

SERVES 8

This recipe was inspired by Elizabeth David. Dried *porcini* (*cèpes*) are simmered slowly in chicken or garlic stock (or a very light chicken stock with lots of garlic) for an hour, and the resulting bouillon has a staggeringly intense flavor. I think making it a day ahead of time enhances its taste. The soup has a tonic quality and makes a great starter, light lunch, or even a between-meals drink. I like it with no enrichment other than a few paper-thin mushroom slices and a sprinkle of chopped fresh chives. But I've given an optional egg enrichment for a more substantial bowl of soup.

2   ounces (2 cups, approximately) dried *porcini* (*cèpes*)

1   quart boiling water

2   quarts chicken stock (page 413) or garlic broth (page 415)

1   pound (about 5 medium) fresh or canned tomatoes, chopped

4   large garlic cloves, minced or put through a press

    salt and freshly ground pepper to taste

    a few thinly sliced mushrooms tossed with a teaspoon of fresh lemon juice for garnish

¼   cup chopped fresh chives

OPTIONAL

4   medium eggs, beaten with a squeeze of lemon juice

8   garlic croutons (page 392)

¼   cup freshly grated Parmesan or Gruyère cheese

Place the dried mushrooms in a bowl and pour on the boiling water. Let sit for 15 minutes. Strain through a cheesecloth. Squeeze the mushrooms over the strainer to extract all of the liquid. Rinse the mushrooms thoroughly and squeeze dry over the strainer. Pour the soaking water into a 4-cup measure and add enough water to measure 5 cups.

    Combine the mushrooms, their soaking liquid, the stock, tomatoes, and garlic in a saucepan or soup pot. Bring to a simmer, cover, and simmer gently over very low heat for 1 hour. Strain and return the liquid to the saucepan. Add salt and pepper. Cool, refrigerate overnight, and reheat before serving. Or serve at once, garnishing each bowl with a few slices of mushrooms and some chopped fresh chives.

If you are serving the soup with the egg and lemon enrichment, beat the eggs in a bowl and squeeze in a little lemon juice. Ladle in some hot soup, then stir this back into the soup. Do not boil. Serve at once, garnished with Parmesan or Gruyère, chives, and the garlic croutons.

ADVANCE PREPARATION: This soup tastes even better if it's made a day ahead.

LEFTOVERS: The soup freezes well and is good to have on hand, to be used as either a soup or a stock.

PER PORTION

Calories	79	Protein		2 G	
Fat	2 G	Carbohydrate		14 G	
Sodium	13 MG	Cholesterol		0	

ASPARAGUS AND HERB LASAGNE

SERVES 8

This lasagne is subtle and elegant. It's a springtime dish, inspired by the arrival of asparagus and fresh herbs in the markets. Don't be disheartened by the length of the recipe; once it's put together, it can sit for hours before being heated through and served. The dish is really very simple, with its delectable layers of homemade pasta, béchamel mixed with fresh herbs, cooked asparagus, more fresh herbs, and Parmesan. In France I use white asparagus, which must be peeled. I must say, it's incredibly succulent with this type of asparagus, but green is marvelous as well. The idea of using olive oil for the béchamel is Provençal, and I think just a little bit of olive oil flavors the béchamel in a very nice way. You could substitute butter if you prefer the taste, or, as I like to do (especially if I'm making a large quantity of this lasagne), you could use half butter and half olive oil. The béchamel should be quite thin, like cream.

It's important that you don't bake the lasagne too long. The noodles are very delicate and will become crunchy if exposed to high heat for too long; the herbs will also lose their color and punch. The dish is really just warmed through in a low oven.

(continued)

FOR THE ASPARAGUS AND THE LASAGNE

- 5 large garlic cloves
- 3 pounds asparagus
- salt and freshly ground pepper to taste
- 2 cups freshly grated Parmesan cheese

FOR THE PASTA

triple recipe egg white pasta (page 403)

FOR THE BÉCHAMEL

- 3 cups skim milk
- 1 cup cooking water from the asparagus
- 2 tablespoons olive oil or unsalted butter *or* 1 tablespoon each
- 2½ tablespoons unbleached white flour
- ¼ cup freshly grated Parmesan cheese
- the garlic from the asparagus
- salt and freshly ground white pepper to taste
- pinch of freshly grated nutmeg
- 2 cups tightly packed fresh herbs and vivid salad greens, such as chervil, parsley, tarragon, chives, arugula, basil, washed, dried, and shredded, not too fine, with scissors

First cook the asparagus (you'll need the stock and garlic for the béchamel). Fill a large pot with water and add the garlic. Bring to a boil and allow to simmer while you prepare the asparagus. Break off the ends and peel if you're using white asparagus or if your asparagus is thick and tough, and tie in 2 bundles. Bring the water back to a rolling boil and add about 1 teaspoon salt and the asparagus. Parboil for about 5 or 6 minutes, until the asparagus is cooked through but still sort of crunchy. Remove the asparagus from the water and plunge into cold water to stop the cooking. Cut the stalks in half lengthwise, then into 1-inch lengths; or, if the asparagus is thin, cut into 1-inch lengths on the diagonal, without cutting in half first. Place in a bowl, salt and pepper lightly, and set aside. Continue to simmer the garlic in the cooking water while you prepare the pasta.

Mix up the pasta dough, following the directions on page 403, and wrap in plastic. Set aside and allow to rest for 30 minutes while you prepare the béchamel.

Make the béchamel. Heat the milk and 1 cup of the cooking water from the asparagus in a saucepan. In another heavy-bottomed saucepan, heat the olive oil and/or butter over medium-low heat. Add the flour and cook with the oil or butter for a couple of minutes over medium-low heat, stirring all the while with a whisk or a wooden spoon. When it is just beginning to brown, slowly add the hot milk and asparagus cooking water mixture, stirring all the while with a whisk. Cook over medium heat, stirring constantly, until the sauce begins to thicken. When it gets to the simmering stage, the sauce should be thickening up like cream. Put your saucepan on a Flame Tamer or into a pan of simmering water or over extremely low heat and let it barely simmer for 20 to 30 minutes, stirring often. Remove from the heat and stir in the Parmesan. Remove the garlic from the simmering asparagus cooking water and squeeze it into the béchamel (set aside the remaining cooking water and use as a stock for another dish). Season to taste with salt, pepper, and a pinch of nutmeg. Cover and set aside. A film will form on the top, but you can whisk it away later.

ROLLING OUT THE PASTA AND ASSEMBLING THE LASAGNE: Roll out the pasta very thin (number 4 setting is best; if it's thinner, it will tear or be too insubstantial in the finished lasagne) and cut into wide strips that will fit your lasagne pan. Allow to dry for 15 minutes on a lightly floured board or kitchen towel. Meanwhile, bring a large pot of water to a boil (the best method is to add some water to the asparagus cooking water and cook the noodles in this).

When you're assembling the lasagne, you need to work fairly quickly, so get everything organized before you begin. Oil or butter your lasagne pan generously and have your béchamel, asparagus, herbs, and Parmesan within reach.

Remove a cup of béchamel from the pot and stir all but a generous handful of the herbs into the rest of the béchamel.

Cook only a few noodles at a time, enough for 1 layer. When the water comes to a boil, add salt if necessary and a drop of oil and cook the lasagne noodles, a few at a time, just until they float to the surface of the pot, about 10 to 20 seconds. Remove from the water and cool in a bowl of cold water. Drain on clean kitchen towels. Don't let the noodles sit too long on the towels once drained or they'll become sticky. Place the noodles in a layer on the bottom of the dish, overlapping very slightly. Spread a thin layer of asparagus over this and top with a layer of the béchamel with the herbs. Spread the béchamel and herbs evenly over the lasagne. Sprinkle on some Parmesan.

Cook the next batch of pasta and repeat the layers. You should have about 4 layers of pasta, asparagus, béchamel with herbs, and Parmesan. The last (5th) layer of pasta will be the top layer of the lasagne. Spread the reserved béchamel without the herbs over the top and sprinkle with Parmesan. Cover with foil or plastic wrap until you're ready to bake.

Preheat the oven to 325 degrees. Bake, uncovered, in the oven for 15 to 20 minutes or until the top is just beginning to brown. You can also warm it in a 250-degree oven for up to an hour. Remove from the heat. Sprinkle on the remaining herbs and serve. You can turn off the oven and keep the lasagne warm in the oven while eating your first course.

NOTE: If you are multiplying this recipe for a crowd, you might find proportions a bit different for the béchamel. When I made it for 30, for instance, I ended up using only about three-quarters of the liquid after I'd multiplied everything by 4, and I had plenty of thin, creamy béchamel, which had to simmer for quite a while to thicken.

ADVANCE PREPARATION: The various components of this dish can be prepared a day ahead of time. The pasta can be mixed up, wrapped in plastic, and refrigerated or frozen. The béchamel will hold for a day in the refrigerator, as will the cooked asparagus. The herbs should be prepped on the day you make the lasagne. You can pick the leaves off the stems and wash them a few hours ahead of time, but make sure they are perfectly dry before you store them.

LEFTOVERS: Cover with foil and reheat in a moderate oven. The lasagne will be good to eat, but not as pretty, for a day or two.

PER PORTION

Calories	332	Protein	23 G
Fat	14 G	Carbohydrate	31 G
Sodium	653 MG	Cholesterol	77 MG

RAW TUNA OR SALMON AND PICKLED GINGER SKEWERS

SERVES 10 AS AN HORS D'OEUVRE

These are marinated sashimilike hors d'oeuvres on toothpicks. They're very easy to put together. Either tuna or salmon would be suitable for this. Make sure the fish is impeccably fresh.

1 pound very fresh tuna, weighed after the bones, dark meat, and skin are removed, cut into ½-inch chunks, *or* salmon fillet, small bones and skin removed, cut into ½-inch chunks

salt and freshly ground pepper to taste

1 tablespoon tamari soy sauce

1 tablespoon rice wine vinegar, cider vinegar, or balsamic vinegar

2 tablespoons mirin *or* 2 teaspoons mild-flavored honey

a 1-inch piece of fresh ginger, peeled and grated or minced

2 tablespoons water

1 tablespoon chopped cilantro

3 ounces (about ½ cup tightly packed) drained pickled ginger

Place the fish chunks in a bowl and sprinkle with salt and pepper. Mix together the soy sauce, vinegar, mirin or honey, ginger, water, and cilantro and toss with the fish. Marinate in the refrigerator for at least 30 minutes.

Make small *brochettes* on toothpicks, alternating tuna or salmon pieces and rolled-up or folded strips of pickled ginger. There should be 2 pieces of fish and 2 pieces of ginger per toothpick. Arrange on a platter and serve.

ADVANCE PREPARATION: The marinade can be made a day ahead of time. The skewers can be assembled an hour or so before serving, but make sure you cover them tightly with plastic wrap and refrigerate until shortly before serving.

PER PORTION

Calories	84	Protein	11 G
Fat	2 G	Carbohydrate	3 G
Sodium	121 MG	Cholesterol	17 MG

CHAPTER THREE

SIT-DOWN DINNER PARTIES AND BUFFETS

SAVORY BAKED TOMATOES

SERVES 8

There are many versions of baked tomatoes. When they're baked *à la Proven-çale,* they're topped with herbs, lots of garlic, olive oil, and bread crumbs. This version is very simple, meant to embellish but not detract from a subtle main dish like the preceding Asparagus and Herb Lasagne or complement but not compete with a redolent fish or chicken dish.

8 medium-size ripe tomatoes

   salt and freshly ground pepper to taste

   crumbled dried or chopped fresh thyme, rosemary, oregano, or *herbes de Provence*

2 tablespoons olive oil

Preheat the oven to 400 degrees. Cut the tomatoes across the top, about ¼ inch down from the stem. Place on a lightly oiled baking sheet. Salt and pepper lightly and sprinkle with herbs. Drizzle with olive oil.

   Bake for 20 minutes, until the skins split and the tomatoes soften. They should not collapse, however. Serve hot.

ADVANCE PREPARATION: The tomatoes can be prepped and sprinkled with the herbs hours ahead of time. Drizzle on the olive oil and bake shortly before serving.

PER PORTION

Calories	58	Protein	1 G
Fat	4 G	Carbohydrate	5 G
Sodium	10 MG	Cholesterol	0

ARUGULA AND LAMB'S LETTUCE SALAD

SERVES 8

This is a lovely side salad with a very light vinaigrette. I hate to interfere with the brilliant flavor of arugula by dressing it with too much vinegar.

> **a couple of generous handfuls of arugula, trimmed, washed, and dried (6 ounces)**
>
> **a couple of generous handfuls of lamb's lettuce, trimmed, washed, and dried (6 ounces)**
>
> 1½ **tablespoons balsamic vinegar**
>
> 6 **tablespoons olive oil**
>
> **salt and freshly ground pepper to taste**

Toss together the arugula and lamb's lettuce. Whisk together the vinegar and olive oil. Add salt and freshly ground pepper to taste. Toss with the salad just before serving.

ADVANCE PREPARATION: The lettuces can be washed and dried hours ahead of time. Store in the refrigerator, wrapped in a kitchen towel and sealed in a plastic bag.

PER PORTION

Calories	78	Protein	0
Fat	8 G	Carbohydrate	I G
Sodium	5 MG	Cholesterol	0

PAN-FRIED RED BELL PEPPERS

SERVES 8

Whenever you need color on a plate, these peppers make a perfect side dish. They can be garlicky and seasoned with thyme or not, depending on what you're serving them with.

- 1 tablespoon olive oil
- 4 medium (about 2 pounds) red bell peppers, seeds and membranes removed, cut into thin lengthwise slices
- 1 garlic clove, minced or put through a press (optional)
- 1/2 teaspoon fresh thyme leaves *or* 1/4 teaspoon crumbled dried (optional)

  salt and freshly ground pepper to taste

Heat the olive oil in a nonstick or well-seasoned frying pan over medium heat and add the peppers. Sauté, stirring often, for about 10 minutes or a little longer, until the peppers are soft and fragrant. If you're using the garlic and/or thyme, add halfway through the cooking. Stir in salt and freshly ground pepper to taste, remove from the heat, and serve.

ADVANCE PREPARATION: These peppers can be prepped and cooked until just about tender (about 8 minutes) and removed from the heat several hours before serving. Finish cooking just before serving.

LEFTOVERS: Leftover sautéed peppers make great toppings for *crostini* or additions to sandwiches. They can also be added to salads.

PER PORTION

Calories	40	Protein	I G
Fat	3 G	Carbohydrate	4 G
Sodium	2 MG	Cholesterol	0

RHUBARB, HONEY, AND BLOOD ORANGE COMPOTE, SOUP, OR SORBET

SERVES 8

This recipe began as the first stage in a sorbet I was making up as I went along. I liked the initial combination of rhubarb, blood orange juice, and honey so much that I decided I'd call it a compote and stop there. Then I thought I might as well see how the sorbet would turn out, so I pureed the mixture. When I tasted the puree, it was good enough to serve as a soup, garnished with fresh mint. But I went ahead and froze it anyway; and I like all 3 versions of this terrific mixture.

Compote

4   pounds fresh rhubarb stalks, washed, trimmed, and sliced into 1-inch lengths

3   cups blood orange juice

2/3 cup lavender or clover honey to taste

Combine all the ingredients in a nonreactive saucepan. Bring to a simmer. Simmer for 6 to 8 minutes, just until the rhubarb is tender when pierced with a fork. Remove from the heat and allow to cool slightly before serving or serve chilled.

Soup

Make the compote as above. Puree in a blender or food processor with the steel blade. Stir in 3 to 4 tablespoons fresh lemon juice, to taste. Chill and serve garnished with fresh mint leaves and sliced strawberries.

Sorbet

Make the soup as above. Freeze in an ice cream maker or in a covered bowl or baking dish in the freezer. Puree again in a food processor fitted with the steel blade when the mixture has just frozen. Transfer to individual serving dishes, a loaf pan lined with plastic wrap, or an attractive mold and freeze. Let soften for 15 minutes in the refrigerator before serving.

The Fish with Veracruzana Sauce is given in two versions for this menu, first with fish fillets baked in foil, then in its traditional form, as a whole fish baked with the sauce. Veracruzana sauce—a pungent mixture of tomatoes, onions and garlic, capers, green olives, and pickled jalapeño—is a Mexican classic and always a hit. (If you make extra, you can use it up later in the week as a topping for pizza or spaghetti. The menu would make a beautiful buffet dinner if you did the whole fish version, with everything laid out on pretty ceramic platters. But each dish makes equally colorful plate servings.

The meal is an easy one to organize, although as always an extra hand is welcome for squeezing limes and making salsa.

Dessert here is a splurge, the only chocolate dessert I make. It was inspired by the minted bitter chocolate sorbet I've eaten at Alain Dutournier's Au Trou Gascon and his Carré des Feuillants in Paris. I am not much of a chocolate lover, but this is irresistible.

Wines are flexible here. Dry whites and rosés, from the south of France or from Alsace (I'm thinking of Riesling), would go with the meal, as would fruity southern French or Spanish reds or light fruity reds from the Beaujolais region or the Loire.

Making This Dinner for a Crowd

All of these dishes multiply easily, although fish isn't easy to do for more than 12 people. If you are serving a large crowd, I suggest doing a buffet, because the dishes will be so pretty on large platters. In this case, don't do *papillotes,* but cook fillets in a baking dish with the sauce (see recipe) or cook large whole fish.

CUCUMBER SALSA SALAD

SERVES 6

Like the Zucchini and Avocado Salsa Salad on page 142, this salad is a light way to begin a Mexican meal. It's also vaguely reminiscent of gazpacho, with its clean, crisp, *picante* flavors.

5 medium-size ripe tomatoes, chopped

1 small red onion, finely minced

2 jalapeño or serrano peppers, seeded and finely chopped

4 to 6 tablespoons chopped cilantro

1 tablespoon balsamic vinegar

   salt and freshly ground pepper to taste

1 European (seedless) cucumber, very finely diced

   juice of 1 large lemon

2 tablespoons olive oil

   leaf lettuce for serving

1 avocado, sliced, and cilantro sprigs for garnish

Combine the tomatoes, onion, chili peppers, cilantro, vinegar, and salt.

Toss the cucumber with the lemon juice and salt and pepper to taste. Combine with the tomato salsa. Toss with the olive oil and adjust seasonings. Refrigerate until ready to serve.

Serve on lettuce leaves and garnish with sprigs of cilantro and avocado slices.

ADVANCE PREPARATION: This salad will hold for a few hours in the refrigerator, but add the cilantro and garnishes close to serving time.

LEFTOVERS: Serve on tortilla chips or Toasted Pita Triangles (page 71), or on red pepper wedges or small lettuce leaves, as an hors d'oeuvre.

PER PORTION

Calories	126	Protein	2 G
Fat	10 G	Carbohydrate	10 G
Sodium	13 MG	Cholesterol	0

FISH WITH VERACRUZANA SAUCE

SERVES 6

In Mexico this sauce is usually served with a whole baked fish. You could do the same here, but I often buy fish fillets and cook them in foil or in a baking dish with the pungent tomato sauce.

FOR THE FISH

1½ pounds whiting, snapper, or bream fillets

juice of 1½ lemons

salt and freshly ground pepper to taste

FOR THE VERACRUZANA SAUCE

1 tablespoon olive oil

1½ onions, sliced into thin strips

3 large garlic cloves, minced or put through a press

2¼ pounds (about 12 medium) fresh or canned tomatoes, peeled, seeded, and chopped

3 tablespoons sliced pitted green olives

2 tablespoons drained capers to taste

1 or 2 canned jalapeño peppers (in *escabeche*) to taste, seeded and sliced

Sprinkle the fish with lemon juice and salt and pepper and set aside while you prepare the sauce.

Heat the olive oil in a heavy-bottomed saucepan, skillet, or casserole and add the onion and garlic. Sauté over medium heat until the onion is tender. Add the tomatoes, olives, capers, and jalapeño and bring to a simmer, stirring occasionally, for 30 minutes. Add salt and freshly ground pepper to taste and remove from the heat.

Preheat the oven to 450 degrees. Cut 6 double thicknesses of aluminum foil, large enough to accommodate the fish fillets. Brush with olive oil and lay the fish on the squares. Spoon about 2 heaped tablespoons of the sauce over each portion. Fold the foil loosely over the fish and crimp the edges together tightly. Place on a baking sheet. Heat any additional sauce in a saucepan.

Bake for 8 to 10 minutes and serve in the foil. Cut each serving open along the crimped edge, place on plates and serve, accompanied with rice and steamed zucchini. Pass the additional sauce.

(continued)

ALTERNATIVE METHOD: Preheat the oven to 425 degrees. Instead of using *papillotes,* lay the fillets in an oiled baking dish. Spoon half the sauce over the fish, cover tightly, and bake for 15 minutes or until the fish flakes. Serve with the remaining sauce.

This would be good with whole whitings or a whole large fish like snapper or porgy. In this case, spoon half the sauce over and around the fish, cover the baking dish tightly with foil, and bake for 15 to 20 minutes for small whitings or 30 to 40 minutes for a large fish, until the fish flakes easily with a fork. Heat the remaining sauce and pour over the fish. Serve hot.

ADVANCE PREPARATION: The Veracruzana sauce will hold for up to a day in the refrigerator. The fish can be prepared in the *papillotes* or baking dish several hours before baking.

LEFTOVERS: Use leftover sauce for *bruschette* (page 77), or toss with pasta (with any leftover fish, broken up with a fork; see recipe, page 238). Leftover fish can also be used in salads.

PER PORTION

Calories	169	Protein	23 G
Fat	5 G	Carbohydrate	10 G
Sodium	325 MG	Cholesterol	76 MG

SAUCE PER ½ CUP

Calories	78	Protein	2 G
Fat	4 G	Carbohydrate	11 G
Sodium	292 MG	Cholesterol	0

STEAMED ZUCCHINI

SERVES 6

As simple as it is, this steamed zucchini, reheated in a little butter or olive oil, is probably what I serve most often as an accompaniment to complex fish or chicken dishes. The flavor of the zucchini is delicate, and the slices look pretty on the plate. As a variation you can use yellow squash or a combination.

1½ pounds (3 medium) zucchini or yellow squash or a combination, sliced about ¼ inch thick on the diagonal

1 tablespoon unsalted butter or olive oil

   salt and freshly ground pepper to taste

2 or 3 tablespoons chopped fresh parsley to taste

Steam the squash until just tender but still bright green, 7 to 10 minutes. Remove from the heat and refresh under cold water. Just before serving, heat the butter or olive oil in a nonstick skillet and reheat the squash, adding salt and freshly ground pepper to taste. Toss with the parsley and serve.

ADVANCE PREPARATION: The squash can be prepped and steamed hours ahead of time and reheated at the last minute.

PER PORTION

Calories	33	Protein	I G
Fat	2 G	Carbohydrate	3 G
Sodium	24 MG	Cholesterol	5 MG

BITTER CHOCOLATE SORBET WITH MINT

MAKES 1 QUART, SERVING 10

I have never been a chocolate eater, but there is a minty chocolate sorbet that Alain Dutournier makes at his two Paris restaurants, Au Trou Gascon and Carré des Feuillants, that I always order. I asked Monsieur Dutournier for his recipe, but he is keeping it a secret, so I set about to figure it out myself. I've never eaten as much chocolate as during the weeks I was working on this recipe; I must say I enjoyed "having" to taste my various tries and adore what I have finally settled on. It's both intensely chocolatey—though less chocolatey than some chocolate sorbets I've tasted in Paris—and minty.

I haven't been able to decide whether I prefer the sorbet with or without vanilla. With vanilla the sorbet is slightly sweeter and rounder; without it's more intensely chocolatey. I'm going to leave it up to you. Try it both ways.

$1/2$ vanilla bean *or* $1/2$ teaspoon vanilla extract (optional)

3 cups very strong brewed peppermint tea (made with $1/4$ cup loose dried peppermint tea or 4 tea bags)

$3/4$ cup sugar

1 tablespoon instant coffee powder

$3/4$ pound bittersweet chocolate, preferably French

$1/2$ teaspoon peppermint extract (optional; omit if you want a subtler mint flavor)

4 medium egg whites

fresh mint sprigs for garnish

If you're using a vanilla bean, scrape the seeds into the peppermint tea and add the sugar. Heat to boiling, stirring with a wooden spoon to dissolve the sugar, and boil for 2 or 3 minutes. Turn off the heat and stir in the instant coffee. Break up the chocolate and add to the tea. Stir until the chocolate has melted. Stir in the vanilla extract if you're using that, along with the peppermint extract if desired. Allow to cool to lukewarm.

Beat the egg whites until they form stiff but not dry peaks. Strain the chocolate mixture into the egg whites. Tap the strainer against the bowl with the egg whites to make sure all the chocolate goes in. Stir together with a whisk or transfer to a food processor and quickly mix together.

Transfer the mixture to a stainless-steel bowl or an ice cream maker. Freeze in the ice cream maker according to the manufacturer's directions. Or cover the bowl and place in the freezer; when the mixture has just frozen solid, remove from the freezer, cut the sorbet into pieces, and transfer to a food processor. Blend, using the pulse action, until you get an icy, smooth mixture.

This menu is easy to shop for and cook all in the same day. It's easy to plan a dinner party based on a large whole fish. The fish will make an attractive and dramatic centerpiece just by virtue of its size, and all the better if it's surrounded by beautiful wisps of carrot, leek, and zucchini, as it is here. Although cutting the vegetables into julienne takes time, cooking them takes only about five minutes, and as for the fish, practically all you have to do is throw it in the baking dish, season it, and make sure it's securely covered before you bake it.

The crunchy curly endive salad with croutons and walnuts is a simple, appetite-whetting way to begin this meal. The fish is served with the slivered vegetables and sautéed oyster mushrooms, which go extremely well with sea trout and salmon. While relatively inexpensive, oyster mushrooms are luxurious. They're also very easy to prepare and don't suffer if they're cooked ahead of time and reheated. I find the vegetables sufficient as side dishes, but you could also serve rice or other grains or potatoes as well. It would be a filling meal.

This is a perfect menu for showing off rich, buttery white wines. The Tokay Pinot Gris d'Alsace is my first choice, although a good Vouvray would be just as good, and a Chardonnay or a rich white Burgundy or Châteauneuf-du-Pape would also work.

Making This Dinner for a Crowd

This isn't a menu I'd choose for a crowd. I'd want to bake only one fish. I suppose if you have two ovens it wouldn't be so difficult, but making julienne with lots of vegetables will take a lot of time.

FRISÉE WITH GARLIC CROUTONS AND WALNUTS

SERVES 6

Crisp, garlicky squares of toasted, preferably sourdough, bread and crunchy walnuts make this simple salad come alive. The walnut oil dressing is great with the bitter curly endive lettuce.

1 large head of curly endive lettuce, tough outer leaves removed, leaves washed and dried, and broken up

1½ cups cubed garlic croutons (page 392)

⅓ cup broken walnut pieces, preferably fresh walnuts

¼ cup torn basil or chervil leaves

1 recipe Low-Fat Walnut Vinaigrette (page 435)

Just before serving, toss all the ingredients together with the dressing in an attractive salad bowl.

ADVANCE PREPARATION: The lettuce and herbs can be washed and dried, the croutons prepared, and the walnuts cracked hours ahead of time. The dressing can be made an hour or 2 ahead of time as well. Store the lettuce in the refrigerator, wrapped in a towel and sealed in a plastic bag. Tear up the herbs shortly before serving.

PER PORTION

Calories	160	Protein	5 G
Fat	9 G	Carbohydrate	16 G
Sodium	193 MG	Cholesterol	0

BAKED WHOLE SALMON OR SEA TROUT WITH SLIVERED VEGETABLES

SERVES 6

There is something dramatic about serving a large whole fish. Pink-fleshed sea trout is much less expensive than salmon and has a milder flavor and lovely, succulent flesh. You will need a baking dish large enough to accommodate the fish, which will be about 18 inches long or longer. But you can always snip off part of the tail, and it's all right if the tail hangs over the edge of the baking dish, as long as the whole fish is covered with foil and the dish well sealed.

1 very fresh large sea trout or salmon (about 4 pounds), cleaned

1 tablespoon olive oil plus another tablespoon for the dish and fish

2 large carrots, peeled and cut into 2-inch-long julienne

2 medium leeks, white part only, cleaned and cut into 2-inch-long julienne

3 medium zucchini, cut into 2-inch-long julienne

3 to 4 tablespoons water, as needed

   salt and freshly ground pepper to taste

$\frac{1}{2}$ cup dry white wine

$\frac{1}{2}$ bunch of fresh dill

2 lemons, cut into wedges

Keep the fish refrigerated until 2 hours before you're ready to bake. Heat 1 tablespoon olive oil in a large nonstick or well-seasoned frying pan. Add the julienned vegetables and cook, stirring over medium-high heat, for a couple of minutes. Add 3 to 4 tablespoons water, as needed, and salt and pepper to taste and continue to cook, stirring or shaking the pan, for another 5 minutes, until just barely soft. Remove from the heat.

    Oil a baking dish that will accommodate the fish. Spread the vegetables around the edge of the dish so that the fish will be in the middle.

    Preheat the oven to 425 degrees. Rinse the fish and pat dry. Rub lightly with olive oil and salt and pepper both sides. Stuff the cavity generously with sprigs of fresh dill. Lay in the baking dish and sprinkle with lots of chopped fresh dill. Pour the wine into the baking dish and cover with foil. Crimp the foil securely around the edges of the baking dish. Bake for 30 minutes or until the fish flakes easily with a fork and is still juicy in the middle. Remove from the heat and serve at once.

(continued)

TO SERVE: You can transfer the fish to a platter and surround it again with the vegetables, or transfer the vegetables to a serving dish, or you can serve from the baking dish, which is easier, and if your baking dish is attractive it will look nice as well. Using a sharp knife, cut lengthwise straight down the middle of the fish. Remove the skin, which should come off easily. Sprinkle the fish with more dill. Now cut crosswise slices from the middle to the back and to the stomach and lift the portions off the bone.

Once you have removed the fish from one side, remove the bones in one piece by lifting from the tail and bending the skeleton toward the head. The bottom flesh should fall off (ease it off with a spatula or knife if it doesn't). Sprinkle the bottom half of the fish with dill. Continue cutting portions from the bottom half and serve, garnishing each portion with the vegetables and lemon wedges. Serve sautéed oyster mushrooms (page 111) on the side, and/or rice or potatoes.

ADVANCE PREPARATION: The vegetables can be prepared and cooked hours ahead of time and left at room temperature. The fish can be prepped and made ready to bake hours ahead of time. Make sure that it is at room temperature when you put it in the oven.

LEFTOVERS: The fish and vegetables would be great tossed with pasta, added to an omelet or added to a salad.

PER PORTION

Calories	411	Protein	48 G
Fat	19 G	Carbohydrate	10 G
Sodium	124 MG	Cholesterol	127 MG

SAUTÉED OYSTER MUSHROOMS

SERVES 6

Oyster mushrooms, called *pleurottes* in France, have a satisfying, succulent, meaty texture and rich flavor. They are now being cultivated and aren't as expensive as many other wild mushrooms, and they make a great side dish with fish and meat, as well as a marvelous topping for grains and pasta. They are so substantial that I like them as a main dish for a light supper. These can be prepared hours ahead of time and reheated just before serving.

1 tablespoon unsalted butter or olive oil

2 large garlic cloves, minced or put through a press

1½ pounds fresh oyster mushrooms, trimmed, briefly rinsed, patted dry, and broken in half if very large

¼ cup dry white wine

1 teaspoon soy sauce or more to taste

salt and freshly ground pepper to taste

½ teaspoon crumbled dried *or* 1 teaspoon fresh thyme leaves

Heat the butter or olive oil in a large nonstick or well-seasoned frying pan and add 1 garlic clove. When it begins to color, add the mushrooms and the remaining garlic and stir over medium-high heat for about 5 minutes, until the mushrooms begin to release their liquid. Add the white wine, soy sauce, and salt and pepper to taste and continue to sauté for about 10 minutes or until about two thirds of the liquid in the pan has evaporated. The mushrooms should be moist. Add the thyme, stir for a couple of minutes longer, and remove from the heat. Adjust seasonings. Serve at once or cover and set aside until just before serving time. Reheat in the frying pan before serving.

ADVANCE PREPARATION: These mushrooms will hold for hours on top of the stove after you cook them.

LEFTOVERS: The mushrooms are great just as they are, reheated. They also make a terrific topping for *crostini* (page 392), a filling for omelets, and a topping for grains and pasta.

PER PORTION

Calories	49	Protein	3 G
Fat	2 G	Carbohydrate	6 G
Sodium	82 MG	Cholesterol	5 MG

AN EASY SIT-DOWN DINNER PARTY

FOR SIX

———

CRÉMANT D'ALSACE, GEWÜRZTRAMINER,
or VOUVRAY PÉTILLANT

·

GRILLED FISH STEAKS with YOGURT CURRY SAUCE
BASMATI RICE
PAN-FRIED CUCUMBERS

·

ARUGULA and MUSHROOM SALAD with FRESH HERBS

·

RASPBERRIES with FROMAGE BLANC

·

ALSACE RIESLING or BROUILLY

This menu grew out of an impromptu dinner party, yet it's also elegant. I went to the market to buy fish to test this recipe, knowing I had house-guests who would be willing eaters. Meanwhile, another friend showed up unexpectedly (with a bottle of Brouilly, which I discovered went beautifully with the meal), and my houseguests had gone out and bought frozen raspber-ries (it was November). Suddenly we had the makings for a real feast. We ate at the kitchen table, but the next time I served this repast in a candlelit dining room. The meal is very simple and quick to make (although the fish needs to marinate for an hour); it's the kind of menu you could serve to guests after a long day at the office, with one quick stop at a fish market and produce stand between work and home.

I serve the salad after the main dish here, because the tart arugula is a nice palate cleanser after the curry, even though the curried yogurt sauce isn't very strong (and it's certainly not rich). You could just as well serve it as a first course if you prefer.

This is definitely a sit-down meal and not a buffet, because of the grilled or broiled fish. Because both the fish and rice are cooked at the last minute, I would make this meal only for people you can leave on their own or invite into the kitchen while you cook.

There are several things you can keep on hand for this meal so that the minimum of shopping is required: yogurt and basmati rice, lemons and garlic, *fromage blanc*, and even frozen raspberries.

A bubbly aperitif is nice here, but a glass of spicy Gewürztraminer would herald the mildly spicy main dish equally well and could even be sipped into the first course. The first time I made this meal I had planned to serve it with an Alsace Riesling; but my friend's bottle of chilled Brouilly, a light, delicate red wine from the Beaujolais region of Burgundy, was also a good match. So you can go with a fruity white wine (such as a Riesling, Gewürztraminer, or Vouvray) or a light, chilled red wine from the Loire or Beaujolais.

This dinner party is really suitable at any time of year. That, and its insouciance, is one of the best reasons I can think of to make it part of your repertoire.

Making This Dinner for a Crowd

I wouldn't make this meal for too many people, because it's too difficult to handle grilling all of those pieces of fish unless you have help. The recipes will multiply easily. Other aspects of the meal make it viable for a crowd, if you can handle the fish and cooking large quantities of rice (you have to have a very big pot). The sauce doesn't have to be heated and can be made hours in advance; the salad, too, can be ready hours in advance, as can the cucumbers and dessert.

GRILLED FISH STEAKS WITH YOGURT CURRY SAUCE

SERVES 6

This sauce is light and pungent and goes well with all kinds of fish as well as with chicken. I've used a light, firm-fleshed fish here, a member of the cod family called pollack. Haddock or cod steaks would also do. A stronger, steakier fish like swordfish is also suitable.

FOR THE FISH

salt and freshly ground pepper to taste

6 fish steaks, such as pollack, haddock, cod, or swordfish, about ¾ inch thick (6 ounces each)

juice of 1 large lemon

1 tablespoon olive oil

1 garlic clove, minced or put through a press

FOR THE SAUCE

6 tablespoons fresh lemon juice

1½ teaspoons mild curry powder

½ to ¾ teaspoon ground cumin to taste

1 teaspoon crushed coriander seeds

salt and freshly ground pepper to taste

1 teaspoon grated fresh ginger

2 cups plain nonfat yogurt

chopped cilantro or cilantro sprigs for garnish

Salt and pepper the fish steaks on both sides. Combine the lemon juice for the fish, the olive oil, garlic, and more salt and pepper. Pour into 1 or 2 flat baking dishes large enough to accommodate all of the fish and add the steaks. Marinate for 1 to 2 hours, in the refrigerator if the weather is hot, turning the steaks over halfway through.

Combine all of the ingredients for the sauce. Taste and adjust seasonings.

Preheat a grill or broiler. Brush the fish on both sides with the marinade and grill or broil for 3 minutes on each side or until the fish is opaque and flakes easily with a fork. Remove from the heat and distribute among plates or set on a platter. Spoon sauce over each steak, garnish with cilantro, and serve. Pass extra sauce at the table; it's good on the rice.

ADVANCE PREPARATION: The sauce and marinade will hold for several hours in the refrigerator.

LEFTOVERS: Use leftover sauce and/or rice for a salad.

PER PORTION

Calories	229	Protein	38 G
Fat	4 G	Carbohydrate	9 G
Sodium	205 MG	Cholesterol	123 MG

BASMATI RICE

SERVES 6

Basmati rice has an earthy, perfumed fragrance all its own. It's a very light, delicate rice and is perfect with curries and for pilafs. You can find it in Indian import stores as well as stores that stock a good selection of grains. These are Julie Sahni's instructions for cooking basmati rice. They are incredibly quick, simple, and fail-safe. The rice should be cooked just before serving. It takes only 5 minutes. Make sure you have a warm serving dish ready.

      2 cups basmati rice
  3½ to 4 quarts water
        salt

First wash the rice in several changes of water, until the water is no longer milky. Do this by first running water over the rice in a strainer. Then place the rice in a bowl and fill with water (note how milky the water becomes). Drain and fill the bowl again. Repeat until the water is relatively clear.

   Now place the rice in the bowl, cover by an inch with water, and let sit for 30 minutes.

   Meanwhile, bring a large pot of water, 3½ to 4 quarts, to a boil and add some salt. Drain the rice and add it to the pot. Stir the rice for about 30 seconds so that it doesn't stick to the bottom of the pot. Bring the water back to a boil and cook the rice, uncovered, for 5 minutes. Drain, shake in the strainer or colander to rid the rice of excess water, and serve at once in a heated dish.

ADVANCE PREPARATION: Even though the rice is cooked at the last minute, you can have your water simmering and ready ahead of time. Remember to allow for 30 minutes of soaking time.

LEFTOVERS: This kind of rice makes a delicious leftover. I like the flavor so much that I often mix it with a yogurt vinaigrette and herbs for a lunchtime salad. Try it, mixed with the vinaigrette of your choice (pages 426–35), herbs, and pine nuts, as a filling for vine leaves. It can also be reheated in the oven or sautéed in a little oil and served with vegetables.

PER PORTION

Calories	225	Protein	4 G
Fat	.40 G	Carbohydrate	49 G
Sodium	3 MG	Cholesterol	0

PAN-FRIED CUCUMBERS

SERVES 6

These delicate sautéed cucumbers go nicely with curries. You can sauté them in olive oil, butter, or margarine. Be careful not to overcook them.

1 tablespoon olive oil, margarine, or butter

1 garlic clove, minced or put through a press (optional)

2 long European (seedless) cucumbers, peeled and sliced $1/4$ inch thick

juice of $1/2$ lemon (optional)

salt and freshly ground pepper to taste

$1^1/2$ tablespoons finely minced fresh parsley or dill

Heat the oil or butter in a large skillet and add the garlic if desired. Sauté over medium heat for 1 minute. Add the cucumbers and sauté over medium-high heat, stirring, for 5 to 10 minutes. They should soften and become translucent but should not brown. Add the lemon juice if desired, salt and pepper to taste, and transfer to a warm serving dish. Sprinkle with chopped fresh parsley or dill and serve.

ADVANCE PREPARATION: The cucumbers can be sliced hours ahead of serving and refrigerated. You could sauté them for about 5 minutes a few hours ahead of time and reheat them, adding the lemon juice and parsley or dill just before serving.

PER PORTION

Calories	55	Protein	I G
Fat	4 G	Carbohydrate	6 G
Sodium	II MG	Cholesterol	0

ARUGULA AND MUSHROOM SALAD WITH FRESH HERBS

SERVES 6

I love the bitter, pungent flavor of arugula. Here it goes nicely with the subtly flavored mushrooms, all enhanced with chervil and/or basil and a very mild vinaigrette.

- ¼ pound mushrooms, trimmed, rinsed, dried, and sliced paper-thin
- juice of ½ lemon
- 1 tablespoon chopped fresh basil or parsley
- 1½ tablespoons sherry vinegar or champagne vinegar
- ½ teaspoon Dijon mustard
- 1 small garlic clove, minced or put through a press (optional)
- salt and freshly ground pepper to taste
- 5 tablespoons olive oil or a combination of olive oil and sunflower or safflower oil
- 6 ounces (about 5 cups) arugula, washed and dried
- 12 fresh chervil sprigs (optional)

Toss the mushrooms with the lemon juice and basil or parsley. Set aside in a covered bowl until ready to toss with the salad.

Mix together the vinegar, mustard, garlic if desired, and salt and pepper. Add the oil and combine well. Just before serving, toss with the arugula, mushrooms, and chervil.

ADVANCE PREPARATION: The washed greens and mushrooms will hold for several hours in the refrigerator. Wrap the arugula in a clean kitchen towel, then seal in a plastic bag. The vinaigrette will hold for a few hours as well.

PER PORTION

Calories	109	Protein	1 G
Fat	11 G	Carbohydrate	2 G
Sodium	25 MG	Cholesterol	0

RASPBERRIES WITH FROMAGE BLANC

SERVES 6

This dessert couldn't be simpler. You can make it in summer with fresh raspberries or in winter with unsweetened frozen raspberries, which will be even juicier. When you mix up the berries, their liquid, and the *fromage blanc*, you get a bright pink puddinglike mixture.

3 cups fresh raspberries or thawed frozen unsweetened raspberries

juice of 1 lemon (for fresh raspberries) *or* 2 tablespoons fresh lemon juice (for frozen raspberries)

1 tablespoon sugar (for fresh raspberries) *or* 2 tablespoons honey or sugar (for frozen raspberries)

3 cups *fromage blanc* (page 417)

fresh mint leaves for garnish

If you're using fresh raspberries, toss in a bowl with the juice of 1 lemon and 1 tablespoon sugar, cover, and chill for 1 to 2 hours. The berries should have released some juice at the end of this time. Place the berries, with their juice, in a large bowl. Crush some of the berries with the back of a wooden spoon.

    If you're using frozen berries, stir in the 2 tablespoons lemon juice and 2 tablespoons honey or sugar. Toss the berries with the *fromage blanc*. Cover and refrigerate for several hours or serve at once in attractive bowls, garnished with mint.

VARIATION:

Raspberries Topped with Fromage Blanc: If you don't want this to be like a pudding, use fresh berries, toss with the lemon juice and honey or sugar (this can be done a few hours in advance), and simply top with large dollops (about 3 to 4 tablespoons) *fromage blanc*. Serve at once.

ADVANCE PREPARATION: This will hold for several hours in the refrigerator.

PER PORTION

Calories	139	Protein	13 G
Fat	1 G	Carbohydrate	20 G
Sodium	367 MG	Cholesterol	4 MG

A SIT-DOWN DINNER FOR FOUR
WITH MEDITERRANEAN FLAVORS

———

CHAMPAGNE

•

TOMATO SALAD

•

MONKFISH in BROTH with POTATOES, BASIL,
and SAFFRON

•

PINEAPPLE with MINT
ORANGE BISCOTTI (PAGE 409)

•

1988 CHÂTEAU DU TRIGNON CÔTES-DU-RHÔNE
BLANC DE BLANCS CÉPAGE VIOGNIER

There are special touches in this menu—the saffron in the fish broth and the champagne and the good white wine, the simple elegance of the opening salad—that make it a dinner to be served to friends who love good food and Mediterranean flavors. This is a spring/summer/early fall meal, when basil abounds and good tomatoes are to be found.

The fish course, which is served in flat wide soup bowls because it consists of pieces of poached fish served in a heady saffron- and *pistou*-flavored broth, has a big taste, and it's filling, but it's filling because of the broth, not because there's anything particularly heavy in it. It requires some advance thought, as you have to make a fish *fumet*. But *fumets* are very quick to make.

For dessert you need something refreshing and light, and the sharp, juicy, sweet pineapple with fresh mint is a perfect choice. It couldn't be easier to prepare.

With this dinner we served a unique white wine that we'd found during our summer wanderings through the Rhône Valley. It comes from one of our favorite vineyards, Château du Trignon, a vineyard that produces some of the best red Côtes-du-Rhône and Gigondas I've ever tasted. This white, from a single, perfumy, flowery grape variety called *viognier,* was unlike any white wine we'd ever tasted—dry, yet fragrant and floral, delicate yet able to stand up to pungent flavors. The grape variety is present in lots of whites from the northern Côtes-du-Rhône (Trignon is in the southern bit).

Red wines would also go well with this meal, either from the Rhône (like the Château du Trignon Côtes-du-Rhône, Gigondas, Sablet, or Rasteau), or from Bandol (such as Domaine Tempier).

This is definitely a sit-down meal and not a buffet. You have to use a knife and fork for the fish, but then you use a spoon for the broth. That's too difficult if you are balancing a plate.

Making This Dinner for a Crowd

Although I have served this dinner to small, intimate groups, you can expand the menus to feed 8 to 10 people, even more. But as with all of my recipes in which individual pieces of fish are served, I find it difficult to deal with a large group unless I have reliable help at the stove.

TOMATO SALAD

SERVES 4

An old woman and her granddaughter, who have a farm outside of Paris and a stand in the Tuesday and Friday market on the Boulevard Raspail, sell the sweetest tomatoes I've ever tasted. They are picked the day before the market, and you can tell. It's difficult to come by good tomatoes these days, even in France. I am so crazy about ripe sweet tomatoes that once I find a source I buy them all through the season and eat tomato salads every day. When friends were visiting from Oregon one fall, we would sit down to a lunch of tomatoes, bread, and cheese every day, and one of them said, "These tomatoes are going to be the most vivid memory I'll have of Paris." That's the kind you want for this salad. All they'll need is a little vinegar and herbs. Balsamic vinegar is the best, as it brings out the sweetness of the tomatoes. I usually don't add anything else, but you could also sprinkle them with garlic or onion if you wish.

1½ pounds red ripe tomatoes (about 2 or 3 medium tomatoes per person)

2 tablespoons balsamic vinegar

salt to taste

a handful of chopped fresh basil

chopped garlic and/or onion (optional)

Slice the tomatoes and place on a platter. Sprinkle with the vinegar and add salt to taste. Top with the basil and garlic and/or onion if you wish and serve.

ADVANCE PREPARATION: The salad can be assembled, without the vinegar, a few hours before serving and held in the refrigerator. But take it out a half hour or so before you serve so the tomatoes aren't too cold.

PER PORTION

Calories	36	Protein	2 G
Fat	.39 G	Carbohydrate	8 G
Sodium	14 MG	Cholesterol	0

MONKFISH IN BROTH WITH POTATOES, BASIL, AND SAFFRON

SERVES 4

This recipe was inspired by a dish I ate at Georges Blanc's restaurant, À La Mère Blanc, in Vonnas, Burgundy. His was much richer, with a buttery broth that was fragrant with saffron. It was billed as monkfish with *pistou* and almonds (*pistou* is Provençal *pesto,* often made with the addition of a tomato), but I found the saffron flavor just as strong as that of the basil. In any case, it was delicious and gave me lots of ideas about fish, basil, and saffron.

1½ pounds monkfish steaks, cut about ¾ inch thick

2 garlic cloves

¼ cup chopped fresh parsley

1 tablespoon olive oil

1 quart Mild Fish *Fumet* (page 416)

1 pound small red new potatoes, scrubbed and sliced about ½ inch thick

salt to taste

½ teaspoon saffron threads

freshly ground pepper to taste

½ cup finely chopped fresh basil leaves

2 tomatoes, peeled, seeded, and finely diced, for garnish

garlic croutons (optional; page 392)

lemon slices for garnish

Cut the monkfish away from the large center bone. Each slice should yield two little steaks. Rinse, pat dry, and set aside. (Use the center bone in making the *fumet.*)

In a mortar and pestle, pound the garlic and parsley to a paste.

Heat the olive oil in a heavy-bottomed casserole or soup pot over medium-low heat. Add the garlic paste and sauté for a couple of minutes. Add the *fumet* and the potatoes with a little salt and bring to a simmer. Simmer for 20 to 30 minutes, until the potatoes are tender.

(continued)

About 10 minutes before serving, add the monkfish to the simmering broth. Be careful not to boil. Simmer the fish until opaque all the way through and remove from the broth with a slotted spoon. Place the fish in warmed wide soup bowls. Now bring the *fumet* to a boil and add the saffron. Simmer for a few minutes and stir in the basil. Adjust seasonings and ladle the broth, with plenty of potatoes, over the fish. Top with finely diced tomatoes. Float a couple of garlic croutons in the soup if you wish and serve with sliced lemon on the side.

ADVANCE PREPARATION: The *fumet* can be made several hours in advance.

LEFTOVERS: You probably won't have fish left over, but you might have broth. Use it the next day for a fish soup. Just add more fish and cook until it's opaque and flakes easily with a fork.

PER PORTION

Calories	346	Protein	29 G
Fat	12 G	Carbohydrate	30 G
Sodium	282 MG	Cholesterol	62 MG

PINEAPPLE WITH MINT

SERVES 4

This is the perfect simple dessert after a pungent meal, whether it be Mexican, Tex-Mex, Provençal, or North African. The mint provides the special touch. Make sure your pineapples are sweet and ripe.

- 2 medium or large ripe pineapples
- 2 to 3 tablespoons fresh mint leaves, either peppermint or spearmint

Break off the stem end of the pineapples. Cut the pineapples lengthwise into quarters. Peel and trim. Cut away the hard inner core and slice the pineapple into small chunks. Refrigerate in a covered bowl. Toss with the mint about 30 minutes before serving.

ADVANCE PREPARATION: The cut-up pineapple will hold all day in a covered bowl in the refrigerator.

LEFTOVERS: The pineapple will keep for a few days in the refrigerator. Eat it for breakfast, lunch, or as a snack.

PER PORTION			
Calories	130	Protein	1 G
Fat	1 G	Carbohydrate	33 G
Sodium	3 MG	Cholesterol	0

A SALMON DINNER FOR SIX

———

PEACH KIRS

∙

ENDIVE and WALNUT SALAD or
TOSSED GREEN SALAD
(PAGE 425)

∙

GRILLED SALMON STEAKS with RED PEPPER SAUCE
POTATO GRATIN with ROSEMARY
STEAMED BROCCOLI or GREEN BEANS

∙

DRIED APRICOT SOUFFLÉ (PAGE 338) or PEACH TART

∙

BANDOL ROUGE DOMAINE TEMPIER or
GIGONDAS CHÂTEAU DU TRIGNON

What a pretty meal this is: pink salmon sauced with a fire-engine red puree of sweet red peppers, bright green steamed vegetables, and golden brown potato gratin. This could be a winter/fall or spring/summer meal. In winter, serve the endive salad—one of my favorites—and the apricot soufflé; in summer, the green salad and the peach tart. Succulent pink salmon steaks are always luxurious; but they lose their magic if they're overcooked, so watch them carefully.

Although the gratin, the red pepper puree, and the tart demand some advance thought and some busywork, this menu is far from intimidating. The dishes have few ingredients, and if you happen to have a piecrust in the freezer, this meal can be thrown together after work.

I'm not including a recipe for steamed broccoli or green beans. In both cases the vegetables are steamed 5 to 10 minutes, until tender and bright, and served with no further adornment.

My husband and I only recently discovered how nice a peach Kir can be. We resisted the fashionable "champagnes aux pêches" that began to appear on the market a few years ago. But on a trip to Burgundy we bought some Crème de Pêches, a peach liqueur, and we were delighted with the subsequent peach Kirs we made with champagne and other bubbly white wines.

I think Bandol reds (especially Domaine Tempier) go very nicely with dishes with red peppers; along with the intense fruit in these wines, there is an earthy, vegetal essence, and sweet red peppers are the closest I can come to a comparison. Other good Rhône reds, like Gigondas, are also good with this meal. If you wanted to go with a white, I would serve a Chardonnay or a Pinot Gris Tokay d'Alsace.

It's easiest to serve this dinner as a sit-down meal, because the fish should be served right away once it's cooked.

Making This Dinner for a Crowd

Forget about making this menu for a crowd unless you have help. If you do, the recipes will multiply successfully.

ENDIVE AND WALNUT SALAD

SERVES 6

Endive keeps for days, even weeks, in the refrigerator. That, as well as the fact that it's one of my very favorite vegetables, is why I keep it on hand all through the winter. I make simple salads like this one and more elaborate salads with apples and cheese or with broccoli and other vegetables. Sometimes when I want a quick, nutritious dinner, I'll make an endive salad and add a poached egg. It's terrific.

FOR THE SALAD

1½ pounds Belgian endives

¼ cup broken walnut pieces

3 tablespoons chopped fresh parsley

FOR THE DRESSING

2 tablespoons red wine vinegar

2 tablespoons fresh lemon juice

1 teaspoon Dijon mustard

salt and freshly ground pepper to taste

¼ teaspoon crumbled dried tarragon *or* ½ to 1 teaspoon minced fresh

2 tablespoons walnut oil

½ cup plain nonfat yogurt

Wash the endives and pat them dry. Either cut them in thick slices or separate the leaves. If the leaves are still wet, dry in a salad spinner. Toss with the other salad ingredients.

Mix together the vinegar, lemon juice, mustard, salt and pepper, and tarragon. Whisk in the oils and yogurt and combine thoroughly. Toss with the salad just before serving.

ADVANCE PREPARATION: All the ingredients and the dressing can be prepared several hours in advance. Dry the endives and seal in a plastic bag. Place the other ingredients in a tightly covered container in the refrigerator.

PER PORTION

Calories	95	Protein	2.8 G
Fat	7 G	Carbohydrate	6.61 G
Sodium	49 MG	Cholesterol	0

GRILLED SALMON STEAKS WITH RED PEPPER SAUCE

SERVES 6

Juicy pink salmon steaks go wonderfully with pungent Sweet Red Pepper Puree. This is a very easy dish, especially if the sauce is on hand. If you can't get fresh salmon, try the same sauce with haddock, swordfish, or snapper.

1 recipe Sweet Red Pepper Puree (page 420), made with *fromage blanc*

1 or 2 garlic cloves

6 salmon steaks, about ¾ inch thick

1 tablespoon olive oil

salt and freshly ground pepper to taste

a handful of chopped fresh herbs, such as basil, parsley, thyme, for garnish

lemon wedges for garnish

Season the red pepper puree with 1 or 2 cloves of garlic, minced or put through a press.

Preheat the broiler or prepare a grill. Brush the salmon steaks on both sides with olive oil and sprinkle on a little salt and pepper. Grill for 3 minutes on each side (it should be very pink in the middle; grill a minute longer if you like it more well done).

Remove the salmon from the heat and place on individual plates or on a platter. Top with the sauce, sprinkle with the herbs, and serve with lemon wedges.

ADVANCE PREPARATION: The Sweet Red Pepper Puree can be made days ahead of time and held in the refrigerator.

PER PORTION

Calories	305	Protein	31 G
Fat	17 G	Carbohydrate	7 G
Sodium	70 MG	Cholesterol	82 MG

Dissolve the yeast in the water and let sit for 5 to 10 minutes. Beat in the honey, egg, sugar, and the butter. Combine the flours and salt and stir in (this can be done in an electric mixer, using the paddle). Work the dough only until it comes together in a coherent mass; shape it into a ball. Place in a lightly oiled bowl, cover with plastic wrap, and let rise in a warm spot for 2 hours or a little longer. It will not rise too much, but it will expand and soften.

When the pastry has risen and softened, punch it down gently and divide into 2 equal-size pieces. Shape each into a ball, cover with plastic wrap, and let rest for 10 minutes.

For each crust, butter a 10- to 12-inch tart pan and roll out the dough very thin to fit the dish. The dough should be easy to handle. Line the dish and pinch a lip around the top edge (at this point the dough can be frozen). Cover loosely with a kitchen towel and let rest for 20 minutes.

Preheat the oven to 375 degrees.

Brush the crust with beaten egg and prebake for 7 minutes before filling and baking the tart. Or bake according to the specific recipe.

ADVANCE PREPARATION: These crusts freeze very well. Transfer directly from the freezer to the oven for prebaking. Prebake for 9 to 10 minutes instead of 7 minutes before filling or bake according to the specific recipe.

PER PORTION

Calories	91	Protein	2 G
Fat	3 G	Carbohydrate	14 G
Sodium	57 MG	Cholesterol	19 MG

PEACH TART

SERVES 8

There is nothing like a peach tart in summer and early fall, when the peaches are ripe and abundant. Make this one close to serving time so that the crust stays crisp. It helps to brush the crust with plenty of beaten egg before you prebake it.

1/2 recipe Yeasted Dessert Pastry (page 131) to make 1 crust

1 medium egg, beaten

juice of 1 large lemon

a sprinkling of ground cinnamon

2 1/2 pounds peaches, pitted, peeled if desired, and thinly sliced

2 tablespoons unrefined brown sugar (turbinado)

2 tablespoons apricot preserves (optional)

Preheat the oven to 375 degrees. Brush the crust generously with the beaten egg and prick with a fork in several places. Prebake for 15 to 20 minutes, until the bottom is cooked through and the edges are beginning to brown. Remove from the oven.

Toss the sliced peaches with the lemon juice in a bowl. Arrange the fruit on the prebaked crust. Sprinkle with the cinnamon and sugar. Reserve any liquid remaining in the bowl. Return the tart to the oven and bake for another 10 to 15 minutes or until the crust is brown.

Transfer the liquid from the fruit to a saucepan and reduce over medium-high heat until you have a thick syrup. Add the apricot preserves if desired and melt together with the syrup.

Remove the tart from the oven and brush the fruit gently with the syrup. Serve warm or cooled.

ADVANCE PREPARATION: The crust can be made weeks ahead of time and frozen or made a day ahead of time and refrigerated. The fruit can be prepped hours ahead of time and held in the refrigerator.

PER PORTION

Calories	151	Protein	3 G
Fat	3 G	Carbohydrate	29 G
Sodium	58 MG	Cholesterol	19 MG

A PROVENÇAL MENU FOR SIX

———

CASSIS or BELLET BLANC (PLAIN OR KIRS)
TOASTED PITA TRIANGLES (PAGE 71)
with HERBED GOAT CHEESE (PAGE 36)
■
A SALAD of SLICED FRESH MUSHROOMS
and GREEN BEANS
■
BAKED FISH FILLETS with TOMATOES
and TAPENADE
WATERCRESS PASTA (PAGE 406)
■
PRUNE ICE CREAM
ORANGE BISCOTTI (PAGE 409)
■
RASTEAU CÔTES-DU-RHÔNE-VILLAGES

This meal's main dish is reason alone for you to keep a stock of tapenade and canned or fresh tomatoes on hand. Any white fish fillet thus becomes a feast. The pasta looks beautiful on the side; it absorbs any sauce not eaten with the fish and adds to the already Niçoise character of the menu. This is a winner of a main course, and it lends itself to both table and buffet service, as does the pretty salad. If you do serve this meal buffet style, naturally you will bring out the dessert just before serving it, after everyone has finished the main dish and plates have been cleared.

A fruity but gutsy southern French wine, to complement these Mediterranean flavors, is the wine to drink with this meal. Nothing too complicated, light but not too light. A Sablet, Gigondas, or a good Vacqueyras would work. If you prefer white or rosé, choose a white from the Coteaux d'Aix or Cassis or a Bandol rosé.

Making This Dinner for a Crowd

All of these dishes multiply easily for up to 30 people.

A SALAD OF SLICED FRESH MUSHROOMS AND GREEN BEANS

SERVES 6

Tender green beans, cooked just until al dente, or until crisp-tender, go nicely with mushrooms in a salad and make a lovely bright green mound on a plate. The beans are crunchy and coated with a tasty vinaigrette, the mushrooms soft and releasing a little vinaigrette with each bite. Try to find thin French green beans and avoid the long, tough gnarly ones that are all too easy to find.

1 pound tender fresh green beans, trimmed and cut into 1½-inch lengths

¼ pound fresh white mushrooms, trimmed, rinsed, dried, and thinly sliced

juice of ½ lemon or more to taste

2 tablespoons chopped fresh chives

1 recipe Lemon-Yogurt Vinaigrette (page 434)

salt and freshly ground pepper to taste

small leaves from the heart of a leaf or Boston lettuce for garnish (optional)

radish roses for garnish (optional)

Steam the green beans for 5 minutes or blanch in salted boiling water for 2 to 3 minutes, just until crisp-tender. Drain and rinse with cold water.

Toss the thinly sliced mushrooms with the lemon juice. Let sit for a few minutes, then toss with the green beans and the chives.

Just before serving, toss the mushrooms and green beans with the vinaigrette. Add salt and pepper.

Place lettuce leaves on plates if you wish and top with a mound of the salad. Garnish with radish roses if desired and serve.

ADVANCE PREPARATION: All of the ingredients can be prepped hours ahead of serving and refrigerated. The mushrooms can be tossed with the lemon juice a few hours ahead of time, but the beans and herbs should be tossed with the rest of the ingredients just before serving, or they'll lose their bright color.

LEFTOVERS: The acid in the vinaigrette will take away the lovely bright green of the beans, but they'll still taste good. They can be added to green salads or salade Niçoise.

PER PORTION

Calories	47	Protein	3 G
Fat	.30 G	Carbohydrate	9 G
Sodium	77 MG	Cholesterol	0

BAKED FISH FILLETS WITH TOMATOES AND TAPENADE

SERVES 6

The inspiration for this recipe comes from a fabulous restaurant in Brussels called L'Ecailleur du Palais. But my real excuse for making it was the fact that one night I found myself with leftover tapenade and tomatoes that were quickly deteriorating in my refrigerator and some fish fillets left over from a cooking class I'd taught that had to be used up. Tapenade is a wonderful condiment as well as an hors d'oeuvre, and this combination is a great one. It also takes just minutes to put together (provided you've got the tapenade).

1	tablespoon olive oil
4	to 5 large garlic cloves to taste, minced or put through a press
1½	pounds tomatoes, seeded and chopped
	salt and freshly ground pepper to taste
6	fish fillets, such as plaice, whiting, snapper, or brill (about ¼ pound each)
	juice of 1½ lemons
6	heaped tablespoons tapenade (page 38)
	chopped fresh parsley for garnish

Preheat the oven to 425 degrees. Oil a baking dish large enough to accommodate the fish fillets.

Make the tomato topping. Heat the oil over medium-low heat in a heavy-bottomed saucepan and add the garlic. Sauté for a few minutes and add the tomatoes. Add salt to taste and cook over medium heat for about 10 minutes, stirring often. Add freshly ground pepper, adjust seasonings, and remove from the heat.

Rinse the fish fillets and pat dry. Place in the baking dish. Salt and pepper lightly on both sides and squeeze on some lemon juice. Spread a heaped tablespoon of tapenade over each fillet. Spoon the tomato sauce around and between the fillets. Cover tightly with foil.

Bake for 10 minutes or until the fish is opaque and flakes easily. Garnish with parsley and serve at once.

ADVANCE PREPARATION: The tapenade should be on hand. The tomato sauce can be made a day in advance and the dish assembled several hours before serving.

LEFTOVERS: Break up the fish with a fork and toss leftovers with pasta.

PER PORTION

Calories	154	Protein	21 G
Fat	6 G	Carbohydrate	3 G
Sodium	219 MG	Cholesterol	76 MG

PRUNE ICE CREAM

SERVES 6 TO 8

Okay, so there's cream in this. But no egg yolks, as in most ice creams, and really not that much cream per serving. It's definitely worth a few extra calories for this marvelous dessert. A real showstopper.

    1   pound prunes
    2   cups boiling water
    1/3 to 1/2 cup mild-flavored honey to taste
    2   tablespoons prune or plum eau de vie
    2   teaspoons vanilla extract
    1/8 teaspoon almond extract
    2   medium egg whites
    1   cup whipping cream

Place the prunes in a bowl and pour on the boiling water. Let sit for 1 or 2 hours.

Drain the water and reserve. Pit the prunes. Transfer them to a food processor fitted with the steel blade or a blender along with the reserved water, honey, eau de vie, vanilla extract, and almond extract and blend until smooth.

Beat the egg whites to soft peaks. Beat into the prune mixture. Transfer to ice cube trays, a shallow pan, or a bowl. Cover and freeze for 2 to 3 hours, until the mixture is just about frozen.

Beat the whipping cream to *chantilly* (soft—but not too stiff—peaks).

Remove the prune mixture from the freezer. Blend again in a food processor or a mixer. The mixture will become light and fluffy. Fold in the whipped cream. Freeze again, in a mold, an attractive bowl, individual ramekins or serving bowls, or a plastic container. Soften for 20 to 30 minutes in the refrigerator before serving.

ADVANCE PREPARATION: This ice cream keeps for weeks in the freezer.

PER PORTION

Calories	293	Protein	3 G
Fat	11 G	Carbohydrate	48 G
Sodium	26 MG	Cholesterol	41 MG

A SIT-DOWN DINNER FOR SIX

WITH MEXICAN FLAVORS

———

MARGARITAS (PAGE 16)

•

ZUCCHINI and AVOCADO
SALSA SALAD

•

GRILLED SWORDFISH with TOMATO SALSA
CORN ON THE COB
STEAMED FRENCH GREEN BEANS

•

NECTARINE SORBET with NECTARINE and
MUSCAT GRAPE GARNISH
MUSCAT DE BEAUMES DE VENISE

•

BANDOL ROSÉ DOMAINE TEMPIER

Late summer or early fall is the most realistic time to serve this bright, vibrant meal, when the fruit and vegetables are at their best. Tomatoes and corn have to be in season, as do nectarines and muscat grapes. Each course will stimulate your eyes as well as your palate, from the pale green margaritas and mosaiclike salad, through the main dish with its bright red, *picante* salsa, yellow corn on the cob, and delicate French green beans (which are simply topped, tailed, and steamed 5 to 10 minutes to taste) to the luscious nectarine sorbet flanked with dark-blue muscat grapes.

The recipes are easy, although a fair amount of prep is involved.

Whenever I'm serving a Mexican meal, I like to kick it off with margaritas. They're always popular. If you prefer wine, serve a clean, dry white wine, such as a Sancerre or a Sauvignon Touraine. As for the wine to serve with the meal, I've chosen an elegant Bandol Rosé from Domaine Tempier, which is complex, fruity, and at the same time dry. It can stand up to the salsa, yet makes a light accompaniment to this light meal. A number of reds would also go well. Choose a light, fruity wine from the south of France, such as a Côtes du Ventoux, a Coteaux du Tricastin, Côtes-du-Rhône, or Roussillon.

A small glass of Muscat de Beaumes de Venise is a perfect complement for the sorbet and the grapes. The wine echoes the flavor of the grapes and makes a beautiful finish to this meal.

Making This Dinner for a Crowd

All of the recipes are easy to stretch here, but when you're serving grilled or broiled fish that is cooked just before serving, it gets to be a bit difficult unless you have help with the cooking, once you go beyond eight or ten.

ZUCCHINI AND AVOCADO SALSA SALAD

SERVES 4 TO 6

It's important for this pretty salad that the zucchini and avocado be cut into very tiny dice. Slice the zucchini lengthwise, paper-thin, then into fine dice. Dice the avocado extra-small inside the skin, then scoop out the fine dice.

5 or 6 medium-size ripe tomatoes, finely chopped

2 jalapeño or serrano peppers, seeded and finely chopped

4 to 6 tablespoons chopped cilantro to taste

1 tablespoon balsamic vinegar

salt to taste

1 medium zucchini, cut into tiny dice

1 avocado, peeled, pitted, and cut into tiny dice

juice of 1 large lemon

romaine or leaf lettuce leaves for serving

Combine the tomatoes, peppers, cilantro, vinegar, and salt.

Toss the zucchini and avocado with the lemon juice and salt to taste. Combine with the tomato salsa. Adjust the seasonings and refrigerate until ready to serve. Serve on leaves of romaine or leaf lettuce.

ADVANCE PREPARATION: This salad can be made a few hours ahead, but add the cilantro shortly before serving.

LEFTOVERS: Serve on tortilla chips, Toasted Pita Triangles (page 71), or wedges of red or yellow bell pepper as an hors d'oeuvre.

PER PORTION

Calories	84	Protein	2 G
Fat	5 G	Carbohydrate	9 G
Sodium	14 MG	Cholesterol	0

GRILLED SWORDFISH WITH TOMATO SALSA

SERVES 6

Grilled fish goes very well with salsa. The steaks are grilled for just a few minutes on each side—don't grill them for a second too long, or they'll be as dry as cotton.

juice of ½ lemon

1 tablespoon olive oil

1 garlic clove, minced

salt and freshly ground pepper to taste

6 swordfish steaks, ¾ inch thick (about 6 ounces each)

1 recipe Tomato Salsa (page 422)

Combine the lemon juice, olive oil, and garlic. Lightly salt and pepper the swordfish steaks and brush both sides with the oil. Let sit while you prepare a grill or preheat the broiler.

Grill the fish or broil 3 to 4 inches from the heat for 2½ minutes on each side, or even less if you like your swordfish very rare. Don't cook longer than this or the fish will be too dry. Remove from the heat and place on serving plates. Spoon the salsa down the side of each swordfish steak, letting a little cover the top. Serve hot or allow to cool and serve.

ADVANCE PREPARATION: The salsa will hold for several hours in the refrigerator.

LEFTOVERS: Salsa can be refrigerated and eaten almost like a salad. Or serve it with scrambled eggs, as a topping for *crostini* (page 392), or as a dip.

PER PORTION

Calories	259	Protein	35 G
Fat	9 G	Carbohydrate	8 G
Sodium	166 MG	Cholesterol	66 MG

CORN ON THE COB

Our family used to have corn on the cob orgies when the sweet corn came in at the end of the summer in Connecticut. My mother would go to a local produce stand, and we would have meals of just corn, tomatoes, and salad. Meat was there for those who wanted it, but most of us just concentrated on corn, it was so sweet and good. "It's a short season," my father would say as he reached for his third or fourth ear.

There is really no secret to perfect corn on the cob. It has to be very young and fresh to begin with. Look for small whitish kernels. And whether you steam it or boil it (I steam it), the main thing is not to cook it too long. Five to seven minutes should suffice. I test it by puncturing a kernel with the tip of a knife. It should pop and be juicy. In my opinion, good corn needs no butter at all. A little salt and pepper will suffice, and possibly some wedges of fresh lime served alongside.

Shuck the corn. Bring a large pot of water to a boil or a small amount of water to a boil in the bottom of a steamer. If you're boiling the corn, add salt and drop in the corn. Boil the corn for no more than 5 minutes. If you're steaming it, place it in the steamer, cover tightly, and steam for 5 minutes. The corn should be a brighter yellow than when the cooking began, and the kernels should be juicy when you puncture them with a knife. If they aren't, chances are you've cooked the corn too long or it was overripe to begin with.

ADVANCE PREPARATION: You can shuck corn hours ahead of cooking it.

LEFTOVERS: See the recipes for Mexican Corn Salad with Tomatillo Dressing (page 366) and Potatoes Filled with Corn and Sage Salad (page 54).

PER PORTION

Calories	77	Protein	3 G
Fat	I G	Carbohydrate	I7 G
Sodium	I4 MG	Cholesterol	0

A SIT-DOWN DINNER FOR FOUR TO SIX

FEATURING RABBIT AND POTATOES

———

CHILLED BANDOL, ROUSSILLON ROSÉ or
WHITE CÔTES DU LUBERON

•

BABY VEGETABLES STUFFED with TAPENADE (PAGE 53)

•

RABBIT SIMMERED in CHICKEN STOCK
with NEW POTATOES

•

TOSSED GREEN SALAD with MUSHROOMS (PAGE 425)

•

ORANGE or BLOOD ORANGE SORBET with a
SALAD of BLOOD ORANGES
ORANGE BISCOTTI (PAGE 409)
or PECAN COOKIES (PAGE 411)

•

WHITE CHÂTEAUNEUF-DU-PAPE, CÔTES-DU-RHÔNE,
or MEURSAULT

Sometimes when I cook a rabbit, a whole dinner party grows up around it. That's what happened here. I came up with this recipe, which grew into a menu, which grew into a dinner party.

The rabbit is a filling dish—not because it's rich but because it's like a hearty soup, with the broth and the potatoes—so I'd begin this meal simply, with some light hors d'oeuvres. Follow the rabbit dish with a tossed green salad. If you can't find little vegetables, you can serve the tapenade on sweet peppers (see the recipe) or crackers. Tapenade is made to go with a crisp, dry rosé or white wine (or champagne) from southern France. Bandol rosé is perfect, but we've also found some terrific rosé from the Roussillon, from a domaine called Mas Chichet. A light, dry Provençal white wine, from the Côtes du Luberon, would also go well.

The rabbit dish, served in wide soup bowls, is simple and comforting. It goes well with a rich but dry white wine, either from the Rhône or from Burgundy. If you prefer a red with this dish, a light, fruity Loire red, either a Bourgueil or a Chinon, would be lovely, as would a Provençal or Rhône red.

I like a light, fruit-based dessert with this meal, raspberries in summer, oranges in winter. A cookie of some kind should be served along with the fruit.

Because the rabbit dish is so much like a soup and must be eaten from bowls, I wouldn't serve this meal as a buffet.

Making This Dinner for a Crowd

All the recipes here multiply very easily. The rabbit is a good party dish, because much of it can be done in advance. Tapenade is very easy to stretch. And there are no tricks to the dessert.

RABBIT SIMMERED IN CHICKEN STOCK WITH NEW POTATOES

SERVES 4 TO 6

One day in June one of my husband's colleagues gave him a 10-pound bag of beautiful little red potatoes called *noir moustier* that she'd brought back from the country. They were like new potatoes with a firmer, waxier texture, and they tasted sweeter than any potatoes I'd ever eaten. We never tired of them over the month that it took to use them up. This was just one of the dishes I made using them. The first time I made this dish I used a turkey stock, which I'd made after Christmas and frozen. It worked as well as chicken stock, yielding a broth for this dish with an agreeable flavor that was stronger than chicken broth. If you can get fresh tarragon, by all means use it along with the parsley.

1	tablespoon olive oil
2	medium onions, finely chopped
6	garlic cloves, minced, put through a press, or sliced
1	3- to 3½-pound rabbit, cut into 8 to 10 pieces
1½	quarts chicken or turkey stock (page 413)
1	bay leaf
	salt and freshly ground pepper to taste
½	teaspoon crumbled dried thyme *or* 1 teaspoon fresh leaves
1	pound small new potatoes, sliced about ½ inch thick
½	teaspoon crumbled dried rosemary *or* 1 teaspoon chopped fresh
¼	cup chopped fresh parsley *or* 2 tablespoons chopped fresh parsley and 2 tablespoons chopped fresh tarragon
	juice of 1 large lemon
½	pound green beans, trimmed, cut into 1- or 2-inch lengths, and steamed or blanched (optional)

Heat the oil over medium heat in a large heavy-bottomed casserole or stockpot. Add the onion and garlic and sauté until the onion is tender and beginning to color. Add the rabbit, stock, bay leaf, salt, pepper, and thyme and bring to a simmer. Reduce the heat, cover, and simmer slowly for 30 minutes. Add the potatoes and rosemary and continue simmering for 30 to 45 minutes or until the potatoes are tender and the rabbit is so tender it's falling off the bone. Adjust the seasonings. Just before serving, stir in the parsley or parsley and tarragon and the lemon juice. Add the green beans if you're using them and heat through. Ladle pieces of rabbit, stock, and potatoes into wide soup bowls and serve at once.

ADVANCE PREPARATION: This dish can be made up to the point of adding the herbs, lemon juice, and beans hours ahead of serving. Reheat gently on the top of the stove shortly before serving and add the herbs, lemon juice, and beans.

PER PORTION

Calories	395	Protein	40 G
Fat	15 G	Carbohydrate	24 G
Sodium	89 MG	Cholesterol	107 MG

ORANGE OR BLOOD ORANGE SORBET WITH A SALAD OF BLOOD ORANGES

SERVES 6

When I got home from the market one day, I realized that I'd mistakenly bought oranges with a touch of red instead of the blood oranges I'd planned to use for a sorbet. There I was, with 10 pounds of sweet, juicy oranges on my hands; so I made a sorbet anyway, and it was delicious. I ended up serving it surrounded by a salad of blood oranges and mint, which made a vivid contrast. This is one of my prize desserts. Serve Orange Biscotti (page 409) or Pecan Cookies (page 411) on the side.

FOR THE SORBET

  ¼ cup unrefined brown sugar (turbinado sugar)

  1 tablespoon mild-flavored honey

  ½ cup water

  3½ cups fresh orange juice (from about 3 pounds oranges)

  ⅓ cup fresh lemon juice

FOR THE BLOOD ORANGE SALAD

    6 blood oranges

    2 to 3 tablespoons Grand Marnier to taste

    2 tablespoons chopped fresh mint leaves

       fresh mint sprigs for garnish

TO MAKE THE SORBET: Combine the sugar, honey, and water in a large saucepan and bring to a boil. Reduce the heat and simmer for 10 minutes. Remove from the heat and allow to cool.

Combine the juices and the syrup in a large bowl. Freeze in either an ice cream maker according to the manufacturer's directions or in a covered bowl. When frozen solid, remove from the bowl and spoon into a food processor fitted with the steel blade. Process until fluffy; this breaks up the ice crystals and gives you a smooth texture.

Spoon into individual serving dishes—I use small gratin dishes—and cover each one with plastic wrap, then foil. Or oil a loaf pan and line with plastic wrap. Pour in the sorbet mixture, cover tightly with plastic or foil, and freeze. Work quickly so that the frozen mixture doesn't melt to a liquid, or ice crystals will form again when it freezes.

TO MAKE THE SALAD: Peel the oranges and cut away all the white pith. Cut the sections out from between the membranes, holding the orange over a bowl so that you catch all the juice. Chill until about an hour before serving.

About an hour before serving, toss the oranges with the Grand Marnier and chopped mint. Return to the refrigerator.

Twenty to 30 minutes before serving, place the sorbet in the refrigerator to soften. If you froze the sorbet in a loaf pan, unmold onto a platter. Cut slices, using a sharp knife, and place in serving bowls. If you froze it in individual molds, unmold into the serving bowls (run a knife around the edges to facilitate unmolding). Spoon the orange salad around the sorbet and garnish each sorbet with a sprig of fresh mint.

ADVANCE PREPARATION: The sorbet can be made several days before you wish to serve it. The garnish can be made several hours ahead of serving time and held in the refrigerator in a covered bowl, without the mint and Grand Marnier, which should be added no more than an hour before serving.

PER PORTION

Calories	180	Protein	2 G
Fat	.51 G	Carbohydrate	42 G
Sodium	1 MG	Cholesterol	0

A FALL / WINTER MEXICAN DINNER PARTY

FOR A FEW OR A CROWD

———

MARGARITAS (PAGE 16) or SAUMUR

·

TOMATO GARLIC SOUP (PAGE 334)

·

CHICKEN BREASTS with GREEN TOMATILLO MOLE

MEXICAN-STYLE RICE

STEAMED ZUCCHINI (PAGE 103) or

PAN-FRIED RED BELL PEPPERS (PAGE 95)

·

TOSSED GREEN SALAD (PAGE 425)

·

PINEAPPLE-MINT SORBET

PECAN COOKIES (PAGE 411)

·

GEWÜRZTRAMINER or SAVENNIÈRES

The main attraction of this meal is the Chicken Breasts with Green Tomatillo Mole (not to mention the refreshing, minty dessert). I came across the tangy sauce when I was researching mole sauces, and now I make it all the time, not just to go with chicken or rabbit as a main dish but also as a dip, with tortilla chips or *crudités*.

I hesitate to serve this meal as a buffet because of the soup, which might slosh around a bit. If you do, you might want to cut the chicken into small pieces, because it's difficult for your guests to wield a knife and fork if they aren't sitting at a table.

For this menu, add cilantro instead of basil or parsley to the soup.

As always, a dinner with Mexican dishes is a good excuse for margaritas beforehand. Or try a bubbly wine from the Loire. There are some good ones from Saumur and from Vouvray.

The chicken with green mole would go with some red wines, like a fruity wine from the Loire (a Bourgueil or a Gamay, for example), but I think it goes best with a spicy white, and that's what I serve with this meal. Gewürztraminer is a brilliant choice; its perfume and complexity don't fight with, but rather complement, the pungent flavors of the sauce. Another great choice would be a Loire white from Savennières. These are supple, very floral whites that go extremely well with delicately spiced food.

Making This Dinner for a Crowd

This meal works well in quantity and is fairly easy to prepare. See the Green Tomatillo Mole recipe for specific instructions for cooking this dish in quantity. The other recipes multiply easily.

CHICKEN BREASTS WITH GREEN TOMATILLO MOLE

SERVES 6

Here you can make the chicken stock that you'll need for the *mole* from the chicken breasts that you'll use for the *mole*. This is easy and fairly quick as *moles* go.

1 small onion, diced

1/2 teaspoon salt or more or less to taste

3 large chicken breasts, halved (about 3³/₄ pounds total), skin removed

6 cups water or chicken stock (page 413), approximately

1 recipe Green Tomatillo Mole (recipe follows)

cilantro sprigs and radishes for garnish

Combine the onion, salt, chicken breasts, and water or stock in a stockpot and bring to a boil. Skim off any foam that rises, reduce the heat, and simmer, partially covered, for 12 minutes, until the chicken breasts are just about cooked through. Remove from the broth and set aside. Strain the broth and use in the *mole* recipe if desired.

Just before serving, bring the *mole* to a simmer and add the chicken breasts. Heat through for a few minutes. Spoon a little sauce onto plates or a platter and transfer the chicken breasts to the platter or plates. Spoon the remaining sauce over the chicken and garnish with cilantro and radishes.

ALTERNATIVE METHOD: You can also prepare the chicken by cooking it directly in the sauce. If you already have chicken stock on hand for the *mole,* this method is a good one. Omit the onion and salt from the recipe and brown the chicken pieces in 1 tablespoon oil for a few minutes on each side. Drain on paper towels. About 20 minutes before serving, bring the sauce to a simmer and add the chicken pieces. Cook for 15 minutes in the sauce, until done, and proceed as above.

ADVANCE PREPARATION: Both the sauce and the chicken will hold for a day in the refrigerator. Keep the meat and the sauce in separate containers.

FOR A CROWD: If you're making this recipe for a crowd, multiply by the correct factor, but see the *mole* sauce recipe for the chicken stock amounts. Finish or cook the chicken in the sauce as directed. Once the chicken is cooked, transfer it to an oval casserole, cover partially with the sauce, and reheat in a low oven just before serving. Have the remaining sauce simmering on top of the stove and spoon over the chicken just before serving.

LEFTOVERS: If you have only sauce left over, see the suggestions on page 157. If you have both chicken and sauce left over, try the following.

Chicken and Green Mole Enchiladas: Shred the chicken and use as a filling for enchiladas. Heat corn tortillas through in a small amount of oil mixed with some of the *mole*. Fill with chicken and a spoonful of *fromage blanc* (page 417) or plain low-fat yogurt. Roll up and place in a lightly oiled baking dish. Pour on the remaining sauce, heat through in a preheated 350-degree oven, garnish with cilantro and additional *fromage blanc* or plain low-fat yogurt, and serve.

Chicken Salad with Green Mole Dressing: Add a little lime or lemon juice or vinegar to the sauce, shred the chicken, and toss with chopped cucumber or jicama, chopped green or red bell pepper, sliced scallions, and the leftover sauce. Serve over lettuce leaves.

PER PORTION

Calories	337	Protein	47 G
Fat	9 G	Carbohydrate	16 G
Sodium	494 MG	Cholesterol	107 MG

GREEN TOMATILLO MOLE

SERVES 6 (ABOUT 3 CUPS SAUCE)

This recipe is based on Rick Bayless's recipe for Green Pumpkinseed Mole with Chicken Breasts (*Authentic Mexican,* Morrow, 1987). I love the tangy flavor of tomatillos, which show up frequently in supermarkets all over the country; canned tomatillos will work if fresh ones aren't available. If hulled pumpkin seeds (*pepitas*) aren't available, as they're not to me, substitute pine nuts. You can't pulverize them in a spice mill, however, as you would *pepitas,* because they'll turn to butter. So I blend them in the blender with stock, then strain the mixture. I've made this with both chicken breasts and rabbit. Once I served Rabbit with Mole Two Ways. Each plate had one piece of meat with dark brown Mole Poblano and one piece with this green sauce. The two sauces went well together, and the plates looked beautiful. I've also made the same combination with chicken breasts.

3 ounces hulled raw pumpkin seeds or pine nuts

3 cups chicken stock (page 413) or more if needed

3/4 pound (8 medium) tomatillos, husked and washed, *or* 1 1/2 13-ounce cans tomatillos, drained

2 to 3 fresh hot green chilies (jalapeños or serranos), to taste, stems, seeds, and membranes removed

1/2 medium onion, roughly chopped

3 garlic cloves, roughly chopped

4 or 5 cilantro sprigs

1/4 teaspoon cumin seeds or ground cumin

3/4 inch cinnamon stick *or* 3/4 teaspoon ground cinnamon

2 cloves *or* a pinch of ground

5 large romaine or leaf lettuce leaves, washed

salt to taste (about 1/2 teaspoon)

1 tablespoon safflower or sunflower oil

Toast the seeds in a dry frying pan, shaking the pan or stirring constantly until they are browned and toasty (for pine nuts) or until they have browned and popped (for pumpkin seeds). Remove from the heat and transfer to a blender jar if you're using pine nuts or to a bowl if you're using pumpkin seeds. If you're using pine nuts, blend with 1 cup of the stock until smooth, then strain through a medium-mesh strainer. If you're using pumpkin seeds, pulverize in a spice mill in batches and sift into a bowl. Stir in 1 cup of the stock and mix well. Set aside.

If you're using fresh tomatillos, simmer in water to cover with the chilies for 10 to 15 minutes. Drain and place in the blender jar. If you're using canned tomatillos, drain and place in the blender jar along with the chilies. Add the onion, garlic, and cilantro. Grind the spices in a spice mill and add to the blender jar. Add the lettuce leaves and salt. Blend until the mixture is smooth.

Heat the oil in a heavy-bottomed saucepan or casserole over medium heat. Add the nut or seed mixture and cook, stirring constantly, until the mixture thickens, about 5 minutes. Add the tomatillo mixture and cook again, stirring for about 5 to 10 minutes, until the mixture is thick. Stir in the remaining 2 cups chicken stock, bring to a simmer, cover partially, and simmer for 30 minutes. Taste and correct seasonings. If the mixture seems too thick, stir in a little more chicken stock.

ADVANCE PREPARATION: This sauce will hold for a day, in or out of the refrigerator.

FOR A CROWD: Multiply all the ingredients *except the chicken stock* by the proper factor. Add half the multiplied quantity of chicken stock, and if the mixture seems too thick, continue to add more until the desired thickness is reached. The *mole* thins out too much with the addition of too much stock.

LEFTOVERS: Use as a dip with *crudités,* as a topping for nachos or enchiladas, as a topping for the polenta squares on page 72, or add a few tablespoons of lime juice, lemon juice, or vinegar and use in place of the Tomatillo Dressing for Quinoa Salad (page 364) or Mexican Corn Salad (page 366). This sauce freezes well.

PER PORTION

Calories	130	Protein	4 G
Fat	6 G	Carbohydrate	15 G
Sodium	192 MG	Cholesterol	0

MEXICAN-STYLE RICE

SERVES 6

This is a Mexican method for cooking white rice. You sauté it until it begins to color, then pour in chicken or vegetable stock. The rice cooks in 20 to 25 minutes and comes out fluffy, all the grains perfectly separated. It's a good method for making rice ahead of time, as the grains don't get mushy or soggy.

   1 tablespoon safflower or peanut oil
1½ cups white long-grain rice
   3 cups chicken or vegetable stock (page 413 or 414)
¼ teaspoon salt

Heat the oil in a medium saucepan over medium heat and add the rice. Cook, stirring, for a few minutes, until the rice begins to color. Add the stock, which will sizzle into a boil quickly, and the salt, reduce the heat, cover, and simmer for 20 to 25 minutes, until the liquid has evaporated. Serve at once.

ADVANCE PREPARATION: You can cook the rice a few hours ahead of time and reheat it in a 350-degree oven in a lightly oiled baking dish for 20 minutes.

PER PORTION

Calories	220	Protein	4 G
Fat	5 G	Carbohydrate	40 G
Sodium	93 MG	Cholesterol	0

PINEAPPLE-MINT SORBET

SERVES 6 TO 8

Here's yet another dessert in which pineapple is paired with mint. They are as great together in this iced version as they are fresh (page 125); the two desserts could be used interchangeably in this menu. But I think a sorbet is welcome at the end of a big meal and is special, even though sorbets are so easy to make.

FOR THE SORBET

- 1/4 cup sugar
- 1 cup water
- 2 cups strained fresh orange juice (from about 2 pounds oranges)
  juice of 1 large lime
- 1 ripe pineapple, peeled, cored, and coarsely chopped
- 3 tablespoons chopped fresh mint leaves

FOR THE PINEAPPLE-MINT GARNISH (optional)

- 1/2 ripe pineapple, peeled, cored, and finely chopped
- 1/4 cup Cointreau (optional)
- 2 tablespoons chopped fresh mint leaves

TO MAKE THE SORBET: Combine the sugar and water in a large saucepan and bring to a boil. Reduce the heat and simmer for 10 minutes. Remove from the heat and allow to cool.

Meanwhile, combine the orange and lime juices.

Puree the pineapple in a food processor fitted with a steel blade or blender along with the mint leaves. Use some of the orange juice to moisten. Combine with the orange-lime juice.

Stir the pineapple mixture into the cooled syrup. Either freeze in an ice cream freezer or freeze in a covered bowl. When frozen solid, remove from the bowl and spoon into a food processor fitted with the steel blade. Process until fluffy; this breaks up the ice crystals and results in a smoother texture. To ensure a very smooth texture, repeat this process one more time after a couple of hours (this step is optional).

Spoon into individual serving dishes, cover with plastic and then foil, and freeze. Or oil a loaf pan or mold and line with plastic wrap. Pour in the sorbet mixture, cover tightly with plastic wrap and then foil, and freeze. Work quickly so that the sorbet doesn't melt, or ice crystals will form again when it freezes.

(continued)

TO MAKE THE GARNISH AND SERVE: Toss together the chopped pineapple and the Cointreau if you're using it. Add the mint leaves. Set aside or refrigerate until ready to serve.

Twenty minutes before serving, place the sorbet in the refrigerator to soften. If you froze it in the loaf pan, unmold on a platter. Cut slices using a sharp knife. If you froze it in individual molds, unmold into bowls. Serve, topping each serving with the garnish.

ADVANCE PREPARATION: This sorbet, like all the others in this book, will hold for weeks, covered tightly, in the freezer. The garnish can be made several hours ahead of serving time and held in a covered bowl in the refrigerator.

PER PORTION

Calories	86	Protein	I G
Fat	.40 G	Carbohydrate	21 G
Sodium	I MG	Cholesterol	0

SPINACH AND MUSHROOM SALAD WITH LEMON-YOGURT VINAIGRETTE

SERVES 6

A simple, lemony salad to serve with a complex main dish.

$1/2$ pound fresh spinach, stemmed, washed, and dried

6 ounces fresh mushrooms, cleaned, trimmed, and sliced

1 tablespoon fresh lemon juice

2 tablespoons chopped fresh parsley

1 recipe Lemon-Yogurt Vinaigrette (page 434)

Tear the spinach leaves into small pieces or cut with scissors. Toss the sliced mushrooms with the lemon juice. Place the spinach in a bowl, top with the mushrooms, and sprinkle with the parsley. Toss with the dressing just before serving.

ADVANCE PREPARATION: The spinach and parsley can be washed and dried hours ahead of time. The mushrooms can be prepped and tossed with lemon juice and the dressing prepared a few hours ahead of time. Store the spinach in the refrigerator, wrapped in a towel and sealed in a plastic bag.

PER PORTION

Calories	30	Protein	2 G
Fat	.27 G	Carbohydrate	5 G
Sodium	75 MG	Cholesterol	I MG

BUCKWHEAT CRÊPES WITH CORN, RED PEPPER, AND GOAT CHEESE

SERVES 6

These crêpes are both earthy and sweet, and they're beautiful to look at, with their colorful mosaic of yellow corn and diced red pepper. The wild rice adds a chewy texture, the cheese a rich, savory taste, and it all goes wonderfully well with the distinctive buckwheat flavor of the crêpes. I find these crêpes very satisfying with no additional sauce. I like them a bit dry on the outside. But if you think they need something, the Sweet Red Pepper Puree on page 420 would be good, as would a fresh Tomato Concassée (page 423).

    12 buckwheat crêpes (page 401)
     2 ears of sweet corn *or* 2 cups frozen corn kernels, thawed
     1 tablespoon olive oil
     1 large red bell pepper, finely diced
     1 to 2 garlic cloves, to taste, minced or put through a press
     2 medium eggs
     3 ounces mild, not too salty goat cheese
     3 tablespoons low-fat cottage cheese or ricotta
     1 ounce Parmesan or Gruyère cheese, grated (about 1/4 cup)
    1/2 cup cooked wild rice
    1/4 cup chopped fresh parsley
     1 teaspoon fresh thyme leaves *or* a pinch of crumbled dried
     1 tablespoon chopped cilantro (optional)
        salt and freshly ground pepper to taste

Set aside the crêpes (they will hold for a couple of days in the refrigerator). Cut the corn kernels off the ears of corn and set aside.

Heat the olive oil in a wide, heavy-bottomed or nonstick frying pan and add the red pepper. Sauté over medium heat for about 5 minutes and add the garlic. Sauté, stirring, for another 3 or 4 minutes. Add the corn and continue to sauté, stirring, for 3 to 5 more minutes. The vegetables should be crisp tender. Remove from the heat and transfer to a bowl.

Beat the eggs in a separate bowl and mash in the goat cheese and cottage cheese or ricotta. Stir in the Parmesan or Gruyère, the corn and pepper mixture, the wild rice, and the herbs. Season to taste with salt and lots of freshly ground pepper.

Preheat the oven to 400 degrees. Brush a baking dish with butter or olive oil. Place 3 tablespoons of the filling down the middle of each crêpe and gently roll up. Place seam side down in the baking dish.

Bake for 20 minutes or a little longer, until puffed and bubbling. Remove from the heat and serve, topped if you wish with a sauce (see note above).

ADVANCE PREPARATION: The crêpes will hold for a couple of days in a plastic bag in the refrigerator, and they freeze well. The filling can be made up to a day in advance and refrigerated. Bring it to room temperature before filling and cooking the crêpes.

LEFTOVERS: If you have any crêpes left over, cut them into slices for beautiful hors d'oeuvres. The slices should be about ¾ inch thick. You can serve them cold or reheat them in a 350-degree oven.

PER PORTION

Calories	282	Protein	13 G
Fat	11 G	Carbohydrate	36 G
Sodium	412 MG	Cholesterol	23 MG

BAKED APPLE AND PEAR COMPOTE

SERVES 6

This dessert can be put together in seconds. Indeed, I made it up one night when my in-laws came to dinner (we'd invited them at the last minute), and I wanted to serve something with the Crème Anglaise I had in my refrigerator, left over from a dinner party. It doesn't *seem* like an impromptu dish, but it easily can be.

  4 tart apples, peeled, cored, and cut into quarters or sixths

  3 ripe but firm pears, peeled, cored, and cut into quarters or sixths

     a handful of raisins

  2 tablespoons mild-flavored honey, approximately

  3/4 teaspoon ground cinnamon

  1/2 teaspoon freshly grated nutmeg to taste

     juice of 1 lemon

  3/4 cup apple juice

  1 tablespoon whiskey

     plain nonfat yogurt for topping or Crème Anglaise (page 436)

Preheat the oven to 375 degrees. Butter a baking dish large enough to accommodate all of the fruit.

Place the fruit in the baking dish along with the raisins. Drizzle on the honey. Sprinkle on the spices. Mix together the lemon juice, apple juice, and whiskey. Toss with the fruit. Place in the oven and bake for 45 minutes to 1 hour, until the fruit is very soft. Stir every 10 to 15 minutes. Remove from the heat. Serve hot or at room temperature, topped if you wish with crème Anglaise or plain low-fat yogurt.

ADVANCE PREPARATION: The compote can be assembled, or assembled and baked, hours ahead of time. Reheat in a 350-degree oven for 15 to 20 minutes.

PER PORTION (WITHOUT CRÈME ANGLAISE)

Calories	172	Protein	1 G
Fat	.72 G	Carbohydrate	44 G
Sodium	3 MG	Cholesterol	0

A BLACK BEAN CHILI DINNER PARTY

———

MEXICAN BEER, MARGARITAS (PAGE 16),
or CÔTES-DU-RHÔNE
JICAMA with LIME JUICE and
CHILI POWDER (PAGE 51)

•

BLACK BEAN CHILI
CORN BREAD (PAGE 393)

•

SPINACH and MUSHROOM SALAD with
LEMON-YOGURT VINAIGRETTE (PAGE 434)

•

ORANGES with COINTREAU and MINT or ORANGE ICE

•

MEXICAN BEER or CÔTES-DU-RHÔNE

This meal focuses on the Black Bean Chili, which is a rich, special chili. It's a long-cooking dish. The goat cheese melts into the steaming chili, adding an earthy, creamy dimension.

After the filling chili, a spinach salad with mushrooms, tossed with a lemony dressing, is a welcome palate cleanser. The dessert is light, whether you serve the oranges or the ice, and also refreshing after the chili.

I choose Mexican beer as my favorite drink with this repast; margaritas, of course, would also make a great aperitif. If you want to serve wine, go with a full-bodied, spicy red, such as a Côtes-du-Rhône or a big red from northern Spain.

This would be an easy meal to serve as a buffet, even though you will be eating the chili from bowls. You don't have to cut anything, so it's not inconvenient. But if you do serve it as a buffet, make sure people know about stirring the crumbled goat cheese into the chili, or they'll miss out on the crowning touch. For this reason you might want to have somebody supervising the serving. If you're serving the Orange Ice, make sure that people are ready for dessert when you bring it out, because it melts quickly.

Making This Dinner for a Crowd

All of the recipes here multiply easily. This is a good dinner for a crowd.

BLACK BEAN CHILI

SERVES 6

Over the years I've lived in Paris, friends from the States have brought me black beans and chili peppers when they've come to town and left me their leftover chili supplies when they've moved back. I'm always grateful, but at a certain point I found I had a small refrigerator full of chili peppers and powders, a pantry shelf filled with black beans that were getting old and hard. So I had no choice but to perfect a chili recipe. I hardly had to buy anything for this one; if you have onions, garlic, beans, spices, and canned tomatoes on hand, little shopping will be required. The deep, rich flavor of the black beans lends itself to this long-cooking, spicy chili. A few sun-dried tomatoes add a kind of smoky, meaty flavor. The goat cheese added at the end is a French touch, just the kind of twist I like to give to my Tex-Mex dishes over here.

Let me repeat the fact that this is a long-cooking dish. The longer it cooks, the better. It's a dish to make on a weekend.

1 pound dried black beans, picked over

3 tablespoons sunflower, safflower, peanut, or corn oil

2 large or 3 medium onions, chopped

6 large garlic cloves or more to taste, minced or put through a press

6 cups water, approximately

1 bay leaf

4 teaspoons cumin seeds or ground cumin

1 tablespoon sweet Hungarian paprika

$1/2$ teaspoon cayenne pepper

2 tablespoons ground dried chilies (preferably a combination of *ancho, pasilla,* and *piquín*) or chili powder

2 teaspoons dried oregano

1 green bell pepper, diced

1 ounce (about 6) sun-dried tomatoes, chopped

1 28-ounce can tomatoes, seeded and chopped, with the juice

2 teaspoons salt or more to taste

$1/2$ teaspoon sugar

freshly ground pepper to taste

1 tablespoon cider vinegar

$1/4$ cup chopped cilantro

6 heaped tablespoons *fromage blanc* (optional; page 417)

$1/4$ pound goat cheese, not too salty

1 recipe Tomato Salsa (page 422)

cilantro leaves for garnish

Soak the beans for at least 6 hours or overnight, using bottled water if your tap water is very hard. Drain.

Heat 1 tablespoon of the oil over medium heat in a large stockpot and sauté 1 of the chopped onions with 2 of the garlic cloves until the onion begins to soften. Add the beans, about 6 cups water, or enough to cover the beans by an inch or 2, and the bay leaf. Bring to a boil. Reduce the heat, cover, and simmer for 1 hour.

Meanwhile, toast the cumin seeds in a dry heavy skillet until they begin to color. (If you're using ground cumin, heat until they just begin to smell fragrant and remove from the heat.) Shake the pan or stir the seeds constantly or they'll burn. Remove from the heat and add the paprika and cayenne. Stir together for about 30 seconds in the hot pan, then transfer to a bowl. Grind the spices together in an electric spice mill. Add the ground chilies or chili powder and the oregano.

In a second large casserole or a bean pot, heat the remaining oil and sauté the remaining onion over medium-low heat until it softens. Add half the remaining garlic and the green pepper and continue to sauté for 5 minutes or so. Add the spices and chopped sun-dried tomatoes and continue sautéing, stirring constantly, for about 3 to 5 minutes, scraping the bottom of the casserole carefully so that the spices don't burn. If they cake on the bottom of the pan, add a little water. Add the tomatoes and their juice, about ½ teaspoon salt, and the sugar and bring to a simmer. Cover and simmer over low heat for 30 minutes, stirring often.

By this time the beans should have been cooking for about an hour. Add them with their liquid to the tomatoes and spices. Add the remaining garlic. If the beans aren't thoroughly covered with water, add a little more so that they are covered by at least an inch. Stir everything together and continue simmering, covered, for an hour or 2, until the beans are thoroughly tender and the broth is thick and fragrant. Add salt and freshly ground pepper to taste and simmer for another 15 minutes. If you want a thicker chili, place the casserole on a Flame Tamer and continue to simmer, uncovered or partially covered, stirring from time to time, for another hour or so, even up to 3 hours. Stir in the vinegar and adjust the seasonings. You may want to add more chili, garlic, salt, or a bit more vinegar. Stir in the ¼ cup cilantro just before serving.

To serve, ladle a generous portion into each of 6 wide, flat bowls and top with a tablespoon of *fromage blanc* if you're using it. Crumble in the goat cheese and top with a generous dollop of salsa. Garnish with a few leaves of cilantro. Serve at once and have your guests stir the goat cheese around so that it melts into the chili.

NOTE: To make chili powder from whole dried chilies, dry them out in a preheated 375-degree oven for about 5 minutes, making sure not to keep them in too long, or they'll burn. Cool and break into small pieces. Remove the seeds and veins and discard. Grind in an electric spice mill.

ADVANCE PREPARATION: The chili will hold for a couple of days in the refrigerator, and it freezes well. But don't stir in the ¼ cup cilantro until just before serving.

LEFTOVERS: You can keep serving the chili as it is, or you can use it as a filling for enchiladas or as a topping for nachos.

Enchiladas: Soften tortillas in a mixture of tomato sauce, cumin, chili powder, and a little sunflower or safflower oil, top with a spoonful of the chili, and sprinkle on goat cheese and cilantro. Roll up and place in a lightly oiled baking dish. Save about a cup of the chili and spoon it over the enchiladas. Sprinkle on additional goat cheese. Heat through in a 350-degree oven and serve.

Nachos: Reheat the chili and top tortilla chips with it. Crumble on goat cheese and serve as an hors d'oeuvre.

PER PORTION

Calories	519	Protein	27 G
Fat	15 G	Carbohydrate	75 G
Sodium	1,163 MG	Cholesterol	18 MG

ORANGES WITH COINTREAU AND MINT

SERVES 6

Oranges with Cointreau and fresh mint is one of my most frequent winter desserts. I have a big pot of mint on my balcony, and I usually have oranges on hand. I like this dessert because it's as welcome at a fancy dinner party as it is at an informal one. The oranges are very refreshing after a filling, savory meal.

6 navel oranges, peeled, white pith cut away, sliced or sectioned

¼ cup Cointreau

3 tablespoons chopped fresh mint

Toss the orange slices or sections, with their juice, in a bowl with the Cointreau and refrigerate until ready to serve. Toss with the mint just before serving.

ADVANCE PREPARATION: This dessert will hold, without the mint, for a few hours in the refrigerator.

PER PORTION

Calories	106	Protein	I G
Fat	.12 G	Carbohydrate	21 G
Sodium	I MG	Cholesterol	0

ORANGE ICE

SERVES 6

This ice couldn't be simpler, yet it's terrific every time. It may seem as though fresh orange juice would be even better, but in this case the concentrate works best.

1½ quarts orange juice made from unsweetened concentrate

Place the orange juice in an ice cream maker and process until frozen.

You can make this without an ice cream maker by freezing the juice in ice cube trays and breaking it up after 1 hour in the freezer in a food processor fitted with the steel blade or in an electric mixer. Return it to the freezer and freeze until just about frozen solid. Break up and freeze once more before serving. Allow to soften in the refrigerator for 20 minutes before serving.

ADVANCE PREPARATION: This ice can be made weeks ahead of time.

	PER PORTION		
Calories	75	Protein	1 G
Fat	.09 G	Carbohydrate	18 G
Sodium	2 MG	Cholesterol	0

TWO FALL/WINTER MENUS WITH
ROAST CHICKEN AND FINE WINES

———

CHAMPAGNE
•
EITHER
ROAST CHICKEN with ROSEMARY and MORELS
SPAGHETTI SQUASH GRATIN
WILD RICE PILAF
•
TOSSED GREEN SALAD (PAGE 425)
CHEESE (OPTIONAL)
•
KIWIFRUIT SORBET
OR
ROAST CHICKEN with ROSEMARY and MORELS
PUREE of POTATO and CELERIAC with a HINT of APPLE
or PLAIN POTATOES, ROASTED with the CHICKEN
STEAMED ZUCCHINI (PAGE 103)
•
TOSSED GREEN SALAD (PAGE 425)
CHEESE (OPTIONAL)
•
KIWIFRUIT SORBET
•
FINE RED WINES from BORDEAUX, BURGUNDY,
or the CÔTES-DU-RHÔNE

For years we'd been trying to get together with our neighbors, the wine writer Jon Winroth and his wife Doreen, to drink a bottle of 1973 Château Lafite that we'd had in our wine closet for some time. Dates had been canceled for one reason or another, but finally we found a night when we'd all be in town. Then all I had to do was decide what to cook. It had to be simple, without much if any garlic, and it couldn't be fish. Roast chicken, dressed up with dried morels, would be perfect—and easy. The rest of the menu could have been simpler—roast or boiled potatoes and steamed zucchini would have been just fine—but I had so many good recipes that would go well with the chicken and not compete with the wines, enough to make two terrific menus. They're fall/winter meals, with autumn colors and sweet-tasting vegetables. And they do justice to very fine wines. But you don't *have* to drink big, fine wines with these menus. A Rhône wine would be great, something like a St.-Joseph; or a light, fruity red wine from the Loire, such as a Bourgueil, Gamay, or Saumur-Champigny, or a Beaujolais Cru would also make a good match. You could also drink a California zinfandel with this meal.

Making This Dinner for a Crowd

All the recipes here are easily multiplied, but I would think it would be difficult to bake more than two chickens at a time, so don't plan on serving this meal for more than eight people. You could serve turkey instead of chicken for a crowd.

ROAST CHICKEN WITH ROSEMARY AND MORELS

SERVES 4

This is really an informal menu. Roast chicken is certainly one of the easiest things to cook. But timing is important, and you have to have a really good chicken to begin with. Try to find a reliable supplier of organic free-range chickens; they have a much richer, more wholesome flavor than battery chickens and are worth the extra cost.

There's nothing new about roast chicken, but this one is particularly fragrant because of the dried morels and sprigs of rosemary that are stuffed into its cavity before baking. If you wish, you could serve the chicken with the Mushroom "Gravy" on page 213. But because this meal was designed to show off some very nice red wines from Bordeaux, I chose to keep the flavors simple. To make a light gravy that isn't loaded with chicken fat, I pour off the drippings and deglaze the pan with a very small amount of butter and the soaking water from the morels. To keep fats down, remove the skin before serving the chicken.

1   ounce (1 cup) dried morels
    boiling water to cover
1   3-pound free-range roasting chicken
1   tablespoon olive oil plus a small amount for the baking dish
    salt and freshly ground pepper to taste
3   fresh rosemary sprigs
1   teaspoon unsalted butter

Place the morels in a bowl and pour on boiling water to cover. Let sit for 20 minutes, until softened. Drain through a cheesecloth-lined strainer, squeeze the mushrooms over the strainer, and reserve the liquid. Rinse the mushrooms thoroughly under cold water and squeeze dry.

Preheat the oven to 425 degrees. Rub the chicken with olive oil and sprinkle with salt and pepper. Place the mushrooms and the sprigs of rosemary in the cavity and truss if you wish.

Lightly oil a flameproof baking dish that isn't too much bigger than the chicken and place the chicken on its side in the dish. (You can put small roasting potatoes in the dish with the chicken if you wish.) Bake for 20 minutes, turn it onto its other side, and bake for another 20 minutes. Finish cooking the chicken on its back, about 20 minutes longer, or until the juice runs clear when pierced with a knife. Baste every 10 or 15 minutes.

Transfer the chicken to a serving platter and cover loosely with foil. Pour off all the fat from the baking dish and discard. Add the butter and ⅔ cup of the strained soaking liquid from the mushrooms. Heat over high heat and stir, using a whisk or a wooden spoon or spatula to scrape up the bits adhering to the bottom of the pan. Reduce by about half and add salt and pepper to taste; transfer to a gravy boat. Remove the morels and the rosemary from the chicken. Discard the rosemary. Carve the chicken (remove the skin first if you wish), garnish with the morels, and serve with the gravy on the side.

ADVANCE PREPARATION: The morels can be soaked and the chicken stuffed and trussed hours before serving. But it should be baked just before serving.

LEFTOVERS: Use for the chicken salads on pages 354 and 356. Make chicken stock (page 413) with the carcass.

PER PORTION

Calories	290	Protein	36 G
Fat	13 G	Carbohydrate	5 G
Sodium	117 MG	Cholesterol	111 MG

SPAGHETTI SQUASH GRATIN

SERVES 4

Spaghetti squash has such a sweet flavor and makes a terrific gratin. The spaghettilike strands of squash catch the milk and egg mixture like noodles so that the dish has a kugellike quality. This could be a main dish or a side dish.

1 large spaghetti squash (about 3 pounds)

¾ cup skim milk

2 medium eggs

2 tablespoons grated Gruyère cheese

   salt and freshly ground pepper to taste

   pinch of freshly grated nutmeg

3 tablespoons medium to fine fresh bread crumbs

2 tablespoons freshly grated Parmesan cheese

1 tablespoon olive oil

First bake the spaghetti squash. Preheat the oven to 400 degrees and pierce the squash in several places with a sharp knife. Place on a lightly oiled baking sheet and bake for 1 hour or until the squash has softened. Remove from the heat and allow to cool. Cut the squash in half lengthwise. Remove the seeds. Scoop out the squash from the skin and place in a bowl. Using a fork, separate the spaghettilike fibers.

Beat together the milk and eggs. Stir in the Gruyère cheese, salt (about ½ teaspoon), lots of freshly ground pepper, and a pinch of nutmeg. Mix thoroughly with the spaghetti squash.

Lightly oil a 12- by 8- by 2-inch baking dish or gratin dish with olive oil and transfer the spaghetti squash mixture to the dish. Top with the bread crumbs and Parmesan, and drizzle on the olive oil.

Bake for 30 minutes or until the gratin is set and browned on the top. Serve hot.

ADVANCE PREPARATION: The entire dish can be assembled hours ahead of the time you wish to bake it. It should be at room temperature when it goes into the oven.

PER PORTION

Calories	205	Protein	9 G
Fat	9 G	Carbohydrate	23 G
Sodium	196 MG	Cholesterol	101 MG

PUREE OF POTATO AND CELERIAC WITH A HINT OF APPLE

SERVES 4

This is a really satisfying combination, and kind of mysterious with its touch of apple. Celeriac (celery root) and potatoes go nicely together, and the apple gives it a slight hint of sweetness and acidity. You can moisten this puree with the cooking liquid from the potatoes, celeriac, and apple. That way none of the flavors are diluted, and there's no added fat.

This puree goes nicely with chicken or fish, but it would also make a great filling for crêpes, with a little Parmesan or Gruyère sprinkled over it before baking.

    1 pound waxy potatoes, peeled
    1 pound celeriac, cut into quarters and peeled
      juice of ½ lemon
    2 Granny Smith apples, peeled, cored, and quartered
      salt and freshly ground pepper to taste

Cut the potatoes into halves or quarters if very large and place in a saucepan. Cover them with water.

Cut the celeriac quarters into pieces roughly equal in size to the potatoes. Place in water acidulated with the lemon juice. Place the apples in the acidulated water with the celeriac.

Drain the celeriac and apples and add to the saucepan with the potatoes. Add enough additional water just to cover everything, along with ¼ to ½ teaspoon salt, to taste. Bring to a simmer and cook over medium-low heat until everything is very tender, about 20 minutes.

Remove the pan from the heat and drain over a bowl, retaining the cooking liquid.

Preheat the oven to 350 degrees. Puree the mixture through the fine blade of a Mouli food mill. Don't use a food processor or the mixture will be too gummy. Add cooking liquid until the mixture is moistened to your taste. Add salt and pepper to taste and transfer to a lightly buttered serving dish. Heat through for 15 minutes in the preheated oven before serving.

NOTE: You can also use low-fat milk or *fromage blanc* (page 417) to moisten the mixture.

(*continued*)

ADVANCE PREPARATION: This dish can be prepared up to a day ahead of time and held in the refrigerator. The cooked vegetables will also hold for a day or two before you puree them.

LEFTOVERS: If you have leftovers, you can make a gratin or a soup.

Potato, Celeriac, and Apple Gratin: Place in a buttered baking dish and sprinkle the top with 2 tablespoons freshly grated Parmesan cheese. Bake at 400 degrees for about 20 minutes or until the gratin begins to brown on the top.

Puree of Potato, Celeriac, and Apple Soup: Thin out to the desired consistency with low-fat milk and heat through in a saucepan. You could add a little curry powder for a different flavor.

PER PORTION

Calories	158	Protein	4 G
Fat	.67 G	Carbohydrate	37 G
Sodium	106 MG	Cholesterol	0

WILD RICE PILAF

SERVES 4

This makes a great side dish with chicken or rich fish like salmon or trout or with vegetable gratins. When I'm serving this with the Roast Chicken with Rosemary and Morels, I omit the morels.

- 1 ounce (1 cup) dried morels (optional)
- 2 cups boiling water
- 2 cups chicken or vegetable stock (page 413 or 414)
- 1 cup reserved morel soaking liquid or water
- 1 cup wild rice, washed
- 1 tablespoon unsalted butter or sunflower oil
- 1 shallot, minced
   salt to taste
   freshly ground pepper to taste
- 1 tablespoon dry sherry (optional)
- 1 tablespoon chopped fresh parsley

Place the morels in a bowl and pour on the boiling water. Let sit for 15 to 20 minutes, until the morels have softened. Strain through a cheesecloth-lined strainer. Squeeze the mushrooms over the strainer and reserve the liquid. Rinse the morels thoroughly under cold water and squeeze dry. Chop coarsely and set aside.

Combine the stock and strained soaking liquid or water in a saucepan and bring to a boil. Add the rice and about ¼ teaspoon salt, bring to a boil again, cover, reduce the heat, and simmer for 40 minutes or until the rice is tender. Remove from the heat and pour off any excess liquid in the pan.

Heat the butter or oil in a nonstick or well-seasoned frying pan and add the shallot. Cook over medium-low heat until it begins to soften and brown; stir in the rice and the mushrooms if you're using them. Stir together over medium heat for a few minutes, add salt and pepper to taste, and the sherry if desired. Heat through, stir in the parsley, and serve.

ADVANCE PREPARATION: You can cook this dish a few hours ahead of serving, transfer it to a baking dish, cover with foil, and heat through in a 350-degree oven.

LEFTOVERS: Use for a salad, such as the Wild Rice and Peas Salad on page 294.

PER PORTION

Calories	217	Protein	7 G
Fat	4 G	Carbohydrate	39 G
Sodium	173 MG	Cholesterol	8 MG

KIWIFRUIT SORBET

SERVES 4

This beautiful tart sorbet sits atop a bright layer of thin kiwifruit slices. It's a great light finish to a savory meal.

2½ tablespoons sugar

¼ cup water

2½ pounds kiwifruit

    juice of 1 orange

    juice of 1 large lemon

    fresh mint leaves for garnish

Combine the sugar and water in a saucepan and bring to a boil. Simmer until the sugar is completely dissolved and the syrup slightly thickened. Remove from the heat and allow to cool while you prepare the kiwifruit.

    Hold 4 of the kiwifruit for later and peel the rest. Remove the stems, quarter, and puree in a food processor fitted with the steel blade. Add the orange and lemon juices and syrup and continue to puree until smooth. Put through a fine strainer, pressing through all of the puree with the back of a spoon or a spatula, and discard the seeds. Transfer to ice cube trays, a stainless-steel bowl, or an ice cream maker. Freeze according to the manufacturer's instructions or until just about set in the ice cube trays or bowl. If you're not using an ice cream maker, puree again when the mixture has just about set, to break up the ice crystals. You can repeat this process one more time for an even smoother sorbet. Freeze until 20 minutes before serving, then allow to soften in the refrigerator.

    To serve, peel the remaining kiwifruit and slice thin. Line 4 dessert plates with the kiwifruit slices. Using a soupspoon, spoon 1 or 2 scoops of the sorbet onto the kiwifruit slices. Decorate with mint leaves and serve.

ADVANCE PREPARATION: This sorbet will keep for weeks in the freezer.

PER PORTION

Calories	191	Protein	3 G
Fat	1 G	Carbohydrate	47 G
Sodium	13 MG	Cholesterol	0

A FESTIVE DINNER FOR SIX

FEATURING LAPIN À LA MOUTARDE

———

DRY WHITE WINE or CHAMPAGNE

CAVIAR

•

LAPIN (ou POULET) À LA MOUTARDE

COOKED SWEET and SOUR RADISHES

STEAMED ZUCCHINI (PAGE 103)

PASTA MADE with EGG WHITES ONLY (PAGE 403)

•

FRISÉE with WALNUTS (PAGE 108; OMIT CROUTONS)

•

RASPBERRIES with FROMAGE BLANC (PAGE 417)

or TANGERINES

•

CÔTES-DU-RHÔNE, GIGONDAS, or PALETTE CHÂTEAU

SIMONE (APPELLATION PALETTE)

If you don't make your own pasta, this is an easy meal to prepare in a couple of hours. You can marinate the rabbit in the morning (chicken doesn't require marinating) and do all the rest after work. The pasta requires extra time, but you don't *have* to make it. The menu is quite a pretty one, with the pinkish red radishes and bright-green zucchini served alongside the rabbit or chicken in its tangy mustard sauce. Rabbit is my first choice for this dish, but chicken also works well.

I served caviar the first time I made this meal because one of my guests had just flown in from Russia, and she brought me a can of it. It made a great start to a fun dinner party. I don't serve a first course with this meal—the caviar is enough—but after the main dish I like to serve a big crisp green salad. My favorite for this meal is the frisée and walnut salad on page 108, but without the croutons. You could also serve a simple tossed green salad. The Raspberries with Fromage Blanc make an easy, light finish to the meal.

A fruity, gutsy red from the south of France or from Italy is perfect with this meal. A Beaujolais Cru would also go well.

Making This Dinner for a Crowd

This is a good menu for a crowd, but be prepared to spend a lot of time at the stove browning all the rabbit or chicken pieces and have somebody to help you prep the radishes. You can multiply the recipe to feed up to 25 people. If you're making a large quantity of the rabbit or chicken, you will probably have to brown the rabbit or chicken in the nonstick frying pan, then add the onions and cook, remove the pan from the heat, coat with flour, then transfer everything to a big stockpot.

LAPIN (OU POULET) À LA MOUTARDE (RABBIT OR CHICKEN IN MUSTARD SAUCE)

SERVES 6

Lapin à la moutarde is one of my favorite French dishes. Until I came across Patricia Wells's recipe in *Bistro Cooking* (Workman Publishing, 1989), I never cooked it myself, because most recipes call for generous amounts of crème fraîche. Hers doesn't; the sauce contains a little flour, and it thickens naturally with the mustard and flour as it cooks. I've adapted Patricia Wells's recipe, marinating the rabbit in the white wine in which it will be cooked, reducing the oil, and adding some chicken stock. I always prefer cooking rabbit practically submerged in liquid so that the meat doesn't dry out. This is terrific with fresh pasta.

> 1 large fresh rabbit, cut into 8 serving pieces, *or* 1½ large fry chickens, cut up and with skin removed (about 3 pounds rabbit *or* chicken)
>
> 1 bottle dry white wine
>
> ½ cup imported Dijon mustard
>
> 2 tablespoons olive oil, as needed
>
> 1 tablespoon unsalted butter
>
> salt and freshly ground pepper to taste
>
> 2 medium onions, chopped
>
> 1½ tablespoons superfine flour (Wondra)
>
> 2½ cups chicken stock (page 413)
>
> 1 teaspoon crumbled dried thyme
>
> 1 bay leaf
>
> a handful of chopped fresh parsley

If you're using rabbit, trim away all excess fat and place in a large bowl. Pour in the wine, cover, and refrigerate for 6 hours or longer. Turn the pieces over from time to time if the rabbit isn't covered with wine.

Remove the rabbit from the marinade, reserving the wine. Brush 1 side of each rabbit or chicken piece generously with mustard.

Heat 1 tablespoon of the oil with the butter over medium heat in a large nonreactive, preferably nonstick frying pan. Brown the rabbit or chicken, mustard side down, a few pieces at a time, in batches, about 10 minutes. Add

(continued)

oil as needed. Transfer to a paper towel–lined platter or baking sheet. Sprinkle with salt and freshly ground pepper.

Deglaze the pan with several tablespoons of the reserved wine (or fresh wine if you're using chicken). Add the onions and cook over medium-low heat, stirring, until golden brown, about 5 minutes. Remove the pan from the heat. Sprinkle the flour over the onions and stir to coat. Return the rabbit or chicken to the pan. Pour in the remaining reserved wine if you're using the rabbit version, or 2 cups wine for the chicken, and add the chicken stock, any remaining mustard, the thyme, and the bay leaf. Return the pan to the stove and simmer over medium-low heat, partially covered, until the meat is very tender and almost falling off the bone and the sauce is thick, about 1 to 1½ hours for rabbit, 20 minutes for the white chicken pieces, 45 for the dark meat. Move the pieces of meat around and turn over from time to time so that they don't dry out. Taste the sauce and correct seasonings. Add a little more mustard if you want a more pungent sauce.

Transfer the rabbit or chicken and sauce to a warm platter and sprinkle with parsley. Serve immediately, over fresh noodles or brown or white rice.

ADVANCE PREPARATION: The rabbit can be marinated and refrigerated the night before serving. The chicken stock can be made 2 days ahead of time.

LEFTOVERS: Remove the meat from the bones. Heat with leftover sauce and toss with pasta or with warm rice.

PER PORTION

Calories	376	Protein	38 G
Fat	19 G	Carbohydrate	10 G
Sodium	707 MG	Cholesterol	112 MG

COOKED SWEET AND SOUR RADISHES

SERVES 6 GENEROUSLY

This recipe comes from my friend Deirdre Simms, who cooked them for a *Lapin à la Moutarde* dinner party at my house. Everybody *raved* about the radishes, which take on the most beautiful pink color when they cook. You'll surprise your guests with this; nobody ever thinks of cooked radishes, and these have such a nice, slightly sweet and sour flavor and a succulent texture.

1 tablespoon unsalted butter

3 large bunches of radishes (about 3 pounds), *or* 4 small bunches, trimmed and washed

  salt and freshly ground pepper to taste

1 tablespoon red wine vinegar

4 teaspoons sugar

1/4 cup water or more as needed

Heat the butter over medium heat in a nonreactive heavy-bottomed lidded saucepan and add the radishes as soon as it foams. Add salt and pepper, turn down the heat, cover, and cook over medium-low heat, stirring often, for 8 to 10 minutes. Add the vinegar and sugar and cook, stirring, for 5 minutes. Add the water, cover, and cook over low heat, stirring from time to time, for another 10 to 15 minutes, until the radishes are tender, pink, and slightly glazed. Add more water during the cooking, if needed. Serve hot.

ADVANCE PREPARATION: The radishes can be prepped a day ahead of time and kept in cold water. However, drain well before cooking.

LEFTOVERS: Leftovers can be reheated gently in a saucepan and served again as a side dish.

PER PORTION

Calories	63	Protein	1 G
Fat	3 G	Carbohydrate	10 G
Sodium	69 MG	Cholesterol	5 MG

A COUSCOUS DINNER FOR EIGHT

———

MUSCAT D'ALSACE

•

THREE MOROCCAN SALADS:
SIMPLE ORANGE SALAD with CINNAMON and MINT
GRATED CARROT SALAD with MINT and ORANGE JUICE
GRATED BEET SALAD with ORANGE JUICE and PARSLEY

•

FISH COUSCOUS
CORN BREAD (PAGE 393)

•

RASPBERRIES with CRÈME DE FRAMBOISE LIQUEUR
ORANGE BISCOTTI (PAGE 409)

•

BANDOL ROSÉ or ROUGE DOMAINE TEMPIER

Couscous is always a good dish for a crowd, because all of its components can be prepared ahead of time.

Once I prepared this menu only to find out a couple of days before that two of the guests were deathly allergic to fish. No matter, in this case; I just kept some of the vegetable soup mixture separate from the fumet and served vegetable couscous to those who preferred it. That's another convenient thing about serving this couscous to a crowd: if you have a mix of fish eaters and vegetarians, or people with allergies, you can make two different versions with no extra trouble.

This meal goes from a very light first course, which will whet your guests' appetites, to a filling, though not rich, main dish, back to a light dessert. Cornmeal-based breads complement the meal nicely. It's suitable for both large and small groups.

A crisp, fruity rosé or a robust red from a Mediterranean climate would be the perfect choice with this meal. Domaine Tempier would be my number-one preference.

Making This Dinner for a Crowd

All of the dishes are easy to make for a crowd. They will multiply easily. It's easiest when serving the fish couscous to a crowd to cook the fish separately, steaming it or poaching it in a little of the broth in advance and setting it aside until ready to serve.

SIMPLE ORANGE SALAD WITH CINNAMON AND MINT

SERVES 8

This is an easy orange salad that can be served as a first course in combination with other salads or as a dessert.

    10 navel oranges
  1½ tablespoons orange flower water
    2 tablespoons fresh lemon juice to taste (optional)
        ground cinnamon to taste
  2½ tablespoons chopped fresh mint
        lettuce leaves for serving
        fresh mint sprigs for garnish

Cut both ends off each orange. Holding the oranges above a bowl to catch the liquid, cut away the peel and pith of the oranges in wide strips, cutting from one end to the other. Cut the orange sections out from between the membranes dividing them. Toss with the orange flower water and lemon juice. Sprinkle very lightly with cinnamon.

Chill until ready to serve. Shortly before serving, toss with the chopped mint. To serve as a salad, line a bowl, platter, or individual serving plates with lettuce leaves and top with the salad. To serve as a dessert, chill and serve in an attractive serving bowl. Garnish with sprigs or leaves of fresh mint.

ADVANCE PREPARATION: The salad will hold in the refrigerator for a few hours, but add the mint shortly before serving.

NOTE: Orange flower water is available in specialty food shops.

PER PORTION

Calories	87	Protein	2 G
Fat	.16 G	Carbohydrate	22 G
Sodium	2 MG	Cholesterol	0

GRATED CARROT SALAD WITH MINT AND ORANGE JUICE

SERVES 8

Everyone is always amazed to taste this salad. The orange juice brings out the sweetness of the carrots, their juices combining in the most delicate way. Mint is the perfect herb to toss with the mixture. With no oil at all, this is one of the lowest-calorie salads I know of.

juice of $2^1/_2$ oranges

juice of 1 lemon

$2^1/_2$ pounds carrots, peeled and grated

2 tablespoons chopped fresh mint

salt and freshly ground pepper to taste (optional)

fresh mint sprigs for garnish

Combine the orange and lemon juices. Toss with the grated carrots and mint. Add salt and freshly ground pepper if you wish. Serve at once, or chill until ready to serve (in which case, hold the mint and toss with the carrots just before serving). Garnish each serving with a sprig or a few leaves of fresh mint.

ADVANCE PREPARATION: The carrots can be grated a day ahead of time and held in a covered container or sealed bag in the refrigerator. They can be tossed with the orange and lemon juice a few hours before serving.

	PER PORTION		
Calories	72	Protein	2 G
Fat	.30 G	Carbohydrate	17 G
Sodium	47 MG	Cholesterol	0

FISH COUSCOUS

SERVES 8

Authentic fish couscous usually calls for striped mullet fish steaks. For entertaining, especially large groups, I prefer fillets, which are much tidier, with no bone problem.

FOR THE FISH STOCK

3 pounds fish heads and bones

2 quarts water

1 onion, peeled and quartered

1 large carrot, thickly sliced

1 celery rib, sliced

2 large garlic cloves, peeled

1 leek, white part only, cleaned and sliced

6 peppercorns

a bouquet garni made with 1 bay leaf, 2 fresh thyme sprigs, and 2 fresh parsley sprigs

1 cup dry white wine

salt to taste

FOR THE VEGETABLE SOUP

1 tablespoon olive oil

1 large *or* 2 small onions, sliced

3 to 4 garlic cloves to taste, minced or put through a press

$1/2$ pound dried chick-peas, washed, picked over, and soaked overnight

1 leek, white part only, cleaned and sliced

2 celery ribs, sliced

1 pound tomatoes, peeled and coarsely chopped, *or* 1 28-ounce can tomatoes, drained and coarsely chopped

1 quart water

1 bay leaf

1 fresh jalapeño or other hot green chili, seeded and sliced

the fish stock

$1/2$ teaspoon saffron threads

$3/4$ pound turnips, peeled and cut into quarters or sixths

GRATED BEET SALAD WITH ORANGE JUICE AND PARSLEY

SERVES 8

Like carrots, beets release a sweet juice that combines beautifully with orange juice. I've served this salad to sworn beet haters (not knowing, before I served it, that they had an aversion to beets—it's not uncommon), and they've loved it. First of all, they didn't know they were eating beets until I told them. Most people who hate beets, it turns out, hate *cooked* beets. They don't know that they might like them uncooked, because they've never tasted them. As beautiful as it is delicious, this is another extremely low-calorie salad, with absolutely no oil.

    juice of 2^1/$_2$ oranges
    juice of 1^1/$_2$ lemons
2^1/$_2$ pounds fresh beets, peeled and grated
 ^{1}/$_3$ cup chopped fresh parsley plus additional for garnish
    salt and freshly ground pepper to taste
    lettuce leaves for serving

Combine the orange and lemon juices and toss with the beets and parsley. Add salt and pepper. Serve at once or chill until ready to serve. To serve, line salad plates, a platter, or a salad bowl with lettuce leaves and top with the beet mixture. Sprinkle on additional parsley.

ADVANCE PREPARATION: This salad can be made a few hours ahead of serving, but in this case hold the parsley and toss it with the beets shortly before serving.

PER PORTION

Calories	60	Protein	2 G
Fat	.19 G	Carbohydrate	14 G
Sodium	74 MG	Cholesterol	0

RASPBERRIES WITH
CRÈME DE FRAMBOISE LIQUEUR

SERVES 8

Here raspberries are tossed shortly before serving with a small amount of Crème de Framboise liqueur, just enough to embellish their already superb sweet flavor.

> 2 pints (about 1 pound) raspberries
>   juice of 1 lemon
> ⅔ cup Crème de Framboise liqueur
>   fresh mint leaves for garnish

Shortly before serving, sprinkle the raspberries with the lemon juice and toss gently with the liqueur. Garnish with mint leaves.

PER PORTION

Calories	111	Protein	1 G
Fat	.37 G	Carbohydrate	16 G
Sodium	1 MG	Cholesterol	0

A FALL/WINTER CANNELLONI FEAST

———

PINOT BLANC D'ALSACE JOSMEYER

•

BROCCOLI and ENDIVE SALAD with
ROASTED RED PEPPERS

•

CANNELLONI with SPINACH and HERB FILLING
SAUTÉED OYSTER MUSHROOMS (PAGE 111)

•

PEAR and RED WINE SORBET

•

MAS CHICHET CABERNET

first served this menu on a particularly dark, rainy, gusty autumn evening; dinner was colorful and warming.

The dinner is a good one for a crowd, because so much of it can be done in advance, and it makes a good buffet as well as a sit-down dinner. The colors (lots of green and red) remind me of Christmas, and in fact it would be perfect for a Christmas Eve buffet.

It's a beautifully balanced feast: the salad is light and pungent, with garlicky roasted red peppers, sharp Stilton cheese, and a nutty vinaigrette. The cannelloni are savory and comforting, with their vibrant fresh spinach and herb filling that contains just enough cheese to make the dish satisfying but not so much as to make it heavy and rich. The cannelloni are gorgeous, whether served from an attractive casserole on a buffet or on individual plates. The pale green pasta contrasts vividly with the bright orange tomato sauce. Earthy sautéed mushrooms fill out the plate and complement the cannelloni. Crusty country bread is a must. Dessert is light and tangy, an intriguing sorbet made with wine and pears.

A light, dry white wine makes a good aperitif to serve before the dinner. The slightly spicy Pinot Blanc d'Alsace is perfect. A Loire Valley white, such as a Sancerre or Sauvignon Touraine, would also be good. The fruity Muscat d'Alsace is another one to try; it tastes like the muscat grape but isn't sweet like Muscat de Beaumes de Venise.

The meal requires a moderately light but gutsy red wine. The ones that go best are from southern France. We've found some good wines from the Roussillon region, down near the Spanish border, and we've especially enjoyed a Cabernet from a small winery called Mas Chichet, near Perpignan. Other wines that I've served successfully with this meal are a Coteaux du Tricastin, Côtes-du-Rhône, and Gigondas. A Bandol would be excellent as well.

Making This Dinner for a Crowd

Each recipe multiplies easily.

BROCCOLI AND ENDIVE SALAD
WITH ROASTED RED PEPPERS

SERVES 6

This is a beautiful salad that can be composed in a large salad bowl or on individual plates. A fall/winter dish, it's a colorful opener for a meal. Each element of the salad has its own delicious character, and they all blend together in perfect harmony.

1 teaspoon salt

1¾ pounds broccoli, separated into florets, stems set aside

2 medium red bell peppers

1 tablespoon red wine vinegar

1 garlic clove, minced or put through a press

salt to taste

4 teaspoons olive oil

1 pound Belgian endives

1½ tablespoons pine nuts

¾ cup Low-Fat Walnut Vinaigrette (page 435) or Low-Fat Yogurt Vinaigrette with Olive Oil (page 433)

2 ounces Stilton cheese, crumbled

freshly ground pepper to taste

2 tablespoons chopped fresh parsley

Bring a large pot of water to a boil. Add the salt and the broccoli and cook for 1 minute. Drain, refresh under cold water, and set aside.

Roast the pepper over a gas flame or under a broiler until uniformly charred. Place in a paper or plastic bag for about 15 minutes or until cool enough to handle. Remove charred skin, rinse, and pat dry. Cut into thin strips, discarding the seeds and inner membranes. Toss with the vinegar, garlic, salt to taste, and olive oil. Cover and set aside.

Rinse the endives and cut off the root end. Break off the leaves. Dry and place in a bowl.

Roast the pine nuts in a dry frying pan over medium heat just until they begin to brown. Remove from the pan at once.

Toss the endives with one third of the vinaigrette.

In another bowl, toss together the broccoli, Stilton, and roasted pine nuts with the remaining vinaigrette. Taste and add salt and freshly ground pepper to taste.

(*continued*)

If you're using individual plates, line with individual endive leaves, radiating out from the center of the plate like petals of a daisy. Top with the broccoli and distribute the red pepper strips over the broccoli. Sprinkle with parsley and serve.

If you're using a large salad bowl or platter, use the same design, lining the bowl or platter with the endive, then filling with the broccoli and topping with the red peppers.

ADVANCE PREPARATION: All of the ingredients can be prepared hours in advance and kept separately. Toss with the vinaigrette and compose the salad just before serving. The red peppers will keep for 2 or 3 days in the refrigerator.

PER PORTION (WITH LOW-FAT WALNUT VINAIGRETTE)

Calories	154	Protein	8 G
Fat	10 G	Carbohydrate	12 G
Sodium	400 MG	Cholesterol	7 MG

PER PORTION (WITH LOW-FAT YOGURT VINAIGRETTE WITH OLIVE OIL)

Calories	128	Protein	8 G
Fat	7 G	Carbohydrate	12 G
Sodium	357 MG	Cholesterol	7 MG

CANNELLONI WITH SPINACH AND HERB FILLING

SERVES 6

These beautiful green cannelloni taste not only incredibly good but also intensely healthy, like a garden of spinach and herbs. The ricotta and eggs give the mixture body; the goat cheese and Parmesan add depth. They're time-consuming to make but can be assembled a day in advance and held in the refrigerator overnight. It helps to make these with a friend.

FOR THE PASTA

2 recipes Herb or Watercress Pasta (pages 405 or 406), made with egg whites only

1 tablespoon salt

1 teaspoon vegetable oil

FOR THE FILLING

1 pound fresh spinach, stemmed and washed

1 cup finely chopped fresh flat-leaf parsley

$1/2$ cup finely chopped fresh basil *or* $1^{1}/2$ cups finely chopped fresh parsley in all

1 pound low-fat cottage cheese

$1/4$ pound goat cheese, not too salty (such as St. Christophe, Ste. Maure, or a fresh local variety)

$1/2$ cup plus 2 tablespoons freshly grated Parmesan cheese

$1/2$ teaspoon crumbled dried thyme *or* 1 teaspoon fresh leaves

$1/2$ to 1 teaspoon minced fresh rosemary, *or* $1/4$ to $1/2$ teaspoon crumbled dried, to taste

2 garlic cloves, minced or put through a press

$1/8$ teaspoon freshly grated nutmeg

1 medium egg, beaten

FOR THE TOMATO SAUCE

    1 tablespoon olive oil

    1 small onion, minced

    3 large garlic cloves, minced or put through a press

    4 pounds fresh tomatoes, peeled and chopped, *or* 4 32-ounce
      cans tomatoes, drained and chopped

$1/4$ teaspoon sugar

    salt to taste

    1 to 2 tablespoons chopped fresh basil

    pinch of ground cinnamon

    freshly ground pepper to taste

FOR THE TOPPING

$1/2$ cup freshly grated Parmesan cheese

    2 to 3 tablespoons chopped fresh parsley to taste

You have a number of choices here since all of the components except the tomato sauce can be made a day in advance. The order listed below works well if you are assembling the pasta a day ahead of time. If you are making a large quantity of the cannelloni and need to stack them, stack them between sheets of aluminum foil, lightly oiled with olive oil, and heat the sauce separately on the stove. Sauce the cannelloni when you serve them. You must have the filling ready before you roll out and cook the pasta, since you fill the pasta as soon as it is cooked. The entire dish is then baked in the oven.

MAKE THE PASTA DOUGH: Knead the pasta dough and allow it to rest for 30 minutes while you make the filling. (See page 403.)

TO MAKE THE FILLING: Wash the spinach and place it in a large dry skillet. Cook over high heat in the liquid left on the leaves after washing, just until it wilts. Remove from the pan, rinse with cold water, and squeeze very dry in a towel. Chop finely, either by hand or in a food processor fitted with the steel blade, and blend together with the remaining ingredients, in a food processor, a mixer, or a large bowl, stirring well with a wooden spoon.

TO ROLL, CUT, COOK, AND FILL THE PASTA: Roll the pasta out into long, wide sheets to the number 4 setting. Cut these into rectangles about $4^{1}/2$ by $5^{1}/2$ inches. Allow to dry on towels for about 20 minutes.
    Bring a large pot of water to a rolling boil and add a tablespoon of salt and a teaspoon of oil. Have a bowl of cold water next to the pot. Drop the pasta rectangles into the boiling water, a few at a time, and cook for about 30 seconds to 1 minute or until they float up to the surface of the boiling water. Remove

from the pot with a slotted spoon and place in the cold water to stop the cooking, then drain on a towel. Continue until you have cooked all the rectangles. (If two of you are doing this together, one can be cooking the pasta while the other fills the cannelloni.)

Oil two 3-quart baking dishes. Place 2 heaped tablespoons of filling along the longer edge of each rectangle and roll up. Place the cannelloni side by side in the baking dish, seam side down.

TO MAKE THE TOMATO SAUCE: (You can do this before you begin the cannellonis if you prefer.) Heat the olive oil in a heavy-bottomed casserole or saucepan and sauté the onion and 1 clove of the garlic over medium-low heat until the onion is golden and translucent. Add the tomatoes, sugar, salt, and remaining garlic and bring to a simmer. Simmer over medium heat, stirring occasionally, for 20 minutes. Add the basil, adjust the salt, and add the cinnamon. Simmer for another 10 minutes and add freshly ground pepper to taste. For the best texture, puree through the medium blade of a Mouli food mill. Taste and adjust the seasonings.

TO ASSEMBLE AND BAKE: Preheat the oven to 375 degrees. Top the cannelloni with a layer of tomato sauce, then a sprinkling of grated Parmesan. Bake for 20 to 30 minutes, until the cheese is melted and the cannelloni are bubbling. Sprinkle with parsley and serve. You can also partially sauce the cannelloni, have the rest of the sauce simmering on top of the stove, and place a bit more sauce on the cooked cannelloni just before serving. Sprinkle with additional Parmesan and parsley.

ADVANCE PREPARATION: The tomato sauce can be made up to a day ahead of time but is best made the day you are serving. The filling can be made a day ahead of time and held in a covered bowl in the refrigerator. The cannelloni can be made and filled a day ahead of time and held in the refrigerator. Oil the baking dish well and cover tightly with lightly oiled foil.

LEFTOVERS: Cover with foil and reheat in a 350-degree oven. They will be good to eat, but not as pretty, for a day or two.

PER PORTION

Calories	450	Protein	31 G
Fat	15 G	Carbohydrate	50 G
Sodium	954 MG	Cholesterol	35 MG

PEAR AND RED WINE SORBET

SERVES 6

Based on a recipe by Richard Olney, this is a beautiful autumn dessert. It's intriguing, with its strong flavor of sweet ripe pears and honey and its deep plum-red color.

2 pounds firm ripe or nearly ripe pears

1 bottle young, deep-hued red wine, such as a cabernet, merlot, or Côtes-du-Rhône

1/3 cup mild-flavored honey

1/2 teaspoon vanilla extract

pinch of freshly ground black pepper

juice of 1 lemon or more to taste

2 tablespoons pear eau-de-vie or more to taste

fresh mint leaves for garnish

Halve or quarter the pears, peel and core them, and place in a large, nonreactive saucepan. Cover with wine (add only enough to cover), add the honey and vanilla, and bring to a simmer. Simmer until softened, about 15 to 20 minutes for nearly ripe pears, longer for hard cooking pears. Add the pepper. Remove the pears from the wine and puree in a food processor fitted with the steel blade. Transfer to a bowl and stir in the lemon juice and eau-de-vie.

Meanwhile, bring the wine to a boil and reduce by about half, until the mixture has the consistency of a thin syrup. Stir into the pears and add any wine remaining in the bottle (there may be none, which is all right). Allow to cool. Taste and add lemon juice or eau-de-vie if desired.

Freeze in an ice cream maker according to the manufacturer's directions or place in ice cube trays, a bowl or a cake pan. Freeze until just about frozen through, then break up by blending in a food processor fitted with the steel blade until smooth. Transfer to individual serving dishes or a bowl, cover, and freeze. Because of the alcohol in the wine, this sorbet will not freeze solid. Serve garnished with fresh mint leaves.

ADVANCE PREPARATION: This sorbet can be made several days ahead of time. It doesn't have to be removed from the freezer before being served, because it will be soft.

PER PORTION

Calories	194	Protein	1 G
Fat	.55 G	Carbohydrate	48 G
Sodium	8 MG	Cholesterol	0

CHRISTMAS DINNER

——

CHAMPAGNE

SMOKED SALMON

BLACK BREAD (PAGE 384), FRENCH SOURDOUGH

COUNTRY BREAD (PAGE 380), or

COARSE WHOLE WHEAT IRISH SODA BREAD (PAGE 295)

BABY LAMB'S LETTUCE (MÂCHE) SALAD

·

ROAST TURKEY

WILD RICE and CHESTNUT STUFFING

MUSHROOM "GRAVY"

STEAMED BRUSSELS SPROUTS or BROCCOLI

BILL'S MASHED POTATOES

BILL'S SLIGHTLY GLAZED CARROTS

CRANBERRY ORANGE RELISH

·

CHÂTEAU DU TRIGNON GIGONDAS

·

GEWÜRZTRAMINER VENDANGE TARDIVE

GOAT CHEESE or ROQUEFORT (OPTIONAL)

·

MAPLE PECAN PIE

Christmas Day is a day to enjoy. We would feel very cheated if we were stuck in the kitchen all day, so we have settled into a menu that's very good but doesn't require too much work. The bird goes into the oven in the afternoon; our Christmas dinner is in the evening, but not too late. There are usually about six of us, although friends visiting from out of town will be invited too. But we try to keep the numbers down.

Although we collaborate on the menu, I think of Christmas dinner as my husband Bill's meal. He likes to oversee the wines, set the table, choose and cook the vegetables, and supervise the turkey. My tasks are the wild rice and chestnut stuffing, the mushroom "gravy," the tangy cranberry relish, the bread, and the pie. The work load is divided evenly, and we're good at delegating tasks to guests.

It looks like there's a lot here, and although our plates are very full, this isn't a difficult menu. I am not giving recipes here for the Baby Lamb's Lettuce Salad or the steamed vegetables. The salad, served alongside the salmon, is a simple one that requires only washing and drying the lamb's lettuce and making a very mild vinaigrette; the broccoli or Brussels sprouts are simply steamed until tender, eight to ten minutes. The other vegetable dishes are all straightforward; Bill cooks his potatoes and mashes them with a fork or potato masher, adding only a little milk and a soupçon of butter. He likes a few roast potatoes as well, thrown into the roasting pan with the turkey. The carrots are simply cooked and very lightly glazed, and the green vegetables are unadorned. For a big holiday meal, with the exception of the pecan pie, there's hardly anything rich; instead of gravy I top the turkey with the mushroom ragout, and the only butter we use beyond the little bit in the mashed potatoes is in the pie.

We particularly enjoy choosing the wines for this meal. We always begin the festivities with champagne, which also goes with the first course of smoked salmon. But if you have a nice white to show off, this is a good opportunity. A Tokay Pinot Gris d'Alsace would also go with the salmon, as would a Riesling or a Côtes-du-Rhône.

We like to drink a full-bodied, fruity red from the south of France with the turkey course. The Gigondas is perfect here; a Bandol red from Domaine Tempier would be equally good, or another good Rhône wine, a Châteauneuf-du-Pape, for example, or a Côte Rôtie. If you really prefer a white wine, I'd lean toward Alsatian whites, a Riesling or a Tokay, for example.

Although people often serve dessert wines with desserts, I have learned from French winemakers that sugary desserts usually fight with sweet wines. They're best with the cheese course; they go especially well with chèvres, with blue cheeses such as Stiltons and Roquefort, and with Gruyères. But they go equally well on their own and can be a dessert in themselves. If you are going to drink them with something sweet, just have some grapes or other fresh fruit. So we serve a very special late-harvest Gewürztraminer as a separate course at our Christmas dinner. We pass the goat cheese and Roquefort and some walnut bread, for those who have room for it, but the wine is just as good on its own. This Gewürztraminer is as aromatic as a bed of roses and somewhat spicy. I like it much better than many of the French sweet wines, which are often too cloying for my palate.

Dessert is the real splurge course here, and I will tell you right now that the pecan pie brings the calories and fat in this menu over the 1,000-calorie, 30-grams-of-fat limit. But I have a weakness for pecan pie; now that my Irish in-laws have tasted it, so do they. You could make a leaner version by using the yeasted piecrust on page 131. But just this once, especially since this is the only real meal we eat on Christmas, I'm advocating going all out. Bill keeps saying he'd like to make a Christmas trifle, but I keep insisting on the pecan pie. Maybe one year, when I don't feel like making a piecrust, I'll defer to him. Or maybe we'll go all out one of these days and serve both.

Making This Dinner for a Crowd

All of these recipes multiply easily, and you can fill an enormous turkey with the stuffing. You might want to go with vegetable dishes you can get done ahead of time in this case, such as a Potato Gratin with Rosemary (page 130) instead of the mashed potatoes; steamed green vegetables won't be too challenging in quantity, nor will glazed carrots, as long as you have a very large steamer and frying pan.

ROAST TURKEY

The turkey we buy for 6 people usually weighs 10 or 11 pounds but might weigh as much as 12. Bill ensures a moist turkey by wrapping it loosely in foil, sort of *en papillote,* and it always comes out succulent. We cook our turkey at high heat for 15 minutes, then turn the oven down for the rest of the cooking time. We like it slightly pink, registering about 162 to 165 degrees on a meat thermometer. If you are using a thawed frozen turkey, you should *not* undercook it. The meat should register 170 degrees on a meat thermometer.

> 1 turkey
>
> **Wild Rice and Chestnut Stuffing (recipe follows)**
>
> olive oil
>
> **salt and freshly ground pepper to taste**

Wash and dry the turkey inside and out. Fill the cavity with the stuffing. Rub the turkey lightly with olive oil, and salt and pepper it lightly.

Cut a long length of aluminum foil, enough to wrap loosely around the turkey. Lay it across the bottom of your roasting pan with the edges overlapping the sides of the pan. Place a rack on top of the foil and set the turkey breast side up on the rack. Bring the ends of the foil up around the turkey and crimp together along the top of the turkey. The foil should be loosely wrapped around the turkey and crimped together at the ends.

Preheat the oven to 450 degrees. Put the turkey in the oven and roast for 15 minutes. Turn the heat down to 375 degrees and cook until done, using the chart below to gauge the time:

> 8 to 10 pounds: 2 to 2½ hours
> 10 to 14 pounds: 2½ to 3 hours
> 14 to 20 pounds: 3½ to 4 hours

During the roasting the bird should be basted occasionally and turned 3 times, that is, rolled onto all of its sides. If your oven is too small to allow this, don't worry, but try to turn the turkey at least once. Open the foil to do this and turn the turkey first on one side, then on another, then upside down. Finally, turn it right side up and remove the foil for final browning. The turkey is done when you stick a fork, knife, or skewer in and clear juice runs out. Do not overcook. Turkey meat should be ever so slightly pink. If you want to roast potatoes with the turkey, throw them into the roasting pan during the last hour.

Remove the turkey from the oven and let sit for 15 to 30 minutes before serving so that the juices will be reabsorbed by the flesh. Remove the stuffing and transfer to a warm serving dish. Carve the turkey and transfer to a serving tray.

(continued)

LEFTOVERS: Salads (see recipes for chicken salads, pages 354 and 356; turkey may be substituted), sandwiches and soup, the usual after-Thanksgiving and after-Christmas fare.

LIGHT MEAT PER PORTION

Calories	131	Protein	25 G
Fat	2 G	Carbohydrate	0
Sodium	58 MG	Cholesterol	59 MG

DARK MEAT PER PORTION

Calories	157	Protein	24 G
Fat	6 G	Carbohydrate	0
Sodium	70 MG	Cholesterol	75 MG

WILD RICE AND CHESTNUT STUFFING

MAKES ENOUGH FOR A 10-POUND TURKEY

The first time Bill and I discussed our Christmas dinner menu, Bill was pretty set on having a chestnut stuffing. But then he'd never tasted wild rice. I suggested a compromise—wild rice and roasted chestnuts combined. Now he won't have anything else. The sweet roasted chestnuts go very nicely with the earthy, savory wild rice. Add fresh sage, mushrooms, garlic, shallots, and sherry and the stuffing becomes irresistible.

You can use leftovers, if there are any, for a marvelous salad (see recipe below).

1/2 pound chestnuts

1 quart vegetable or chicken stock (page 414 or 413)

1 1/2 cups wild rice

salt to taste

2 tablespoons olive oil

1 onion *or* 3 large shallots, chopped

3 garlic cloves, minced or put through a press

1/2 pound mushrooms, trimmed, cleaned, and sliced

2 teaspoons unsalted butter

5 tablespoons dry sherry

1/2 teaspoon crumbled dried thyme

freshly ground pepper to taste

1/2 cup chopped fresh parsley, approximately

3 heaped tablespoons chopped fresh sage

TO ROAST THE CHESTNUTS: There are lots of different ways to roast chestnuts; for me the easiest way is the following: Preheat the oven to 425 degrees. Using a sharp knife, cut an incision in the shape of an X on the flat side of the chestnuts. (You need to slash them so they don't explode when they expand in the oven.) Place the chestnuts on a baking sheet and bake for 10 to 15 minutes, until browned and toasty. Remove from the heat and transfer to a bowl. Allow to cool until you can handle them. As they cool they will shrink away from both the outer shell and the bitter inner peel—just what you want. Peel the chestnuts, making sure that they are free of the dark brown inner shell (the papery part). Cut in half and set aside.

Bring the stock to a boil in a large saucepan. Rinse the wild rice and add to the stock. Add a little salt if the stock isn't salted. Bring to a boil again, reduce the heat, and cover. Simmer for 35 to 40 minutes, until the rice is tender. Remove from the heat, drain off any remaining stock, and set aside.

Heat the olive oil over medium heat in a large frying pan and add the onion or shallots. Cook gently for 10 to 15 minutes, stirring often, until beginning to brown. Add the mushrooms, garlic, and butter and sauté over medium-high heat until the mushrooms begin to release their liquid. Add the sherry, thyme, salt, and pepper and cook, stirring, for a few minutes longer. Stir in the cooked wild rice, chestnuts, parsley, and sage and mix together well. Adjust the seasonings. Remove from the heat and allow to cool before stuffing the turkey. Heat any stuffing that won't fit in the turkey in a 350-degree oven in an oiled baking dish, covered.

ADVANCE PREPARATION: The chestnuts can be roasted and peeled and the rice cooked a day ahead of time. The entire stuffing will hold for a day in the refrigerator.

LEFTOVERS:

A *Salad Made with Leftover Wild Rice and Chestnut Stuffing:* This leftover makes a terrific salad. Make a dressing with walnut oil and red wine or balsamic vinegar, about 1 part vinegar to 4 parts oil (or use a combination of walnut oil and olive or vegetable oil). Add lemon juice or Dijon mustard if you want a tangier dressing. I like it mild so that the flavors of the walnut oil and the stuffing dominate. Add steamed broccoli and more chopped parsley or other herbs to the wild rice mixture if you wish, along with plenty of freshly ground pepper. Half a cup of dressing will suffice for 2 or 3 cups of the stuffing.

PER PORTION

Calories	339	Protein	9 G
Fat	8 G	Carbohydrate	61 G
Sodium	36 MG	Cholesterol	3 MG

MUSHROOM ''GRAVY''

MAKES ABOUT 1 QUART, SERVING 16

This sensuous mushroom ragout is what I use as a gravy for turkey. With hardly any fat, it moistens and embellishes the meat, and it makes versatile leftovers. The recipe makes more than you'll need for 6 people. See leftover suggestions for how to use up the rest.

> 1 ounce (1 cup, approximately) imported dried wild mushrooms, such as *porcini* (*cèpes*), or *chanterelles*
>
> boiling water to cover
>
> 2 tablespoons olive oil or more if needed
>
> 2 large shallots *or* 1 medium onion, minced
>
> 1/2 pound fresh wild mushrooms, such as *porcini,* oyster mushrooms, or *chanterelles,* if available, washed and shaken dry and thickly sliced
>
> 1/2 pound cultivated mushrooms (use 1 pound cultivated mushrooms in all if fresh wild mushrooms are unavailable), cleaned, stems trimmed at the bottom, and thickly sliced
>
> 3 to 4 garlic cloves, to taste, minced or put through a press
>
> 1/2 cup dry red wine
>
> 1 to 2 tablespoons soy sauce to taste
>
> 2 cups vegetable stock (page 414) or bouillon
>
> 1 teaspoon fresh thyme leaves *or* 1/2 to 1 teaspoon crumbled dried
>
> 1 teaspoon chopped fresh rosemary *or* 1/2 teaspoon crumbled dried
>
> salt and freshly ground pepper to taste

Place the dried mushrooms in a bowl and cover them with boiling water. Let sit for 30 minutes while you prepare the remaining ingredients.

Heat the olive oil in a large heavy-bottomed saucepan and add the shallots or onions. Cook over low heat, stirring often, for about 20 minutes, or until golden brown. Add the sliced fresh mushrooms. Stir together and sauté for 5 to 10 minutes, until they begin to release their liquid. Add half the garlic.

Meanwhile, drain the dried mushrooms and reserve the liquid. Rinse the mushrooms thoroughly to remove sand, squeeze dry, and add to the saucepan along with the remaining garlic. Stir together and sauté for a few minutes, adding oil if necessary. Add the wine and soy sauce and bring to a simmer.

Strain the soaking liquid from the mushrooms through a strainer lined with cheesecloth or through a coffee filter. Measure out 1 cup and add to the mushrooms along with the stock, thyme, and rosemary. Bring to a simmer, cover, and simmer for 20 minutes. Uncover and raise the heat to high. Reduce the liquid by half. Taste and adjust seasonings, adding salt, pepper, garlic, or herbs to taste.

Remove 1 cup of the mushrooms and puree in a blender or food processor, then stir back into the ragout.

ADVANCE PREPARATION: This dish holds well and can be made up to 2 days in advance and kept in the refrigerator in a covered bowl. Reheat before serving.

LEFTOVERS: I serve leftover mushroom ragout as a starter or side dish or as a sauce for pasta. One cup makes enough sauce for 2 large or 3 medium portions of pasta. Add a little Parmesan for a real feast. The ragout also makes a good topping for *crostini* (page 392).

PER ¼ CUP PORTION

Calories	33	Protein	1 G
Fat	2 G	Carbohydrate	4 G
Sodium	100 MG	Cholesterol	0

BILL'S MASHED POTATOES

SERVES 6

Bill sometimes doesn't add any butter at all to his mashed potatoes, and they are absolutely scrumptious. He uses waxy potatoes and peels some of them, but not all, and cooks them until tender in salted water. Then he drains them and mashes them in the saucepan with a potato masher or a fork, adding warm milk until they reach the consistency he likes, which is neither too dry nor too moist. Be sure to use waxy potatoes; all-purpose or baking potatoes soak up a lot more milk and beg for butter too. The important thing is to mash the potatoes just before you eat and not to mash them too much, so that they have some texture. They have a little salt and lots of pepper, and they are wonderful. If you want to add a small amount of butter, you can, but they really do work without it.

> 2 pounds waxy potatoes, some peeled, some scrubbed (or all peeled if you wish)
>
> salt to taste
>
> 1 cup skim milk, approximately
>
> 1 tablespoon unsalted butter (optional)
>
> lots of freshly ground pepper

Boil the potatoes in salted water until tender. Drain and return to the saucepan. Meanwhile, warm the milk in another saucepan. Mash the potatoes with a potato masher or fork with the butter if desired and add the milk gradually until the mixture is moistened to your taste. Add salt and lots of freshly ground pepper. Transfer to a warm serving dish and serve at once.

ADVANCE PREPARATION: The potatoes can be peeled hours ahead of serving and kept in a bowl of cold water. They can also be cooked and held in the cooking water for a few hours.

PER PORTION

Calories	137	Protein	4 G
Fat	.35 G	Carbohydrate	29 G
Sodium	33 MG	Cholesterol	1 MG

BILL'S SLIGHTLY GLAZED CARROTS

SERVES 6

These sweet carrots are cooked in water to which a small amount of honey has been added. They absorb the sweetened water, which brings out their own inherent sweetness, and are very slightly glazed in a tiny amount of butter. Cooked carrots have never been my favorite vegetable, but I do have a weakness for these. They always appear on our Christmas menu.

2 pounds carrots, peeled and cut into lengthwise quarters if large, then into 3-inch lengths

1 tablespoon mild-flavored honey

pinch of salt

2 teaspoons unsalted butter

chopped fresh parsley for garnish (optional)

Place the carrots in a saucepan and barely cover with water. Add the honey and salt and bring to a boil. Reduce the heat and simmer, uncovered, until the carrots are tender. Turn up the heat and boil off any water that remains. Remove the pan from the heat and let cool a little, then add the butter. Heat the carrots through, stirring, transfer to a warm serving dish, and serve at once, garnishing if you wish with chopped fresh parsley.

ADVANCE PREPARATION: The carrots can be prepped and kept in a bowl of cold water hours or even a day before cooking.

PER PORTION

Calories	80	Protein	I G
Fat	2 G	Carbohydrate	I7 G
Sodium	82 MG	Cholesterol	3 MG

CRANBERRY ORANGE RELISH

SERVES 6

This tart cranberry sauce is one of my favorite Christmas (and Thanksgiving) dishes, and I'm always asking myself why I don't make it throughout the rest of the year. It takes just a few minutes to make.

    1 12-ounce bag fresh cranberries
    1 navel orange, skin included, washed and cut into eighths
    1/4 cup mild-flavored honey
    1/2 cup shelled walnuts or pecans

Place all the ingredients in a food processor fitted with the steel blade and pulse until you have a uniform, very finely chopped mixture. The texture will be crunchy. Chill until ready to serve.

ADVANCE PREPARATION: This relish will hold for a day in the refrigerator.

LEFTOVERS: Eat leftovers for breakfast, with plain nonfat yogurt.

PER PORTION

Calories	138	Protein	2 G
Fat	6 G	Carbohydrate	23 G
Sodium	2 MG	Cholesterol	0

MAPLE PECAN PIE

MAKES 12 SMALL SERVINGS

I've always loved maple-pecan ice cream, and maple-pecan pie is just as wonderful a combination. The pie is probably the richest single recipe in this book (though it's light compared to other pecan pies) and is highly unsuitable for people with high cholesterol levels. I serve it for special occasions, and cut it into very thin slices or small squares.

    1   Sweet Dessert Crust (page 398)
    4   medium eggs, beaten
  ¹/₄   cup unsalted butter
  ¹/₃   cup mild-flavored honey
    3   tablespoons maple syrup
 1¹/₂   teaspoons vanilla extract
    1   tablespoon whiskey or bourbon
  ¹/₄   teaspoon freshly grated nutmeg
  ¹/₄   teaspoon salt
    2   cups shelled pecans
        whipped cream flavored with nutmeg for topping (optional)

Preheat the oven to 375 degrees. Brush the crust with a little of the beaten egg, prick it all over with a fork, and bake for 5 minutes. Remove from the oven.

Cream together the butter, honey, and maple syrup. Beat in the remaining beaten egg and add the vanilla, whiskey or bourbon, nutmeg, and salt. Combine well. Fold in the pecans.

Turn the filling into the prebaked piecrust. Bake for 35 to 45 minutes, until a knife inserted in the center comes out clean. The pie will puff up almost like a soufflé, but then it will fall.

Remove from the oven and cool on a rack. For a real splurge, serve with whipped cream flavored with nutmeg.

ADVANCE PREPARATION: The pie can be made hours ahead of serving, and held at room temperature.

PER PORTION

Calories	369	Protein	6 G
Fat	27 G	Carbohydrate	29 G
Sodium	162 MG	Cholesterol	114 MG

A NEW YEAR'S EVE BUFFET FOR 20

———

CHAMPAGNE
CUCUMBERS and RED PEPPERS with HUMMUS (PAGE 39)
GARLIC CROUTONS (PAGE 392)
CROSTINI and RED PEPPERS with ESCALIVADA
HORS D'OEUVRE (PAGE 42)
·
WARM BLACK-EYED PEAS VINAIGRETTE
CORNMEAL BLINIS
SAUTÉED FENNEL in RED PEPPER BOATS
ENDIVE, APPLE, and WALNUT SALAD with STILTON
·
GAMAY DE TOURAINE or CHAMPAGNE
·
TANGERINES
SLICED PEARS POACHED in RED WINE

We usually throw a huge party on New Year's Eve, mostly because we don't like going out that night, but we do like a party. I plan my menu with certain criteria in mind. First, the meal must be compatible with champagne from beginning to end, as many people will not switch to wine. Second, the buffet must require no difficult last-minute preparations and little tending once set out, because I intend to be *at* the party, and the party often goes on for quite some time, with some people filling their plates more than once. Third, the menu will not require days of preparation and won't be an expensive one: I'm still recovering from Christmas, after all. And last, because I believe in the southern tradition of eating black-eyed peas on New Year's Day for good luck, they have to figure prominently in the menu. Since black-eyed peas are so filling and delicious, they are the main dish. They require no soaking, and I cook them up and toss them with the vinaigrette on the afternoon of the party.

Everything here can be made well ahead of time. All of the dishes will hold for several hours, so I am usually out of the kitchen long before my friends are due to arrive.

Shortly before the party begins, I pipe the *hummus* onto the cucumber rounds and peppers, spread the *escalivada* on croutons and red peppers, and turn the oven on at about 300 to 325 degrees with the blinis and fennel-filled pepper boats in it.

The party doesn't start until 10:00 P.M., and when guests arrive there are platters filled with garnished *crudités* and *crostini*, placed here and there around the living room, something to nibble on with first glasses of champagne. By about 11:00 it's time to set the rest of the feast out on the buffet, where plates, silverware, napkins, and serving utensils are already attractively arranged. I heat through the warm black-eyed peas vinaigrette, place the blinis on a platter, toss the salad, and run everything out to the buffet. Guests serve themselves, and when the bowls get low, I transfer the food to smaller dishes so that the buffet continues to look fresh.

When you're having a big party like this, and you don't have help (I usually don't on New Year's Eve), there are a few things you can do so that the party goes along smoothly and the place continues to look relatively neat:

- Place a few bottles of champagne in buckets and bottles of mineral water at different places in your home. That way there won't be a bottleneck at the bar or buffet.

- Call on family or friends to be in charge of circulating drinks, making the rounds so that guests are well looked after and you can concentrate on the food and on hosting.

- Place waste cans, or the boxes your wine and champagne came in, lined with plastic bags, under tables (hidden by tablecloths) for easy disposal of empty bottles and dirty napkins, etc.

- Make rounds regularly to empty ashtrays and remove empty plates, napkins, and empty bottles. These messy details are the things that can make a party look like it's been going on for weeks.

- Replenish the buffet when it looks low or remove the food. Or you can transfer the food to smaller dishes so that people can help themselves again if the party continues until very late.

Making This Dinner for a Smaller Group

To make smaller amounts, just divide the recipes by the appropriate factor.

WARM BLACK-EYED PEAS VINAIGRETTE

SERVES 20

This is a very satisfying combination of flavors. The earthy black-eyed peas contrast nicely with the balsamic vinegar-based vinaigrette. It's extremely easy to make this dish, and it will keep for days, although the fresh herbs will have to be replenished. If you can't find chervil, use fresh tarragon, parsley, basil, or cilantro.

FOR THE BEANS

- 1 tablespoon safflower, sunflower, or olive oil
- 3 large onions, chopped
- 12 garlic cloves or to taste, minced or put through a press
- 3 pounds dried black-eyed peas, washed and picked over
- 6 quarts water
- 2 bay leaves

  salt to taste

FOR THE VINAIGRETTE

- 1/2 cup balsamic vinegar
- 3 garlic cloves, minced or put through a press
- 1 heaped tablespoon Dijon mustard

  salt and freshly ground pepper to taste
- 1/2 cup olive oil

FOR THE ADDITIONAL SEASONING

- 1/2 cup chopped fresh chervil leaves
- 1/4 to 1/2 cup chopped fresh chives to taste
- 1/2 to 1 cup chopped fresh parsley to taste

TO COOK THE BEANS: Heat the safflower, sunflower, or olive oil in a large heavy-bottomed saucepan or Dutch oven and sauté the onions with half the garlic over medium-low heat until the onion is tender. Add the black-eyed peas and water and bring to a boil. Reduce the heat, add the bay leaf and remaining garlic, cover, and cook for 35 to 45 minutes or until the beans are tender but not mushy. Add salt to taste. Drain the beans over a bowl and reserve the cooking liquid.

TO MAKE THE VINAIGRETTE: Mix together the vinegar, garlic, mustard, salt, and lots of freshly ground pepper. Whisk in the olive oil and 1 cup of the liquid from the beans. Stir the vinaigrette into the beans. Taste and adjust the seasoning; you may want to add a little more vinegar or salt and pepper. Cover the pot and keep warm until ready to serve. If the beans have cooled down, heat through gently before serving. They should be warm but not bubbling hot.

Just before serving, stir in the fresh herbs. Taste once more, adjust the seasonings, and serve.

ADVANCE PREPARATION: The vinegar acts as a kind of preservative, so the beans can be cooked up to 2 days in advance and marinated in the dressing. Refrigerate in a covered bowl and heat through before serving.

LEFTOVERS: The salad can be served as is over several days, or you can add the beans to other salads, like salade Niçoise. You can also use the beans as a filling for crêpes.

PER PORTION

Calories	298	Protein	17 G
Fat	7 G	Carbohydrate	44 G
Sodium	43 MG	Cholesterol	0

CORNMEAL BLINIS

MAKES 40 BLINIS

These blinis have a grainy texture, a beautiful golden color, and a rich flavor.

2 cups stone-ground cornmeal

1½ teaspoons salt

3 cups boiling water

4 medium eggs

2 cups skim milk

1 cup sifted unbleached white flour

3 tablespoons unsalted butter, melted

unsalted butter for the pan

Combine the cornmeal and salt in a large bowl. Whisk the boiling water into the cornmeal, making sure there are no lumps. This can be done in a food processor fitted with the steel blade or in an electric mixer (combine the cornmeal and salt in the food processor or mixer and pour in the boiling water with the motor running). Let sit for 10 minutes. Beat in the eggs, milk, flour, and butter and beat until smooth. Let sit for 30 minutes.

Heat a well-seasoned crêpe pan or griddle and brush with butter. Ladle in the batter, about 2 tablespoons for each blini (they should be approximately 2½ inches in diameter). Cook 1 minute, then turn and cook for about 30 seconds on the other side. Turn out onto a plate and continue to cook the blinis, brushing the pan with butter after every 3 or so.

If you're not serving the blinis right away, stack them between pieces of wax paper or parchment. Wrap tightly in foil and refrigerate or freeze.

To serve, reheat for 30 minutes (1½ hours if frozen) in a 325-degree oven. Remove from the foil and arrange on a platter or on individual plates.

If you're serving the blinis with the warm black-eyed peas vinaigrette, place the peas on the blinis.

ADVANCE PREPARATION: These blinis can be frozen for several months and will keep for a few days in the refrigerator.

PER PORTION

Calories	54	Protein	2 G
Fat	I G	Carbohydrate	8 G
Sodium	95 MG	Cholesterol	21 MG

SAUTÉED FENNEL IN RED PEPPER BOATS

SERVES 20

I love the anise flavor of the fennel, which is sautéed until tender and presented beautifully in the little half-pepper "boats."

    3 tablespoons olive or safflower oil
    4 garlic cloves, minced or put through a press
    6 pounds fennel, trimmed and chopped
    1 cup water
       salt and freshly ground pepper to taste
   10 small red bell peppers, cut in half lengthwise and seeded

Preheat the oven to 325 degrees.

Heat the olive oil and sauté the garlic and fennel together over medium-low heat for 10 minutes, until the vegetables have begun to soften. Add the water and continue to sauté for 30 to 45 minutes to an hour, until the fennel is very tender and fragrant. Add salt and pepper. Stir often.

While the fennel is cooking, bring a large pot of water to a boil, add a teaspoon of salt, and blanch the peppers. Drain, rinse, and pat dry.

Spoon the fennel into the pepper shells and place in an attractive oven-proof serving dish. Heat through in the preheated oven for 20 minutes before serving.

ADVANCE PREPARATION: The pepper boats can be assembled hours in advance and held in a covered dish. Heat through in the oven shortly before serving.

LEFTOVERS: Scrape out leftover fennel and transfer to a lightly oiled gratin dish. Sprinkle with a little grated Gruyère or Parmesan and bake in a 400-degree oven until the cheese melts and begins to bubble. Sauté leftover peppers (page 95).

PER PORTION

Calories	41	Protein	1 G
Fat	2 G	Carbohydrate	4 G
Sodium	93 MG	Cholesterol	0

ENDIVE, APPLE, AND WALNUT SALAD WITH STILTON

SERVES 20

This endive salad is a variation on the one on page 128. The apples and Stilton go nicely with the slightly bitter greens. I love the textures and sweet and nutty combinations of flavors.

FOR THE SALAD

- 5 pounds Belgian endives
- 8 tart apples, peeled, cored, and sliced
- juice of 2 large lemons
- 1 cup broken walnut pieces
- 1/2 pound Stilton cheese, crumbled
- 2 tablespoons chopped fresh parsley

FOR THE DRESSING

- 1/2 cup red wine vinegar
- juice of 1 large lemon
- 1 tablespoon Dijon mustard
- salt and freshly ground pepper to taste
- 1 teaspoon crumbled dried tarragon
- 3/4 cup walnut oil
- 1 1/4 cups plain nonfat yogurt or olive or safflower oil

Wash the endives and pat them dry. Either cut them into thick slices or separate the leaves. If the leaves are still wet, dry in a salad spinner.

Toss the apples with the lemon juice and set aside in a small bowl until you're ready to toss the salad.

Toss together the endives, apples, walnut pieces, Stilton, and parsley.

Mix together the vinegar, lemon juice, mustard, salt and pepper, and tarragon. Whisk in the oils or oil and yogurt and combine thoroughly. Toss with the salad just before serving.

ADVANCE PREPARATION: All the ingredients can be prepared several hours in advance. Wrap the endives in clean kitchen towels and seal in plastic bags. Place other ingredients in a tightly covered container. The dressing will hold for several hours.

LEFTOVERS: Chop up the salad and fill endive leaves with it for an hors d'oeuvre.

PER PORTION

Calories	209	Protein	5 G
Fat	16 G	Carbohydrate	15 G
Sodium	200 MG	Cholesterol	9 MG

SLICED PEARS
POACHED IN RED WINE

SERVES 20

These poached pears are perfect for a buffet because they will hold for hours—they have to be made several hours in advance—and continue to look good. The peppercorns give them the spicy taste.

10 large ripe but firm Comice pears
     water acidulated with the juice of 1 lemon
 3 bottles Gamay or Beaujolais
 ¾ to 1 cup mild-flavored honey to taste
 2 vanilla beans, split in half
 2 tablespoons peppercorns, tied in a cheesecloth
 1 3-inch cinnamon stick

Peel, core, and slice the pears. To keep the pears from turning brown, drop them into a bowl of acidulated water.

Combine the remaining ingredients and bring to a simmer. Simmer for 10 minutes. Drain the pears and add to the wine. Simmer, never letting the wine boil, for 5 minutes and remove from heat. Remove the cinnamon stick, vanilla beans, and peppercorns, cover, and chill for several hours.

Serve in wide bowls or sherbet dishes, with some of the wine ladled over the top.

ADVANCE PREPARATION: You can keep these pears in the refrigerator for a day.

LEFTOVERS: If you have a lot left over, you might want to try making the pears into a sorbet, which will keep for several months. Puree leftovers in a food processor fitted with the steel blade or a blender. Freeze in an ice cream maker or in ice trays. If you use ice trays, break up in the food processor just after the sorbet sets and freeze again.

PER PORTION

Calories	149	Protein	I G
Fat	.42 G	Carbohydrate	26 G
Sodium	4 MG	Cholesterol	0

A PASTA DINNER FOR FOUR

———

GEWÜRZTRAMINER

•

PENNE with TUNA, TOMATO SAUCE, and OLIVES

•

GRATED CARROTS VINAIGRETTE

•

FRESH FRUIT

•

CHIANTI CLASSICO

This is a meal my husband whipped up one night. He got home from work at 7:00, I had a meeting that lasted until about 9:00, and we had friends in from out of town. We had the spicy Alsatian Gewürztraminer in the refrigerator, as well as carrots and Parmesan. Everything else was in the pantry. When I got home, the kitchen was redolent with the sauce— tomatoes, tuna, olives, capers, and lots of garlic, plus a few spicy touches; the carrots had been grated and tossed with their vinaigrette. All we had to do was make croutons, open the nice Gewürzt—always a welcome aperitif—and set the table. The apples, pears, and tangerines we had in the fruit bowl were just right for dessert, welcome after the heady pasta.

We chose one of our favorite Italian Chiantis, from Villa Antinori, to accompany this pungent food. The wine is big and smooth, fruity, and not too complex. Like the southern French wines we love, Villa Antinori Chianti Classico goes well with garlicky, spicy food.

PENNE WITH TUNA, TOMATO SAUCE, AND OLIVES

SERVES 4

This is a bit like a classic *puttanesca* sauce, with tuna added along with the typical hot peppers, tomatoes, olives, capers, and garlic. It should become a standby in your house, because all of the ingredients are easy to stock. With the exception of people who don't like garlic, everyone loves this dish.

    1 tablespoon olive oil

    1 small onion, minced

    3 or 4 garlic cloves to taste, minced or put through a press

$1\frac{1}{2}$ pounds fresh or canned tomatoes, seeded and chopped

      salt and freshly ground pepper to taste

      pinch of sugar

    1 $6\frac{1}{2}$-ounce can water-packed tuna, drained

    8 imported black olives, pitted and coarsely chopped

    1 tablespoon capers, rinsed and drained

$^{1}/_{4}$ teaspoon hot red pepper flakes *or* a few dashes of cayenne pepper (optional)

$^{1}/_{2}$ teaspoon crumbled dried thyme or oregano

$^{3}/_{4}$ pound penne

$^{1}/_{4}$ cup freshly grated Parmesan cheese

Heat the olive oil in a heavy-bottomed saucepan over low heat and add the onion and 1 clove of the garlic. Sauté, stirring, until the onion is tender, and add the tomatoes and remaining garlic. Bring to a simmer. Add the salt, pepper, and sugar and simmer over medium heat for 15 minutes, stirring often. Stir in the remaining ingredients except the pasta and cheese and continue to simmer, covered, for another 10 to 15 minutes. Taste, adjust the seasonings, and remove from the heat.

Bring a large pot of water to a boil, add salt, and cook the pasta until al dente. Drain and toss with a ladleful of the sauce. Spoon onto warm plates, top each serving with the remaining sauce, and serve, passing the Parmesan on the side.

ADVANCE PREPARATION: The sauce can be made hours ahead of serving and held in or out of the refrigerator, in a covered saucepan.

LEFTOVERS: Toss, with or without salad greens, with vinaigrette of your choice (pages 426–35) and serve as a salad.

PER PORTION

Calories	330	Protein	19 G
Fat	6 G	Carbohydrate	50 G
Sodium	307 MG	Cholesterol	16 MG

GRATED CARROTS VINAIGRETTE

SERVES 4

Grated carrots with a vinaigrette dressing is one of the most common French salads, yet it never loses its appeal. A number of dressings go well with carrots. This yogurt-based vinaigrette, sharp with mustard and tangy with lemon juice, is one of the happiest of marriages. Because carrots will last a long time in the refrigerator, this is one of the most convenient—not to mention healthful—salads I can think of.

1 pound carrots, peeled and grated

1 recipe Lemon-Yogurt Vinaigrette (page 434)

2 to 3 tablespoons finely chopped fresh parsley to taste

lettuce leaves for serving

tomato wedges for garnish (optional)

Grate the carrots and toss with the vinaigrette and the parsley. Refrigerate until ready to serve and give the carrots a toss again just before serving. Serve on lettuce leaves, garnished, if you wish, with tomato wedges.

ADVANCE PREPARATION: This salad will hold, without the parsley, for several hours in the refrigerator. Toss with the parsley shortly before serving.

LEFTOVERS: Add to mixed green salads.

PER PORTION

Calories	76	Protein	4 G
Fat	.43 G	Carbohydrate	16 G
Sodium	144 MG	Cholesterol	1 MG

A PASTA MENU WITH A CHOICE OF TOMATO SAUCES

—

BANDOL ROSÉ

•

A SALAD of SLICED FRESH MUSHROOMS,
PARMESAN, and HERBS

•

PASTA with LEFTOVER FISH, PEAS, and TOMATO SAUCE
or PASTA with TOMATOES VINAIGRETTE

•

APRICOT and STRAWBERRY SALAD
MUSCAT DE BEAUMES DE VENISE
GINGER and HONEY REFRIGERATOR COOKIES
(PAGE 408) (OPTIONAL)

•

BANDOL ROSÉ
GAMAY TOURAINE
or CÔTES-DU-RHÔNE

This menu can be served at any time of year, provided you choose the first pasta dish, which you can make with tomato sauce made from canned tomatoes. The Pasta with Tomatoes Vinaigrette requires sweet, fresh tomatoes, so it's more of a summer/early fall dish. Whichever you choose, the meal is easy to put together. The delicate mushroom salad is one of my favorites: thinly sliced mushrooms, Parmesan, and chopped herbs tossed with lemon juice and olive oil. It couldn't be simpler, and it's bursting with flavor. Other flavors burst forth in the pasta dish. Afterward, sit back and enjoy a cool glass of Muscat de Beaumes de Venise, some fruit, maybe one or two cookies.

I've listed a number of wines that will go well with this meal. You could continue drinking rosé, which would be my first choice; or you could go on to a light, fruity red, from the Loire or the south of France.

A SALAD OF SLICED FRESH MUSHROOMS, PARMESAN, AND HERBS

SERVES 4

I don't know which bit I like best here—the thinly sliced mushrooms, the garden of fresh herbs, or the paper-thin slices of Parmesan. Together, they make a great marriage. It's important to have excellent Parmesan for this salad.

- $1/2$ pound mushrooms, trimmed, cleaned, and very thinly sliced
  juice of $1/2$ lemon or more to taste
- 2 handfuls of chopped fresh herbs, such as chervil, tarragon, thyme, parsley, basil
  salt and freshly ground pepper to taste
- 3 tablespoons olive oil
- 1 to 2 ounces aged Parmesan to taste, sliced paper-thin

Toss the mushrooms with the lemon juice. Add the remaining ingredients, toss together, and serve.

ADVANCE PREPARATION: The ingredients can all be prepped a few hours ahead of serving, although the mushrooms will discolor slightly. Toss them with the lemon juice. Combine all the ingredients just before serving.

PER PORTION

Calories	151	Protein	5 G
Fat	13 G	Carbohydrate	4 G
Sodium	178 MG	Cholesterol	7 MG

PASTA WITH LEFTOVER FISH, PEAS, AND TOMATO SAUCE

SERVES 4

I made this pasta with leftovers from a class in which I'd taught the fish with Veracruzana sauce on page 101. That night I tossed penne with the leftover fish and sauce and threw in some peas for color. It was terrific. This pasta would also be good with other leftover fish and tomato sauce of any kind.

2   red bell peppers, cut into 2-inch pieces

12   ounces cooked white-fleshed fish (such as cod, whiting, or snapper), flaked

2   cups Veracruzana Sauce (page 101) or any tomato-based sauce in this book

    salt to taste

1/2   pound penne

1   cup shelled fresh or thawed frozen peas

    a handful of chopped fresh herbs, such as parsley or basil

    freshly ground pepper to taste and salt if needed

Steam the red peppers for 5 to 10 minutes, until just tender. Combine with the fish and sauce in a saucepan and heat through gently.

Bring a large pot of water to a boil and add a generous amount of salt and the pasta. Cook until al dente, about 10 minutes. Toward the end of the cooking time, add the peas.

Drain the pasta and peas and toss in a warm serving bowl with the sauce and herbs. Add freshly ground pepper to taste and salt if needed. Serve at once.

ADVANCE PREPARATION: The fish (as it can be left over from another meal) can be cooked a day in advance, and the tomato sauce can be cooked up to 3 days ahead of time.

PER PORTION

Calories	472	Protein	33 G
Fat	6 G	Carbohydrate	72 G
Sodium	410 MG	Cholesterol	47 MG

PASTA WITH TOMATOES VINAIGRETTE

SERVES 4

This is a dish you can assemble quickly, provided you have the tomatoes. I make it frequently during the summer and early fall. It's always a hit.

          salt to taste
   3/4   pound spaghetti, spaghettini, or fusilli
     1   recipe Tomatoes Vinaigrette (page 424)
     2   ounces (1/2 cup) freshly grated Parmesan cheese

Bring a large pot of water to a boil and add salt and the pasta. Cook until al dente. Drain and toss at once with the Tomatoes Vinaigrette. Serve, passing the Parmesan for everyone to sprinkle on as desired.

ADVANCE PREPARATION: The Tomatoes Vinaigrette will hold for several hours in the refrigerator.

LEFTOVERS: Serve cold, with chopped fresh herbs, as a salad.

PER PORTION

Calories	475	Protein	18 G
Fat	12 G	Carbohydrate	74 G
Sodium	251 MG	Cholesterol	10 MG

APRICOT AND STRAWBERRY SALAD

SERVES 4 TO 6

You need really good, ripe apricots for this dessert. If you can't find them, use good-quality canned apricots in syrup and drain off the syrup.

    1 pound apricots, washed and sliced
    1 pint strawberries, hulled and sliced
      juice of 1 orange
      juice of ½ lemon
      chopped fresh mint for garnish

Combine the fruit and toss with the juices. Refrigerate until ready to serve. Sprinkle with mint just before serving.

ADVANCE PREPARATION: This salad will hold in the refrigerator for several hours.

PER PORTION

Calories	85	Protein	2 G
Fat	.74 G	Carbohydrate	20 G
Sodium	2 MG	Cholesterol	0

Place the *porcini* in a bowl and pour on boiling water to cover. Let sit for 20 to 30 minutes while you prepare the remaining ingredients. When the mushrooms have softened, drain through a strainer lined with paper towels or cheesecloth, reserving the liquid, and squeeze out the liquid over the strainer. Rinse the mushrooms thoroughly and squeeze again. Chop if very large and set aside.

Bring a large pot of water to a boil.

Meanwhile, heat the olive oil in a medium saucepan over low heat and add the garlic. Sauté gently until it begins to color, about 5 minutes. Add the mushrooms and sauté for a few minutes over medium heat, then stir in the wine, $1/2$ cup liquid from the mushrooms, and the soy sauce. Sauté, stirring, until the liquid has been reduced by half or a little more, and add the herbs and sorrel. Stir together for just a minute or 2 over medium heat. Add salt and lots of pepper. Turn off the heat.

When the water is boiling, add salt and a little oil, and cook the pasta until al dente. When the pasta is just about done, add the *fromage blanc* to the sorrel mixture and heat through without boiling (or the *fromage blanc* will curdle).

Drain the pasta, toss immediately with the sauce and the Parmesan, and serve at once.

ADVANCE PREPARATION: The mushroom and sorrel mixture can be prepared up to the point of adding the *fromage blanc* hours ahead of time and held in the pan.

PER PORTION

Calories	465	Protein	19 G
Fat	13 G	Carbohydrate	68 G
Sodium	314 MG	Cholesterol	87 MG

FIG CRUMBLE WITH CRÈME ANGLAISE

SERVES 8

This dessert is truly luxurious. If it didn't have so little sugar and relatively little fat, I'd call it decadent. But that's just because figs to me are such a sensual fruit.

You have to marinate the optional dried figs the day before you make this dish, but it's very quick to put together. The crème Anglaise is best cool or at room temperature with this dish, so you should make it before assembling the crumble.

I am also giving a low-fat version of this recipe, without the topping. See Baked Fig Compote on the next page.

FOR THE FIGS

6 dried figs, cut into sixths (optional)

1 cup fresh orange juice (optional)

2 pounds fresh dark figs, cut in half lengthwise

3 tablespoons mild-flavored honey, approximately

2 to 3 tablespoons fig eau-de-vie, prune eau-de-vie, or kirsch, approximately

FOR THE TOPPING

1/4 cup chopped shelled pecans

3/4 cup rolled oats

1/2 cup whole wheat pastry flour

1/4 cup unrefined brown sugar (turbinado sugar)

1/4 teaspoon freshly grated nutmeg

1/4 teaspoon salt

6 tablespoons cold unsalted butter

finely chopped zest from 1/2 orange

1 recipe Créme Anglaise (page 436) for serving

TO PREPARE THE FIGS: The day before you wish to make the crumble, place the optional dried figs in a bowl and pour the optional orange juice over them. Cover and refrigerate overnight.

Preheat the oven to 375 degrees. Butter a 2-quart baking dish.

Drain the dried figs. The orange juice will be very sweet, so set it aside for another use. It will make a nice sauce with dried fruit, or you can marinate more figs in it.

Place the fresh figs in the prepared baking dish, cut side up. Sprinkle on the dried figs, placing them in the gaps between the fresh figs. Drizzle on the honey and sprinkle on the eau-de-vie.

TO PREPARE THE TOPPING: Place the pecans in a dry skillet and toast over medium heat just until they begin to brown and smell toasty, stirring constantly. Remove from the heat.

Mix together the oats, flour, sugar, nutmeg, and salt. Cut in the butter and work to a crumbly consistency. Stir in the pecans and orange zest (this can all be done in a food processor fitted with the steel blade). Sprinkle the topping over the figs in an even layer.

Bake for about 45 minutes, until crisp and beginning to brown on the top. To finish browning the top, run under the broiler, watching closely, for 2 to 3 minutes. Serve warm, with crème Anglaise.

NOTE: You can cut this recipe in half to serve 4.

VARIATION:

Baked Fig Compote: Proceed as above, but omit the topping, except for the sugar. Sprinkle the figs with the sugar and bake for 30 to 40 minutes in the preheated oven. Serve warm, with crème Anglaise.

ADVANCE PREPARATION: The crème Anglaise can be made a day in advance. Allow to cool, cover, and refrigerate. Serve it cold or at room temperature with the crumble. Do not bake the crumble too far ahead of time so the topping remains crunchy. You can warm it in a low oven before serving.

LEFTOVERS: The crumble is great for breakfast, topped with plain low-fat yogurt.

PER PORTION

Calories	432	Protein	7 G
Fat	14 G	Carbohydrate	73 G
Sodium	97 MG	Cholesterol	120 MG

ANOTHER GREAT PASTA DINNER:
PENNE WITH ROASTED VEGETABLES
AND PEAS

———

CÔTES DU LUBERON BLANC
•
PENNE with ROASTED VEGETABLES and PEAS
•
TOSSED GREEN SALAD (PAGE 425)
•
PEACHES with RIVESALTES
•
COTEAUX DES BAUX-DE-PROVENCE
or COTEAUX DU TRICASTIN

This is a menu for spring and summer. Only the sweetest tomatoes will do, and there's nothing like this pasta when you have sweet baby peas to add to the sauce. Although the pasta with the roasted vegetables does take time—you need about 45 minutes for the roasted vegetables—it's unsupervised cooking. So I consider this a menu you can put together without too much notice—you just need the time to go to a fruit and vegetable stand. A fruity, not overly complicated red wine from southern France goes well with this meal.

PENNE WITH ROASTED VEGETABLES AND PEAS

SERVES 4

This easy, colorful dish can be prepared at your leisure, even at different times of the day. It can be served at room temperature or hot. What's essential is ripe, sweet tomatoes and lots of garlic.

- 2 red bell peppers
- 1 medium eggplant, cut in half lengthwise
- 2 tablespoons olive oil plus 2 teaspoons for the baking sheet
- 6 (about 1¼ pounds) medium-size ripe tomatoes
- 4 large garlic cloves, minced or put through a press
  coarse salt to taste
- 12 to 20 large basil leaves to taste, cut into slivers
  leaves from 4 fresh thyme sprigs (omit if fresh thyme is not available)
  freshly ground pepper to taste
  pinch of cayenne pepper (optional)
- ¾ pound penne or rigatoni
- ½ pound fresh peas, shelled, *or* ½ cup frozen petite peas, thawed
- 1 to 2 ounces Parmesan cheese to taste, grated (about ¼ to ½ cup)

Preheat the oven to 450 degrees.

Roast the red peppers directly over a burner flame or under a broiler, turning often, until uniformly charred. Remove from the heat and place in a plastic bag or wrap in a towel; set aside until cool enough to handle.

Score the eggplant flesh a couple of times, down to the skin but not through it. Brush a baking sheet with the 2 teaspoons olive oil and place the eggplant on it, cut side down. Cut the stems out of the tomatoes and place on the baking sheet with the eggplant. Bake for 30 to 45 minutes or until the eggplant is soft and the skin shriveled (this may take a little longer, depending on the size of your eggplant). The tomatoes will be very soft and may have collapsed. Remove from the heat and allow to cool.

Meanwhile, remove the blackened skin from the red peppers, rinse, and pat dry. Remove the seeds and cut into thin strips. Cut the strips in half if the peppers are very long. Place in an earthenware serving dish and toss with the garlic, 2 tablespoons olive oil, and coarse salt.

When the eggplant is cool enough to handle, cut into dice, removing the flesh from the skin if desired, and toss with the peppers. Pull the skins off the tomatoes and cut into pieces or mash with the back of a spoon (they will be very soft) and toss with the eggplant and peppers. Add the basil, thyme, salt and pepper to taste and the optional cayenne. Correct the seasonings, adding more garlic or basil if desired. Set aside at room temperature until shortly before serving time.

Shortly before serving, bring a large pot of water to a boil. Add salt, a little oil, and the pasta. Cook until al dente, about 10 to 15 minutes. Five minutes before the end of the cooking, add the peas to the water and cook with the pasta. They should remain bright green.

When the pasta is al dente, drain with the peas and toss at once with the roasted vegetables. Add the Parmesan and salt and pepper to taste and serve.

ADVANCE PREPARATION: The vegetables can be prepared hours ahead of time—the tomatoes and eggplant baked and cut up and the peppers roasted— and tossed with the herbs and seasonings.

LEFTOVERS: Toss with a vinaigrette (pages 426–35) and serve as a salad.

PER PORTION

Calories	533	Protein	19 G
Fat	14 G	Carbohydrate	85 G
Sodium	196 MG	Cholesterol	7 MG

PEACHES WITH RIVESALTES

SERVES 4

We first discovered the sweet, fruity wines from Rivesaltes on a trip to the Roussillon region of France, near the Spanish border and the Mediterranean. Rivesaltes is a small wine region located in the vicinity of the tiny village bearing that name. It is famous for 2 kinds of sweet wine, a grapey Muscat de Rivesaltes, made from the muscat grape, and another natural sweet wine called simply Rivesaltes. The latter tastes a little like a sweet vermouth, but it's a natural wine with no additives (as the winemakers from the region are quick to point out). It makes a lovely aperitif and goes especially well with peaches. This quick summer dessert is always popular at my house.

4 ripe peaches, sliced
1/2 cup Rivesaltes or marsala
    a few fresh mint sprigs

Toss the sliced peaches with the wine and refrigerate until you're ready to serve. Serve garnished with a few sprigs, or the leaves from a few sprigs, of fresh mint.

ADVANCE PREPARATION: This, without the mint, will hold for a few hours in the refrigerator.

PER PORTION

Calories	102	Protein	1 G
Fat	.11 G	Carbohydrate	18 G
Sodium	3 MG	Cholesterol	0

A FALL/WINTER PASTA DINNER

———

A SALAD of RED and GREEN CHICORY with WALNUTS

■

FETTUCCINE with OYSTER MUSHROOMS
and BROCCOLI

■

DRIED APRICOT SOUFFLÉ (PAGE 338)
or MANGO COMPOTE

■

GAMAY TOURAINE, GIGONDAS,
or CÔTES DU ROUSSILLON

Here are three of my favorite dishes, all easy and quick. The only foresight needed is for soaking the apricots in boiling water; they need at least 2 hours.

The nutty salad is tossed with a balsamic vinegar–based dressing, which makes a sweet contrast with the slightly bitter salad greens. The combination of oyster mushrooms and broccoli makes a fabulous dish on its own and a luxurious topping for pasta. You could also serve the vegetable combination with rice or other grains. Dessert is light and sweet.

Once again we have a menu that lends itself to both white and red wines. We usually drink a light, fruity Gamay Touraine, slightly chilled, or a not-too-big red wine from the Rhône or Roussillon. But a floral Tokay d'Alsace or a not-too-big Chardonnay would also go, or a drier, simpler Sauvignon Touraine.

A SALAD OF RED AND GREEN CHICORY WITH WALNUTS

SERVES 4

There is an old woman in the Boulevard Raspail market who sells the best tomatoes I've ever tasted in summer and terrific greens in winter. She piles her red chicory and green chicory together in a beautiful big mound, and I buy it every week. The tough green and red leaves taste very much the same, slightly bitter and very healthful. They keep better than most lettuces, go well with walnut dressings, and make a very pretty salad. This is a nice salad to serve before or after pasta.

FOR THE DRESSING

> 2 tablespoons balsamic vinegar
>
> ½ to 1 teaspoon Dijon mustard to taste
>
>   salt and freshly ground pepper to taste
>
> 2 tablespoons walnut oil
>
> ¼ cup plain nonfat yogurt

FOR THE SALAD

> 6 to 8 ounces mixed green and red chicory or radicchio, washed and torn
>
> a handful of broken walnut pieces
>
> a handful of chopped fresh chervil or parsley

Mix together the vinegar, mustard, and salt and pepper. Whisk in the oil and yogurt and combine well.

Toss the chicory with the walnuts, herbs, and dressing just before serving.

NOTE: A half cup of Low-Fat Walnut Vinaigrette (page 435) could also be used for this salad.

ADVANCE PREPARATION: The lettuce can be washed, dried, and refrigerated and the dressing made hours before serving.

PER PORTION

Calories	132	Protein	3 G
Fat	12 G	Carbohydrate	5 G
Sodium	64 MG	Cholesterol	0

FETTUCCINE WITH OYSTER MUSHROOMS AND BROCCOLI

SERVES 4 GENEROUSLY

Oyster mushrooms, called *pleurottes* in France, are large, downy-textured wild mushrooms. They are now being cultivated and are not too hard to come by, and they are much less expensive than most other wild mushrooms. With their "meaty" consistency and rich earthy flavor, oyster mushrooms are a real treat, either sautéed on their own with garlic and herbs or tossed with pasta as they are here. The broccoli adds bright color and a crunchy dimension to this dish.

> 1 tablespoon olive oil
>
> 1 large *or* 2 or 3 small shallots, minced

1/2 pound fresh oyster mushrooms, rinsed, wiped dry, trimmed, and thickly sliced

3 large garlic cloves, minced or put through a press

3 tablespoons dry red wine

2 to 3 teaspoons soy sauce to taste

1/2 to 1 teaspoon crumbled dried thyme *or* 1 to 2 teaspoons fresh to taste

1/2 to 1 teaspoon crumbled dried rosemary *or* 1 to 2 teaspoons fresh leaves to taste

salt and freshly ground pepper to taste

2 or 3 tablespoons chopped fresh parsley

3/4 pound whole wheat or semolina fettuccine

1 small bunch of broccoli, broken into florets, stems peeled and sliced (about 1 pound in all)

1/3 cup freshly grated Parmesan cheese

Begin heating a big pot of water for the pasta.

Heat the olive oil over medium heat in a heavy-bottomed frying pan or wide saucepan and add the shallot. Sauté until it is beginning to color and add the mushrooms and garlic. Sauté, stirring over medium heat, until the mushrooms begin to release liquid and add the wine, soy sauce, thyme, rosemary, and salt and pepper to taste. Sauté, stirring often over medium heat, for 10 minutes, until the mushrooms are cooked through and the mixture is fragrant. Stir in the parsley. Taste and adjust the seasonings. Keep warm while you cook the pasta.

When the pasta water comes to a boil, add salt and the fettuccine. Cook until al dente, 7 to 10 minutes. About 3 to 5 minutes before the pasta is done, add the broccoli to the cooking water.

Drain the pasta and broccoli and toss at once with the mushrooms. Serve at once, passing the Parmesan to sprinkle on top.

ADVANCE PREPARATION: The cooked oyster mushrooms will hold for several hours on top of the stove or can be made a day ahead of time and held, covered, in the refrigerator.

PER PORTION

Calories	455	Protein	20 G
Fat	10 G	Carbohydrate	72 G
Sodium	418 MG	Cholesterol	87 MG

MANGO COMPOTE

SERVES 4 TO 6

Mango goes very nicely with sweet white wine, something like a Sauternes but not necessarily as fancy. There is a sweet wine from the Loire called Coteaux du Layon that is quite good, and a particularly suitable Moelleux from Gaillac, in southwestern France, made by Robert Plageoles.

    2 large ripe mangoes, peeled and diced or sliced
    2 pints (1 pound) strawberries, hulled and cut in half, or raspberries
       juice of 1 lime
    ¾ cup sweet white wine

Toss the fruit with the lime juice. Pour on the wine, toss, and chill. Remove from the refrigerator about 15 minutes before serving so the fruit won't be too cold.

ADVANCE PREPARATION: This compote will hold for several hours in the refrigerator.

PER PORTION

Calories	203	Protein	2 G
Fat	.93 G	Carbohydrate	39 G
Sodium	8 MG	Cholesterol	0

TWO RISOTTO DINNERS

TO MAKE WITH GUESTS IN THE KITCHEN

———

(1)

CHAMPAGNE or PROSECCO

CHERRY TOMATOES STUFFED with TAPENADE (PAGE 53)

•

ZUCCHINI RISOTTO

•

HERB SALAD with GRUYÈRE and MUSHROOMS

•

RHUBARB, HONEY, and BLOOD ORANGE
COMPOTE or SORBET (PAGE 96), or
FRESH STRAWBERRIES TOSSED with
ORANGE JUICE and MINT

(2)

CHAMPAGNE or PROSECCO

CHERRY TOMATOES STUFFED with TAPENADE (PAGE 53)

HERB BRUSCHETTE (PAGE 77)

•

RISOTTO with FRESH HERBS

•

TOSSED GREEN SALAD (PAGE 425)

•

RHUBARB, HONEY, and BLOOD ORANGE
COMPOTE or SORBET (PAGE 96), or
FRESH STRAWBERRIES TOSSED with
ORANGE JUICE and MINT

•

CÔTES-DU-RHÔNE VIOGNIER, GAVI DI GAVI, or BAROLO

CÔTES-DU-RHÔNE, ST.-JOSEPH, CORNAS, or CÔTE RÔTIE

These menus are practically identical, with a choice of *risotti*. Whichever *risotto* you choose, the same spirit prevails. Guests can sit around sipping bubbly wine and eating stuffed cherry tomatoes or herbed *bruschette* while you make the *risotto*. If you like being with your guests, then you have to insist that they keep you company while you stir the *risotto*. They should be ready to eat the moment it's done, when the sensuous *risotto* is at its unctuous, al dente best. I like both versions equally, the first one brimming with diced zucchini and the herb risotto bursting forth with the heady flavors of all the chopped herbs.

After the *risotto* you need a crisp salad before going on to a light, refreshing dessert. The *risotti* are filling, so desserts should be fruity and uncomplicated.

Both menus would go equally well with a flowery white wine, such as a Viognier from the south of France or an Italian Gavi di Gavi. Red wines with body and fruit, a Chianti or Barolo, a Rhône wine or a Roussillon, would be quite suitable as well. A light, fruity, slightly chilled Gamay Touraine would also be good with this meal, particularly with the herb *risotto*.

ZUCCHINI RISOTTO

SERVES 6 AS A MAIN DISH

My inspiration for this delicate combination of zucchini and rice comes from Provence rather than Italy. There is a Provençal rice and zucchini dish called *tian de courgettes*, a combination of zucchini and rice that is baked together in a *tian*, or baking dish. I love that combination so much I decided to combine some of the same ingredients in a *risotto*, and it's a marvelous dish—good for impromptu entertaining if you have zucchini, rice, and Parmesan on hand.

7 cups vegetable stock (page 414), garlic broth (page 415), or chicken stock (page 413), approximately

2 tablespoons olive oil

1/2 small onion *or* 1 shallot, minced

1 1/2 pounds zucchini, finely diced

salt to taste

2 to 3 large garlic cloves to taste, minced or put through a press

1/2 teaspoon crumbled dried thyme

HERB SALAD WITH GRUYÈRE AND MUSHROOMS

SERVES 6

I first ate a salad of nothing but herbs at a restaurant called Arpège in Paris. What a great idea! Herbs are what bring a green salad to life, so why not make them the focus? The aromas jump off the plate. You could make this salad with herbs alone, but the small amount of Gruyère and thinly sliced mushrooms makes a nice combination.

3 cups chopped fresh herbs, such as parsley, chervil, basil, tarragon, dill, fennel, lovage, marjoram (best if snipped with scissors)

1 cup thinly sliced fresh mushrooms tossed with 1 tablespoon fresh lemon juice

¼ cup grated Gruyère cheese

1 additional tablespoon lemon juice

1 tablespoon balsamic vinegar

5 tablespoons olive oil

salt and freshly ground pepper to taste

Toss together the herbs, mushrooms, and Gruyère cheese. Whisk together the lemon juice, balsamic vinegar, and olive oil. Add salt and pepper. Toss with the salad just before serving.

ADVANCE PREPARATION: The herbs can be prepared hours before serving and held in a covered container in the refrigerator. The cheese can be grated a day before, and the dressing will hold for a day.

PER PORTION

Calories	153	Protein	4 G
Fat	14 G	Carbohydrate	3 G
Sodium	44 MG	Cholesterol	10 MG

2 cups Arborio rice, washed

¼ cup dry white wine

½ cup chopped fresh parsley

1 medium egg, beaten

½ cup freshly grated Parmesan or to taste

freshly ground pepper to taste

Have the stock simmering in a saucepan.

Heat the oil in a wide heavy-bottomed frying pan and sauté the onion over medium-low heat until the onion is golden. Add the zucchini, a little salt, and the garlic and sauté for about 3 to 5 minutes, until the zucchini is coated with oil and becoming translucent. Add the thyme and the rice and continue to sauté, stirring, until all the grains are separate and coated with oil.

Stir in the white wine and cook over medium heat, stirring all the while. The wine should bubble, but not too quickly. You want some of the flavor to cook into the rice before it evaporates.

When the wine has just about evaporated, stir in a ladleful of the stock. It should just cover the rice and should bubble slowly like the wine. Cook, stirring constantly, until it is just about absorbed. Add another ladleful of the stock and continue to cook in this fashion, not too quickly but not too slowly, adding more broth when the rice is almost dry. Add the parsley with a ladleful of stock toward the end of the cooking. After 25 to 35 minutes the rice should be cooked al dente.

Beat together the egg and the Parmesan. Add another ladleful of stock to the rice, so that the rice is not completely dry, and remove from the heat. Stir half a ladleful of stock into the egg and cheese mixture and immediately stir this into the rice. Combine well, taste, and adjust seasonings, adding salt and freshly ground pepper to taste. Return to the heat and stir for a few seconds, then serve at once.

ADVANCE PREPARATION: The onion and zucchini mixture can be prepared several hours ahead of time, up to the point where you add the rice. Reheat with a little extra oil and proceed with the recipe.

LEFTOVERS: Use leftover *risotto* as the basis for a flat omelet. Mix with beaten eggs and cook in a nonstick pan as for the flat omelets on pages 30–34. Or stuff mushrooms with it and serve as an hors d'oeuvre (page 66).

PER PORTION

Calories	350	Protein	11 G
Fat	8 G	Carbohydrate	58 G
Sodium	176 MG	Cholesterol	38 MG

RISOTTO WITH FRESH HERBS

SERVES 6 AS A MAIN DISH

This *risotto* explodes with fresh herbs, which are added at the last minute. It makes a perfect main dish but could also be a starter or side dish (in which case, halve the recipe).

7 cups vegetable stock (page 414), garlic broth (page 415), or chicken stock (page 413)

4 cups chopped fresh herbs and vivid-tasting salad greens, such as arugula, chervil, dill, parsley, basil, chives

4 large garlic cloves or more to taste, minced or put through a press

2 tablespoons olive oil

1 small onion, minced

2 cups Arborio rice, washed

½ cup dry white wine

salt to taste

1 medium egg, beaten

½ cup freshly grated Parmesan or to taste

freshly ground pepper to taste

Have the stock simmering in a saucepan. Have the fresh herbs in a bowl, and add to them ¼ of the minced garlic.

Heat the oil in a wide heavy-bottomed frying pan and sauté the onion and remaining garlic over medium-low heat until the onion is golden. Add the rice and continue to sauté, stirring, until all the grains are separate and coated with oil.

Stir in the white wine and salt to taste and cook over medium heat, stirring all the while. The wine should bubble, but not too quickly. You want some of the flavor to cook into the rice before it evaporates.

When the wine has just about evaporated, stir in a ladleful of the stock. It should just cover the rice and should bubble slowly like the wine. Cook, stirring constantly, until it is just about absorbed. Add another ladleful of the stock and continue to cook in this fashion, not too quickly but not too slowly, adding more broth when the rice is almost dry. After 25 to 35 minutes the rice should be cooked al dente.

Add another ladleful of stock, along with the fr... together for a minute or so, and remove the rice from the egg and Parmesan and stir into the rice. Taste ... adding salt and pepper. Return to the heat and stir fo... serve at once.

ADVANCE PREPARATION: All the ingredients can be ... sured out ahead of time, but the *risotto* must be served as s...

LEFTOVERS: Use leftover *risotto* as the basis for a flat om... beaten eggs and cook in a nonstick pan as for the flat omelets on... Or stuff mushrooms with it and serve as an hors d'oeuvre (p...

PER 1-CUP PORTION

Calories	337	Protein	9 G
Fat	7 G	Carbohydrate	57 G
Sodium	178 MG	Cholesterol	6 MG

2 cups Arborio rice, washed

1/4 cup dry white wine

1/2 cup chopped fresh parsley

1 medium egg, beaten

1/2 cup freshly grated Parmesan or to taste

    freshly ground pepper to taste

Have the stock simmering in a saucepan.

Heat the oil in a wide heavy-bottomed frying pan and sauté the onion over medium-low heat until the onion is golden. Add the zucchini, a little salt, and the garlic and sauté for about 3 to 5 minutes, until the zucchini is coated with oil and becoming translucent. Add the thyme and the rice and continue to sauté, stirring, until all the grains are separate and coated with oil.

Stir in the white wine and cook over medium heat, stirring all the while. The wine should bubble, but not too quickly. You want some of the flavor to cook into the rice before it evaporates.

When the wine has just about evaporated, stir in a ladleful of the stock. It should just cover the rice and should bubble slowly like the wine. Cook, stirring constantly, until it is just about absorbed. Add another ladleful of the stock and continue to cook in this fashion, not too quickly but not too slowly, adding more broth when the rice is almost dry. Add the parsley with a ladleful of stock toward the end of the cooking. After 25 to 35 minutes the rice should be cooked al dente.

Beat together the egg and the Parmesan. Add another ladleful of stock to the rice, so that the rice is not completely dry, and remove from the heat. Stir half a ladleful of stock into the egg and cheese mixture and immediately stir this into the rice. Combine well, taste, and adjust seasonings, adding salt and freshly ground pepper to taste. Return to the heat and stir for a few seconds, then serve at once.

ADVANCE PREPARATION: The onion and zucchini mixture can be prepared several hours ahead of time, up to the point where you add the rice. Reheat with a little extra oil and proceed with the recipe.

LEFTOVERS: Use leftover *risotto* as the basis for a flat omelet. Mix with beaten eggs and cook in a nonstick pan as for the flat omelets on pages 30–34. Or stuff mushrooms with it and serve as an hors d'oeuvre (page 66).

PER PORTION

Calories	350	Protein	11 G
Fat	8 G	Carbohydrate	58 G
Sodium	176 MG	Cholesterol	38 MG

RISOTTO WITH FRESH HERBS

SERVES 6 AS A MAIN DISH

This *risotto* explodes with fresh herbs, which are added at the last minute. It makes a perfect main dish but could also be a starter or side dish (in which case, halve the recipe).

7 cups vegetable stock (page 414), garlic broth (page 415), or chicken stock (page 413)

4 cups chopped fresh herbs and vivid-tasting salad greens, such as arugula, chervil, dill, parsley, basil, chives

4 large garlic cloves or more to taste, minced or put through a press

2 tablespoons olive oil

1 small onion, minced

2 cups Arborio rice, washed

1/2 cup dry white wine

salt to taste

1 medium egg, beaten

1/2 cup freshly grated Parmesan or to taste

freshly ground pepper to taste

Have the stock simmering in a saucepan. Have the fresh herbs in a bowl, and add to them 1/4 of the minced garlic.

Heat the oil in a wide heavy-bottomed frying pan and sauté the onion and remaining garlic over medium-low heat until the onion is golden. Add the rice and continue to sauté, stirring, until all the grains are separate and coated with oil.

Stir in the white wine and salt to taste and cook over medium heat, stirring all the while. The wine should bubble, but not too quickly. You want some of the flavor to cook into the rice before it evaporates.

When the wine has just about evaporated, stir in a ladleful of the stock. It should just cover the rice and should bubble slowly like the wine. Cook, stirring constantly, until it is just about absorbed. Add another ladleful of the stock and continue to cook in this fashion, not too quickly but not too slowly, adding more broth when the rice is almost dry. After 25 to 35 minutes the rice should be cooked al dente.

Add another ladleful of stock, along with the fresh herbs, to the rice, stir together for a minute or so, and remove the rice from the heat. Beat together the egg and Parmesan and stir into the rice. Taste and adjust seasonings, adding salt and pepper. Return to the heat and stir for a few seconds, then serve at once.

ADVANCE PREPARATION: All the ingredients can be prepped and measured out ahead of time, but the *risotto* must be served as soon as it's ready.

LEFTOVERS: Use leftover *risotto* as the basis for a flat omelet. Mix with beaten eggs and cook in a nonstick pan as for the flat omelets on pages 30–34. Or stuff mushrooms with it and serve as an hors d'oeuvre (page 66).

PER I-CUP PORTION

Calories	337	Protein	9 G
Fat	7 G	Carbohydrate	57 G
Sodium	178 MG	Cholesterol	6 MG

HERB SALAD WITH GRUYÈRE AND MUSHROOMS

SERVES 6

I first ate a salad of nothing but herbs at a restaurant called Arpège in Paris. What a great idea! Herbs are what bring a green salad to life, so why not make them the focus? The aromas jump off the plate. You could make this salad with herbs alone, but the small amount of Gruyère and thinly sliced mushrooms makes a nice combination.

3 cups chopped fresh herbs, such as parsley, chervil, basil, tarragon, dill, fennel, lovage, marjoram (best if snipped with scissors)

1 cup thinly sliced fresh mushrooms tossed with 1 tablespoon fresh lemon juice

$1/4$ cup grated Gruyère cheese

1 additional tablespoon lemon juice

1 tablespoon balsamic vinegar

5 tablespoons olive oil

salt and freshly ground pepper to taste

Toss together the herbs, mushrooms, and Gruyère cheese. Whisk together the lemon juice, balsamic vinegar, and olive oil. Add salt and pepper. Toss with the salad just before serving.

ADVANCE PREPARATION: The herbs can be prepared hours before serving and held in a covered container in the refrigerator. The cheese can be grated a day before, and the dressing will hold for a day.

PER PORTION

Calories	153	Protein	4 G
Fat	14 G	Carbohydrate	3 G
Sodium	44 MG	Cholesterol	10 MG

FRESH STRAWBERRIES TOSSED WITH ORANGE JUICE AND MINT

SERVES 6

Fresh strawberries taste marvelous when they're tossed with a little orange juice and fresh mint. People always want to know why these strawberries taste so good: the orange juice brings out their sweetness. If you can find blood oranges, the kind you find in Italy in spring, they will add another dimension to the dish.

1½ pounds (3 pints) fresh strawberries, hulled and cut in half
   juice of 1½ large oranges or 3 small blood oranges
2 tablespoons fresh mint leaves to taste, cut into slivers with scissors

Place the strawberries in a pretty bowl. Just before serving, toss with the orange juice and mint.

ADVANCE PREPARATION: The strawberries can be hulled and cut in half hours ahead of time, but they should be tossed with the juice and mint just before serving.

LEFTOVERS: Serve with yogurt for breakfast.

PER PORTION

Calories	42	Protein	1 G
Fat	.43 G	Carbohydrate	10 G
Sodium	1 MG	Cholesterol	0

A SOUFFLÉ DINNER

———

KIRS ROYALES

·

PUREED RED PEPPER and POTATO SOUP

·

CHEESE SOUFFLÉ

TOSSED GREEN SALAD (PAGE 425) with LOW-FAT YOGURT
VINAIGRETTE (PAGE 433)

·

TANGERINES and GREEN MUSCAT GRAPES

·

CHÂTEAU DE BEAUCASTEL CHÂTEAUNEUF-DU-PAPE

I had been cooking all week, we had a house full of guests, and we were having yet another party. But my friends (Alexis Halmy, Sabine Boulongne, and Mary Collins) took over; Alexis made her terrific Pureed Red Pepper and Potato Soup, Sabine made her cheese soufflé, which is always a winner, and Mary made the salad. I stayed out of the kitchen and sat in the living room with the rest of the guests while my husband served Kirs. It was a restful, fun evening for me. I didn't even set the table. And did we eat well! The combination here is perfect, not just because of the nice contrast of flavors but also because of the colors—the tomato-red soup, the bright yellow, golden-crusted soufflé, and the green salad, which is eaten along with the soufflé. All you need for dessert is fresh fruit. Of course I stole the menu.

This meal is meant to be eaten with a special wine, and the special one we served was a Château de Beaucastel Châteauneuf-du-Pape 1986. It's rich and extremely fruity, with a beautiful dark hue. You could also drink a good red Bordeaux or Burgundy with this meal; I'd go with a lighter Burgundy, maybe a Mercurey. A round, fruity white wine would also go well.

PUREED RED PEPPER AND POTATO SOUP

SERVES 6

This is an adaptation of my friend Alexis Halmy's recipe. It's a thick, intriguing, comforting soup, very easy to make (no peeling of peppers necessary; everything is pureed in the end), and it has the most beautiful tomato-red color.

- 1 tablespoon olive oil
- 1 medium onion, chopped
- 1 celery rib, finely chopped
- 1 carrot, finely chopped
- 3 garlic cloves, minced or put through a press
- 1½ pounds new potatoes, peeled and sliced or chopped
- 4 large (about 2 pounds) red bell peppers, seeds and membranes removed, cut into 1-inch squares
- 6 cups chicken stock (page 413) or garlic broth (page 415)
- salt and freshly ground pepper to taste
- garlic croutons (page 392) and fresh basil leaves or parsley for garnish
- 6 tablespoons plain nonfat yogurt for garnish (optional)

Heat the olive oil in a large heavy-bottomed soup pot and sauté the onion, celery, and carrot slowly over low heat for about 10 minutes, stirring all the time. Add the garlic after the first 5 minutes. If the vegetables begin to stick, add 2 tablespoons water. When the vegetables have softened, add the potatoes, red peppers, and stock and bring to a boil. Add a little salt, reduce the heat, cover, and simmer for 1 hour or until the vegetables are thoroughly softened.

Puree in batches in a blender or a food processor fitted with the steel blade, until smooth. Return to the pot and heat through. Add salt and freshly ground pepper to taste. Serve, drizzling a spoonful of the optional yogurt over each bowlful and topping with a couple of croutons and a few basil leaves.

ADVANCE PREPARATION: This soup can be made a day ahead of serving (in fact it's best if you *do* make it a day ahead of time). It freezes well.

PER PORTION

Calories	189	Protein	4 G
Fat	5 G	Carbohydrate	34 G
Sodium	27 MG	Cholesterol	0

CHEESE SOUFFLÉ

SERVES 6

My friend Sabine Boulongne, who is half Swiss and half French, makes a marvelous cheese soufflé with a rich, nutty flavor. Her recipe reflects her mixed heritage, for her secret, she says, is using 2 cheeses, a Swiss Gruyère called Fribourg (or Fribourg Vacherin) and a French Gruyère called Comté. The Fribourg has a spicy, strong flavor that sets off the nutty, fruity Comté, and they really do complement each other well. Since it's not always so easy to find Fribourg and Comté, I'm giving you both Sabine's recipe and my own mixture, which includes a little Parmesan to give the soufflé the deep flavor that Sabine's mixture of cheeses has. Sabine uses 1 egg per person; I throw in a couple of extra egg whites for added lightness. The béchamel shouldn't be too heavy, and a perfect soufflé should be runny in the middle.

Although it's a delicate item, a soufflé is quite a convenient dish for a dinner party—not for a large party, but for a small group that you can get to the table all at once. Components of the dish can be prepared hours ahead of time, and it's such an uncomplicated dish that you can make it with your guests around you. The main thing is to be ready for it when it comes from the oven, because a puffed-up soufflé will fall quickly. Put it in the oven during the first course, or if the soufflé *is* the first course, get everyone to the table before it's finished baking; if it's ready before you are, turn off the oven without opening the oven door.

This is high in fat, but the rest of the menu is low.

FOR THE BÉCHAMEL

> 1½ cups skim milk
>
> 3 tablespoons unsalted butter
>
> ¼ cup unbleached white flour
>
> salt and freshly ground pepper (preferably white pepper) to taste
>
> pinch of freshly grated nutmeg

FOR THE EGGS AND CHEESE

> 1/4 **pound French Gruyère (Comté), grated (1 cup)**
>
> 2 **ounces Fribourg Vacherin, grated (1/2 cup),** *or* **all Gruyère plus 2 tablespoons freshly grated Parmesan cheese**
>
> 6 **medium eggs, at room temperature, plus 2 egg whites**
>
> 1/4 **teaspoon cream of tartar**
>
> **pinch of salt**

Preheat the oven to 375 degrees.

First prepare your soufflé dish. Butter a 2-quart mold and dust it with 2 tablespoons Parmesan if you wish. Using wax paper or aluminum foil, make a collar by wrapping a cylinder of the paper around the dish and taping or tying it; the cylinder should extend 2 to 3 inches above the edge of the soufflé dish. The collar is optional—few of my French friends go to the trouble (I've never seen Sabine use one)—but it does help guarantee a high-rising soufflé. Set the dish aside.

Heat the milk just to simmering in a saucepan.

In another, heavy-bottomed saucepan, melt the butter and, when it is bubbling, stir in the flour. Cook the *roux* for a few minutes over medium-low heat, stirring with a wooden spoon. It should bubble and cook but not brown.

Whisk the milk into the *roux*. You can do this gradually, whisking all the while, or all at once and whisk very vigorously so that all of the *roux* is incorporated into the milk and no lumps remain. Continue to stir over moderate heat until the thick sauce comes to a simmer.

Simmer very gently for 5 minutes, stirring and bringing the sauce up from the bottom and sides of the pan. The sauce will be very thick, but you're about to thin it out considerably with the egg yolks. Remove the sauce from the heat and continue to stir for a minute. Season with salt (1/2 to 1 teaspoon), pepper, and the nutmeg.

Mix together the 2 cheeses in a bowl.

Separate the eggs, one by one, and stir 6 egg yolks into the sauce, 1 at a time. Transfer the egg whites to a mixing bowl. Add 2 extra whites to the bowl. Set the sauce aside.

Beat the egg whites until they begin to foam. Add the cream of tartar and the salt and continue beating until the egg whites are satiny and form peaks when lifted with the spatula or beater. Do not overbeat; the egg whites should remain smooth.

Now stir one quarter of the egg whites into the sauce base with a spatula. This will lighten up the sauce and facilitate folding in the remaining egg whites and cheese. Pour the sauce base into the middle of the bowl of egg whites. Fold the egg whites into the sauce with your spatula by gently scooping the sauce from the middle of the bowl, under the egg whites to the side of the bowl, up over the egg whites, and back to the middle of the bowl. With each fold, sprinkle in a handful of the cheese mixture, and give the bowl a quarter turn. You should continue this folding process until the mixture is homogenous. Work rapidly yet gingerly; the process should take a couple of minutes at most.

Gently spoon the soufflé mixture into the prepared dish. At this point you may set the mixture aside for up to 2 hours, inverting a large bowl over it.

Bake the soufflé in the preheated oven for 35 to 40 minutes. If you wish, you can stick a thin skewer in to see if it's done. If it comes out with just a little bit of the mixture on it, and the top of the soufflé is golden, the soufflé is done. If it comes out very wet, bake for another 5 minutes. Remove from the oven, detach the collar, and serve immediately.

VARIATIONS:

Cheese Soufflé aux Truffles: If you just happen to have a few truffles about, slice up 1 or 2 and add to the béchamel. Proceed as above.

Cheese Soufflé aux Mirolles: Morels are savory wild mushrooms that you can buy dried in the United States. Place about 5 or 6 morels in a bowl and cover with boiling water. Let sit for 20 minutes, then drain and rinse thoroughly. Squeeze dry and slice. Add to the béchamel and proceed as above.

Soufflé aux Légumes: Fold in 1 or 2 cups of blanched chopped vegetables— asparagus, spinach, broccoli—along with the cheese and proceed as above.

ADVANCE PREPARATION: You can make the béchamel several hours ahead of time, and you can also grate the cheeses. You can beat the egg whites up to 2 hours ahead of time, and put the soufflé mixture into the dish with a large bowl inverted over it, but I recommend beating the whites and mixing the soufflé just before you bake it.

PER PORTION

Calories	288	Protein	18 G
Fat	20 G	Carbohydrate	8 G
Sodium	237 MG	Cholesterol	237 MG

A WARMING FALL DINNER FOR SIX

———

DRY SHERRY (SUCH AS A FINO)

∙

PUREED WINTER SQUASH and GINGER SOUP

SORREL FLAN

ENDIVE and WALNUT SALAD (PAGE 128)

∙

DRIED FIGS in ORANGE JUICE with YOGURT

∙

ALSACE RIESLING or VOUVRAY

When the weather gets cold, I start getting cravings for a glass of cold, dry sherry in the evenings. I know that sherry is just as good a hot-weather as cold-weather tipple, but it's in the fall and winter that my husband and I seem to make it our standard aperitif.

Here sherry is followed by a beautiful orange-hued soup made from winter squash or pumpkin (among my favorite fall and winter vegetables) and subtly seasoned with ginger. The warming, slightly spicy soup always gets raves. The sorrel flan is tangy and rich-tasting, and all it needs to go with it is a salad. You could just as easily serve a tossed green salad (page 425) or a mixed one here.

The colors of fall continue with the dessert, an easy concoction my husband made up. Dried figs marinating in orange juice are very nice to have on hand in the refrigerator, for desserts or for breakfast, mixed with yogurt.

An aromatic white wine, like an Alsatian Riesling or even a Gewürztraminer, or a not-too-sweet Vouvray, would be just right with this meal. These wines complement the spicy soup and aren't overwhelmed by the tangy sorrel in the flan.

PUREED WINTER SQUASH AND GINGER SOUP

SERVES 6 TO 8

I make this soup with a deep orange pumpkinlike squash called "Potimarron" in French. It's a winter squash, a little starchier than pumpkin, with a rich flavor. This is a nice fall soup, very easy, warming, and tangy.

        1 to 2 tablespoons safflower or sunflower oil, as needed

        1 leek, white part only, cleaned and sliced

        1 medium onion, chopped

        3 garlic cloves, minced or put through a press

        2 teaspoons chopped fresh ginger

     1¹/₂ pounds winter squash or pumpkin, peeled and chopped

        2 tart apples, peeled and sliced

      ¹/₂ pound new potatoes, peeled and chopped

        1 quart water or defatted chicken stock (page 413)

           salt to taste

      ¹/₂ to 1 cup skim milk, as needed (optional)

           lots of freshly ground pepper

FOR THE GARNISH

        sliced apple

        fresh lime juice

        plain nonfat yogurt or *fromage blanc* (page 417)

Heat 1 tablespoon of the oil in a large heavy-bottomed soup pot or casserole and add the leek and onion. Sauté, stirring often, over low heat until they begin to soften. Add the garlic and ginger and continue to sauté for another 5 minutes or so, until the garlic begins to color. Add more oil if necessary. Add the squash, apples, potatoes, and water and bring to a boil. Add about 1 teaspoon salt (or to taste), reduce the heat, cover, and simmer for 45 minutes, until all the vegetables are thoroughly tender and aromatic.

   Puree the soup in batches in a blender or a food processor fitted with the steel blade and return to the pot. Thin out as desired with milk. Add lots of freshly ground pepper and adjust the salt. Heat through and serve, garnishing each bowlful with a few slices of apple, a squeeze of fresh lime juice, and a dollop of yogurt or *fromage blanc*.

ADVANCE PREPARATION: This soup keeps for a few days in the refrigerator and can easily be served to guests the day after you make it.

PER PORTION

Calories	93	Protein	2 G
Fat	3 G	Carbohydrate	17 G
Sodium	6 MG	Cholesterol	0

SORREL FLAN

SERVES 6

Inspired by a much higher-fat version of a sorrel flan, this one has been toned down quite a bit, although a small amount of cream is still necessary. Without it the milk would curdle and the flan would be runny because of the high acid content of the sorrel. This recipe would work equally well as a tart, using the Yeasted Olive Oil Pastry on page 395. It has a terrific tangy, savory flavor, and I think it's as good cold as hot.

1 tablespoon olive oil

1 small onion, finely chopped, *or* 2 to 3 shallots, finely chopped

2 garlic cloves, minced or put through a press

1/2 pound sorrel, stemmed and washed

5 medium eggs

1 1/4 cups skim milk

1/4 cup crème fraîche

1/2 cup chopped fresh parsley

pinch to 1/4 teaspoon freshly grated nutmeg to taste

1/4 teaspoon crumbled dried thyme

salt to taste and lots of freshly ground pepper

1/3 cup freshly grated Parmesan cheese

3 ounces Gruyère cheese, grated (about 1 cup)

271

Preheat the oven to 350 degrees. Brush a 10-inch ceramic tart pan or a 6- by 10-inch or 8- by 10-inch baking pan with olive oil or melted butter.

Heat the tablespoon of olive oil in a large frying pan and sauté the onion or shallots over medium heat until translucent. Add the garlic and sauté for a minute or 2 more, stirring. Add the sorrel and cook, stirring often, until it wilts and the leaves begin to melt together, about 3 to 5 minutes. Turn up the heat and boil off the liquid that will have accumulated in the pan. This will take another minute or so. Stir to make sure the sorrel doesn't stick to the pan and burn. Remove from the heat and transfer to a bowl.

Beat together the eggs, milk, and crème fraîche. Mix in the parsley, nutmeg, and thyme. Add salt and pepper.

Toss the sorrel and onion mixture with the cheeses in the bowl. Pour in the milk and egg mixture and combine well. Transfer to the prepared baking dish.

Bake in the middle of the preheated oven for 45 minutes to an hour, until beginning to brown on the top and firm to the touch. Serve hot or let cool and serve at room temperature or chilled.

NOTE: If you wish to make this as a tart, use the Yeasted Olive Oil Pastry on page 395. Brush the pastry with beaten egg and prebake for 7 minutes at 375 degrees, then pour in the filling and proceed as above.

ADVANCE PREPARATION: You can grate the cheese and prep and cook the onions and sorrel hours before assembling and baking the flan. Because this flan is good at room temperature or cold, you can also bake it several hours ahead of time.

LEFTOVERS: Cut into squares and serve as hors d'oeuvres.

PER PORTION

Calories	222	Protein	14 G
Fat	16 G	Carbohydrate	6 G
Sodium	228 MG	Cholesterol	190 MG

DRIED FIGS IN ORANGE JUICE WITH YOGURT

SERVES 6

This recipe was my husband Bill's idea. The figs and orange juice make a great combination, nice to have around to mix with yogurt or *fromage blanc*, either for breakfast or as an after-dinner treat. The figs should be marinated in the orange juice for at least a day.

1 pound dried figs, cut into quarters

3 cups fresh orange juice (from about 7 oranges)

3 cups plain nonfat yogurt or *fromage blanc* (page 417)

The day before serving this dish, or in the morning if you're serving it at night, cover the figs with the orange juice. Cover and refrigerate for 8 to 12 hours.

Divide the yogurt or *fromage blanc* among bowls, spoon on the fig mixture, and serve.

ADVANCE PREPARATION: You can make the fig and orange juice mixture 2 days ahead of serving.

LEFTOVERS: Blend leftovers and mix with yogurt or (more extravagant and fattening but *good*) whipped cream and freeze to make ice cream, 1 part cream (unwhipped) or yogurt to 1 part blended figs. Or blend with yogurt for breakfast.

PER PORTION

Calories	312	Protein	10 G
Fat	1 G	Carbohydrate	71 G
Sodium	96 MG	Cholesterol	2 MG

A SIMPLE MENU FOR FRIENDS:

PIPERADE AU BASILIC

———

PIPERADE AU BASILIC

CHRISTINE'S BAKED NEW POTATOES

.

TOSSED GREEN SALAD (PAGE 425)

.

FRESH FRUIT or APRICOT TART

.

CÔTES DU ROUSSILLON, ZINFANDEL,

or CHIANTI

This light, easy menu would make a nice brunch, lunch, or supper. Make it with your friends around you, seated and ready for the *piperade*, a savory dish of eggs scrambled with red and green peppers (and traditionally ham, which I've left out). Even if you don't do anything in advance, the dish doesn't take very long to prepare from start to finish, which is why it's so good for informal entertaining.

Follow the main dish with a salad and fresh fruit, a big bowl of strawberries dressed with orange juice and lemon juice, or an apricot tart.

I always serve a fruity red wine or a rosé with this meal, something from the Mediterranean. If you really prefer white, choose something dry and simple such as a muscadet or fumé blanc or an Alsace Pinot Blanc.

PIPERADE AU BASILIC

SERVES 4 GENEROUSLY

This is a Provençal *piperade*, the Nicoise name for a savory mix of peppers, onions, eggs, garlic, and basil.

2 tablespoons olive oil

2 medium onions, chopped

2 medium red bell peppers, seeds and membranes removed, diced

2 medium green bell peppers, seeds and membranes removed, diced

3 tomatoes, seeded and chopped

3 or 4 large garlic cloves to taste, minced or put through a press

salt and freshly ground pepper to taste

8 large eggs *or* 4 large eggs and 8 large egg whites

2 to 3 tablespoons chopped fresh basil to taste

Heat the olive oil in a large heavy-bottomed frying pan and add the onion. Sauté over medium heat until the onions begin to color. Add the peppers and continue to sauté, stirring often, until the peppers are just beginning to color. Add the tomatoes and garlic and continue to sauté over medium heat for 15 to 20 minutes, stirring often. Remove from the heat and season with salt and pepper.

Beat the eggs or the eggs and egg whites in a bowl. Add some salt and pepper. If you have prepared the *piperade* mixture ahead of time, stir it into the eggs. If you have just prepared the *piperade* mixture and the pan is still hot, stir the eggs into the *piperade*. If you have added the *piperade* to the eggs, you will have to heat about 2 teaspoons of olive oil in the frying pan. Cook like scrambled eggs, over very low heat, until almost set. The mixture should be runny. Stir in the basil and serve.

NOTE: For a *picante* version, add a seeded, chopped jalapeño to the pepper mixture, cooking it along with the peppers and onions.

ADVANCE PREPARATION: The *piperade* mixture will keep for a few days in the refrigerator. Let it come to room temperature before adding it to the eggs.

LEFTOVERS: Fill little mushroom caps and serve as hors d'oeuvres (see page 63) or use as a filling for pocket breads.

PER PORTION

Calories	246	Protein	13 G
Fat	16 G	Carbohydrate	13 G
Sodium	122 MG	Cholesterol	374 MG

CHRISTINE'S BAKED NEW POTATOES

SERVES 4

This is how my friend Christine Picasso bakes her potatoes, and they are the tastiest baked potatoes I've ever eaten. It's amazing that there is no fat whatsoever here, yet they turn out crispy, as if they've been sautéed. The moisture that remains on their skins after washing, plus the natural moisture of the halved potatoes, creates steam in the oven, and the cut surface of the potatoes puffs up and becomes a bit crispy as the potatoes bake.

1 pound new or Russet potatoes

salt and freshly ground pepper to taste

dried *herbes de Provence,* or a combination of crumbled dried thyme and crumbled dried rosemary

Preheat the oven to 400 degrees. Scrub the potatoes well and cut them in half lengthwise. Place the halves cut side up on a baking sheet. Sprinkle with salt, pepper, and herbs.

Bake for 20 to 30 minutes, until the cut surfaces are puffed and browned and the potatoes are tender. Serve.

ADVANCE PREPARATION: The potatoes can be scrubbed and cut hours before baking. Keep in a bowl of cold water.

LEFTOVERS: I eat the leftovers cold, like fruit, or toss them with olive oil for a salad.

PER PORTION

Calories	92	Protein	2 G
Fat	.21 G	Carbohydrate	20 G
Sodium	9 MG	Cholesterol	0

APRICOT TART

SERVES 8

The fruit is barely cooked in this tart, which is as pretty as it is good to eat.

- ½ recipe Yeasted Dessert Pastry (page 131)
- 1 medium egg, beaten
- 2 pounds apricots, halved and pits removed
- 2 tablespoons unrefined brown sugar (turbinado sugar)
- 2 tablespoons apricot jam

Preheat the oven to 375 degrees. Roll out the piecrust and line a buttered 12-inch tart pan. Brush the surface of the pastry generously with the beaten egg. Prick in several places with a fork and bake for 15 to 20 minutes, until the surface and edges are light brown. Remove from the heat. Raise the oven temperature to 400 degrees.

Arrange the apricot halves, rounded side up, on the prebaked piecrust. Sprinkle with the sugar. Bake the tart for 10 to 12 minutes, until the crust is a rich brown color. Meanwhile, heat the jam in a heavy-bottomed saucepan over medium-low heat. Remove the tart from the heat and brush the fruit gently with the melted apricot jam. Serve cool or warm.

ADVANCE PREPARATION: The crust can be made a day ahead of time and refrigerated or weeks ahead of time and frozen. The cut-up fruit will hold for a few hours.

PER PORTION			
Calories	169	Protein	4 G
Fat	5 G	Carbohydrate	29 G
Sodium	99 MG	Cholesterol	35 MG

AN IMPROMPTU SOUP

AND SALAD DINNER PARTY

———

CHAMPAGNE

CRACKERS with GOAT CHEESE SPREAD and

SUN-DRIED TOMATOES (PAGE 73)

•

ROASTED PEPPERS with TUNA and ANCHOVIES

•

LETTUCE and POTATO SOUP

•

RHUBARB and STRAWBERRY CRUMBLE with CRÈME

ANGLAISE

•

BANDOL ROUGE DOMAINE TEMPIER

If you have some champagne in the refrigerator and a good bottle of wine like Domaine Tempier around, a really simple menu can become a *fête*.

The first course is quite pretty, as dishes made with glistening roasted red peppers usually are. If I have some nice tender greens for a little side salad, I'll serve both, but the roasted red peppers with tuna and anchovies alone will really suffice.

Once you've worked the lettuce soup into your repertoire, you will never have to worry about lettuce getting too old in the refrigerator, and you will always have a quick and nourishing dinner at your fingertips. Everybody loves this soup.

For dessert you can splurge. The rest of the meal is low enough in calories and fat to allow for this magnificent crumble.

ROASTED PEPPERS WITH TUNA AND ANCHOVIES

SERVES 4

This is a pretty, easy combination based on a southern Italian dish that traditionally contains clams as well. I've simplified the dish and come up with one that you could make with ingredients on hand (as long as you have red peppers). This makes a delightful starter or lunch dish.

- 2 large red bell peppers
- 1 tablespoon olive oil
- 2 garlic cloves, minced or put through a press
  salt and freshly ground pepper to taste
- 2 6½-ounce cans water-packed tuna, drained
  juice of 1 large lemon
- ½ cup plain nonfat yogurt
- 6 anchovy fillets, rinsed and chopped
- ¼ cup chopped fresh parsley or basil or a combination
  pinch of hot red pepper flakes (optional)

Roast the red peppers directly over a gas burner or under the broiler, turning often, until uniformly charred. Place in a paper or plastic bag and allow to cool.

Remove all of the blackened skins from the peppers, rinse, and pat dry. Cut in half lengthwise and carefully remove the seeds and membranes. Cut the halves again lengthwise down the middle. Place on 4 serving plates. Combine the olive oil and 1 garlic clove and brush the peppers with the mixture. Sprinkle with salt and pepper.

Mix together the tuna, lemon juice, yogurt, anchovy fillets, remaining garlic, parsley and/or basil, and freshly ground pepper to taste. Add hot red pepper flakes if desired. Top the peppers with the tuna, garnish with fresh basil or parsley, and serve, or chill until ready to serve.

ADVANCE PREPARATION: The peppers will hold for a few days in the refrigerator. In this case, marinate them in olive oil with garlic. The tuna will also hold for a day or 2, but mix in the herbs no more than an hour or 2 before serving. The assembled peppers with the tuna will hold for a few hours in the refrigerator.

LEFTOVERS: Both components of this dish, the roasted peppers and the tuna, make great additions to salads or can be tossed with pasta.

PER PORTION

Calories	185	Protein	28 G
Fat	5 G	Carbohydrate	7 G
Sodium	538 MG	Cholesterol	38 MG

LETTUCE AND POTATO SOUP

SERVES 4 TO 6

Sometimes I buy a big head of romaine lettuce or curly endive and end up with most of it a few days or a week later. This lettuce soup is the answer. Easy to make, pretty and delicious, this is best made with a tough, bitter lettuce.

- 1 tablespoon olive oil
- 1 onion, chopped
- 1 pound waxy potatoes, peeled and diced
- 6 garlic cloves, chopped
- 5 cups chicken or vegetable stock (pages 413 and 414)

    salt to taste
- ³/₄ pound lettuce, such as romaine or curly endive, leaves separated, washed, and chopped
- 1 cup skim milk

    lots of freshly ground pepper
- 4 to 6 tablespoons freshly grated Parmesan cheese

Heat the oil in a heavy-bottomed soup pot and sauté the onion over medium-low heat until it begins to soften. Add the potatoes, garlic, and stock and bring to a boil. Reduce the heat, add some salt, cover, and simmer for 45 minutes. Add the lettuce and continue to simmer, covered, for another 20 to 30 minutes, until the lettuce is thoroughly tender. Remove from the heat and puree in batches in a blender or a food processor fitted with the steel blade until thoroughly smooth. Return to the pot, add the milk, season to taste with salt and pepper, and heat through but don't boil.

Serve, topping each bowlful with freshly grated Parmesan.

ADVANCE PREPARATION: This soup can be made up to a day ahead of time and held in the refrigerator.

PER PORTION

Calories	157	Protein	6 G
Fat	6 G	Carbohydrate	21 G
Sodium	136 MG	Cholesterol	5 MG

RHUBARB AND STRAWBERRY CRUMBLE WITH CRÈME ANGLAISE

SERVES 8

Of all the desserts I've served in my life, I think this one has gotten the biggest raves. The tart rhubarb and strawberry combination, sweetened with lavender honey, is set off by the nutty, crunchy topping and smoothed over with a honey crème Anglaise. Blood oranges come into the market at about the same time as rhubarb and strawberries, and they make a distinct contribution to the dish. Make sure you bake this long enough for the topping to be crisp through and through, and if you're increasing the recipe, make sure your dish is quite deep so that the rhubarb mixture doesn't bubble over as it bakes.

A lower-fat alternative baked compote, without the topping, follows.

FOR THE CRÈME ANGLAISE

4 medium egg yolks

$^1/_3$ cup mild-flavored honey

$1^1/_4$ cups skim milk

$^1/_2$ teaspoon vanilla extract *or* 1 vanilla bean, split in half

FOR THE RHUBARB AND STRAWBERRIES

2 pounds rhubarb, trimmed and sliced into $^1/_2$-inch pieces

$^1/_2$ pound strawberries, hulls removed, sliced

$^1/_2$ cup mild-flavored honey, such as clover, acacia, or lavender

$^1/_2$ teaspoon ground cinnamon

1 blood orange or regular orange, if blood oranges aren't available

FOR THE TOPPING

$^1/_4$ cup chopped shelled pecans

$^3/_4$ cup rolled oats

$^1/_2$ cup whole wheat pastry flour

$^1/_4$ cup unrefined brown sugar (turbinado sugar)

$^1/_4$ teaspoon freshly grated nutmeg

$^1/_4$ teaspoon salt

6 tablespoons cold unsalted butter

finely chopped zest of $^1/_2$ orange

First make the crème Anglaise. Beat the egg yolks and honey together until very thick and lemon-colored. Meanwhile, combine the milk and vanilla bean if you're using a bean: split the bean in half and scrape the inside of the bean into the milk; heat together in a heavy-bottomed saucepan to the simmering point. Remove the vanilla bean pod. Being careful that the milk is not boiling, beat it into the egg-honey mixture. Return this mixture to the saucepan and heat over medium-low heat, stirring constantly with a wooden spoon. Do not allow the mixture to boil. The crème Anglaise is ready when it reaches the consistency of thick cream and coats both sides of your spoon evenly. Remove from the heat and strain into a bowl. Whisk in the vanilla now if you're using vanilla extract. Set aside.

Preheat the oven to 375 degrees. Butter a 2-quart baking dish.

In a large bowl, toss together the rhubarb, strawberries, honey, and cinnamon. Peel the orange over the bowl, cut away the pith, and cut the sections out from between the membranes. Toss with the rhubarb mixture. Transfer all of this to the baking dish.

Place the pecans in a dry skillet and toast over medium heat just until they begin to brown and smell toasty, stirring constantly. Remove from the heat and chop coarsely.

Mix together the oats, flour, sugar, nutmeg, and salt. Cut in the butter and work to a crumbly consistency. Stir in the pecans and orange zest (this can all be done in a food processor). Sprinkle the topping over the rhubarb mixture in an even layer.

Bake for about 45 minutes, until crisp and beginning to brown on the top. To finish browning the top, run under the broiler, watching closely, for 2 to 3 minutes. Serve warm, with the cooled crème Anglaise.

ADVANCE PREPARATION: The crème Anglaise can be made a day in advance. Allow to cool, cover, and refrigerate. Serve it cold or at room temperature with the crumble. Do not bake the crumble too far ahead of time so the topping remains crunchy. You can warm this in a low oven before serving.

LEFTOVERS: This crumble is great for breakfast, topped with plain nonfat yogurt.

VARIATION:

Strawberry-Rhubarb Compote: Omit the topping except for the brown sugar. Prepare the rhubarb as directed. Sprinkle with the sugar and bake for 30 to 40 minutes, until bubbling. Serve with crème Anglaise.

PER PORTION

Calories	361	Protein	6 G
Fat	14 G	Carbohydrate	56 G
Sodium	98 MG	Cholesterol	120 MG

A SPRING / SUMMER FISH DINNER

THAT CAN BE INFORMAL OR FANCY

———

HERB BRUSCHETTE (PAGE 77)
BANDOL ROSÉ or MUSCAT D'ALSACE
∎

TOSSED GREEN SALAD (PAGE 425)
∎

BROILED or GRILLED TUNA LARDED with GARLIC
FRESH TOMATO CONCASSÉE (PAGE 423) or
GREEN YOGURT/MAYONNAISE SAUCE
A GRATIN OF POTATOES and CHARD STALKS
∎

PRUNEAUX AU VIN ROUGE
ORANGE BISCOTTI (PAGE 409)
∎

MUSCADET, CÔTES-DU-RHÔNE BLANC or
ROUGE, CHINON

This spring or summer menu is nice enough for a formal sit-down dinner party, easy enough for something more relaxed. None of the dishes takes long to make, although the dessert requires some advance thought.

The evening begins with a chilled glass of Bandol rosé (another dry rosé or a white wine could be substituted) accompanied by herb bruschette.

White, rosé, or red can be drunk with the tuna. I always prefer red wine with tuna, because tuna has a steaklike nature to me (especially since I always cook it rare). But that doesn't preclude white or rosé. A chilled Loire red, like a Chinon, would go, as would a Rhône wine or a Barolo.

BROILED OR GRILLED TUNA LARDED WITH GARLIC

SERVES 4

This dish is very easy to make and tastes so good, the garlic infusing the lightly cooked tuna. It can also be served with Tomatoes Vinaigrette (page 424), or with nothing more than lemon. Just sear the tuna so that it remains pink inside.

> 4 large *or* 8 small garlic cloves, peeled
>
> 2 1-inch-thick tuna steaks (about 12 to 16 ounces each)
>
> salt and freshly ground pepper to taste
>
> juice of 1 lemon
>
> 2 tablespoons olive oil
>
> 1 cup Fresh Tomato Concassée (page 423) or ⅓ cup Green Yogurt/Mayonnaise Sauce (recipe follows)

Cut the garlic into lengthwise slivers. If the cloves are very large, cut them in half lengthwise first, then lay the flat side down and cut lengthwise slivers. Stick the slivers of garlic into the tuna steaks, distributing them evenly. Salt and pepper the steaks, sprinkle with lemon juice and drizzle 1 tablespoon olive oil onto each of them. Let sit for 15 minutes or longer before cooking.

Preheat your broiler or prepare a grill. Cook the tuna for only 1½ to 2 minutes per side. It should be seared on the outside and pink inside.

Remove the tuna from the heat and cut into 2 pieces. Distribute among plates. Top with the sauce of your choice or serve simply with lemon wedges.

ADVANCE PREPARATION: The tuna can be larded with the garlic hours before cooking. The sauces will hold for several hours.

LEFTOVERS: Add to salads or toss with pasta.

PER PORTION

Calories	353	Protein	47 G
Fat	16 G	Carbohydrate	2 G
Sodium	78 MG	Cholesterol	75 MG

GREEN YOGURT/MAYONNAISE SAUCE

MAKES 1¼ CUPS, SERVING 5

This sauce makes a nice accompaniment to grilled or broiled fish. It can be thinned out by blending the ingredients together in a food processor or blender.

- ½ cup finely chopped fresh herbs, such as tarragon, basil, parsley, dill
- ½ cup plain nonfat yogurt
- ⅓ cup Olive Oil Mayonnaise (page 418)
- 2 tablespoons fresh lemon juice
- salt and freshly ground pepper to taste

Stir the herbs into the yogurt and mayonnaise. Stir in the lemon juice and add salt and pepper. For a thinner sauce, blend everything together in a food processor fitted with the steel blade or a blender.

ADVANCE PREPARATION: This sauce will hold for several hours in the refrigerator.

LEFTOVERS: Leftovers can be used as a salad dressing.

PER PORTION

Calories	105	Protein	2 G
Fat	10 G	Carbohydrate	3 G
Sodium	79 MG	Cholesterol	9 MG

PRUNEAUX AU VIN ROUGE

SERVES 6 TO 8

This is a classic French dessert, and there are many versions of it. In some versions the prunes are soaked for 24 hours in water. In my more impromptu version they are soaked for 2 hours in boiling water. It works both ways. It's a great dessert when you want something sweet but not too filling after a meal. Serve this with Orange Biscotti (page 409) so you can dip the cookies in the wine.

1 pound prunes, pitted

2 cups boiling water or to cover

2 cups full-bodied red wine, such as a Côtes-du-Rhône

2 or 3 tablespoons mild-flavored honey to taste

1½ teaspoons ground cinnamon (optional)

juice of ½ lemon

2 or 3 slices of lemon or orange zest to taste

Place the prunes in a bowl and pour on boiling water to cover. Let sit for 2 hours. Drain the water.

Combine the prunes with the remaining ingredients in a saucepan and bring to a boil. Boil for a minute, then remove from the heat and allow to cool. Chill if desired.

ADVANCE PREPARATION: This dessert can be made a day ahead of serving.

PER PORTION

Calories	143	Protein	1 G
Fat	.25 G	Carbohydrate	38 G
Sodium	5 MG	Cholesterol	0

IN CELEBRATION OF

GOOD THINGS FROM IRELAND

———

GUINNESS STOUT

·

WILD RICE and PEAS SALAD

·

SMOKED SALMON and SMOKED TROUT

COARSE WHOLE WHEAT IRISH SODA BREAD

STEAMED or BOILED NEW POTATOES with

FRESH HERBS

·

BAKED APPLES with WHISKEY and HONEY (PAGE 343)

·

CHAMPAGNE or ALSACE RIESLING

My husband, Bill Grantham, was born in Ireland to an Irish mother and an American father. His family moved to England when Bill was 10, and his parents now live in France, but if I had to describe what Bill is, I'd say he's Irish. Somehow Bill didn't get around to returning to Ireland until fairly recently, and the two of us didn't get there together until we'd been married for almost two years. What a discovery it was! The country is gorgeous, the people incredibly friendly, generous, and fun. And contrary to what we'd been told, we ate very well, because we stuck to simple things.

I knew how good the brown Irish soda bread is, as every time Bill's mother goes to Ireland she brings me a loaf. And I knew how good the smoked salmon can be, because we have it every Christmas. But I didn't know how good the Irish Guinness is; you really have to taste it there, in the pubs, to appreciate it. Nonetheless, we bought some at a duty-free shop on our way back, and it tasted pretty good back home, too.

We had bought smoked salmon and whole wheat soda bread at a super-market on our last day in Dublin. As soon as we got back home, we invited Bill's parents over for a nostalgic meal, maybe not exactly Irish through and through (no stew), but one in which we could celebrate some of the best Irish delicacies. And because we were celebrating, we drank champagne with the dinner. It goes so well with smoked salmon. A Riesling is also a good choice. The potatoes are optional, but I couldn't have a sort-of Irish meal without throwing in some spuds.

WILD RICE AND PEAS SALAD

SERVES 4

This is sort of like a wild rice *tabouli*, with lots of parsley and lemon. I made it the night after I got back from two days of heavy eating on the *Orient-Express*, and it made me feel well nourished and light.

²⁄₃ cup wild rice

2 cups chicken stock (page 413), vegetable stock (page 414), or water

salt to taste

1 pound fresh peas, shelled, *or* 1 cup thawed frozen petite peas

2 bunches of fresh parsley, stemmed, washed, and chopped

¹⁄₃ long European (seedless) cucumber, diced, *or* ¹⁄₂ ordinary cucumber, peeled if desired and diced

juice of 1¹⁄₂ large lemons or more to taste

1 garlic clove, minced or put through a press

1 teaspoon Dijon mustard

¹⁄₄ cup plain nonfat yogurt

freshly ground pepper to taste

2 ripe tomatoes, thinly sliced, for garnish

chopped fresh basil for the tomatoes (optional)

Wash the rice. Bring the stock or water to a boil and add the rice. Add salt to taste, bring to a boil again, reduce the heat, cover, and simmer for about 40 minutes, until the rice is tender. Five minutes before the end of the cooking, add the peas and cook with the rice until bright green. Drain, pouring off any excess liquid, and set aside.

Toss the parsley and cucumber with the rice and peas.

Mix together the lemon juice, garlic, mustard, and yogurt. Toss with the rice mixture. Add pepper and more salt to taste.

Serve on individual plates, surrounded by thinly sliced tomatoes sprinkled with basil if available.

ADVANCE PREPARATION: You can cook the rice several hours ahead of time, without adding the peas, and toss with the dressing. Steam the peas and add the herbs and remaining vegetables just before serving.

PER PORTION

Calories	196	Protein	10 G
Fat	.96 G	Carbohydrate	40 G
Sodium	94 MG	Cholesterol	0

COARSE WHOLE WHEAT
IRISH SODA BREAD

MAKES 1 ROUND OR RECTANGULAR LOAF
(9 BY 4½ BY 2½), PROVIDING 15 SLICES

It's amazing how easy it is to make a good loaf of bread with no yeast at all. This Irish soda bread has a very dense, highly textured crumb due to the coarse whole wheat flour I use. It is fairly crumbly. A lighter bread can be achieved with finer whole wheat flour, whole wheat pastry flour, or a little more unbleached white flour in place of whole wheat. But this one best resembles the bread I've eaten in Ireland, a country where you can always find terrific bread.

³/₄ **pound (2¹/₂ cups) coarse whole wheat flour**

¹/₄ **pound (⁷/₈ cup) unbleached white flour**

1¹/₂ **teaspoons salt**

³/₄ **teaspoon baking powder**

1 **teaspoon baking soda**

1¹/₂ **to 2 cups buttermilk or sour skim milk, as needed**

Preheat the oven to 375 degrees.

Mix together the flours, salt, baking powder, and baking soda in a large bowl. Blend thoroughly so that the soda and baking powder are distributed evenly throughout.

Add 1¹/₂ cups of the buttermilk or sour milk and stir together to make a soft but firm dough. Add a little more if the dough seems dry and stiff. If you are using very coarse flour, the dough will be wet.

(continued)

Knead the dough gently on a floured board for about 3 minutes, until the dough is smooth. Form into a round loaf and place on a well-buttered baking sheet. Cut an X across the top with a sharp knife or razor. Or form into a loaf and place in an oiled loaf pan.

Bake for 35 to 45 minutes, until nicely browned and the loaf responds to tapping with a hollow sound. Remove from the heat and cool on a rack. Slice very thin.

NOTE: Soda bread will not keep for a long time—3 days is about the limit. Store in the refrigerator in plastic bags.

VARIATION:

White Irish Soda Bread: Substitute unbleached white flour for the whole wheat flour and proceed as above.

PER PORTION

Calories	116	Protein	5 G
Fat	.74 G	Carbohydrate	24 G
Sodium	327 MG	Cholesterol	1 MG

SMOKED SALMON AND SMOKED TROUT

SERVES 4

There are no secrets here. All you need is very good-quality smoked fish. We find that the smoked trout we get in Ireland and in Scotland is quite good. If you can't find the trout, serve just smoked salmon. Figure on about 3 to 4 ounces of fish per person. Serve it with lemon wedges and *fromage blanc* (page 417) or plain nonfat yogurt on the side (or crème fraîche if you're splurging). Either lay the fish out on a platter and garnish with the lemon wedges and fresh parsley sprigs or serve individual plates. Serve the steamed new potatoes on the side and pass the bread (see preceding recipe) in a basket.

ADVANCE PREPARATION: The salmon can be arranged on the platter or plates several hours ahead of serving. Cover tightly with plastic wrap so it doesn't dry out.

STEAMED OR BOILED NEW POTATOES
WITH FRESH HERBS

SERVES 4

Sweet little new potatoes are one of my great weaknesses. I like to cook more than I need so that the next day I can eat leftovers for lunch. When they are really good, sweet and fragrant, I eat them as if they were apples.

Sometimes I boil potatoes; sometimes I steam them. They lose their soluble vitamins when you boil them, so steaming is better from a nutritional standpoint.

1¼ pounds small waxy potatoes, preferably new potatoes, unpeeled

2 tablespoons chopped fresh herbs, such as parsley, thyme, dill, basil, rosemary (if you are going to use just one, use parsley)

salt and freshly ground pepper to taste

1 tablespoon olive oil or unsalted butter (optional)

Scrub the potatoes well and cut out any green spots or sprouts. If they are somewhat large—larger than a golf ball—cut them into halves or quarters. Place in a steaming basket or in a pot of salted water and bring the water to a boil. Reduce the heat, cover if steaming, and cook 15 to 25 minutes, or until tender, depending on size. Remove from the heat.

Toss the potatoes with the herbs, salt and pepper, and olive oil or butter if desired. Serve hot.

ADVANCE PREPARATION: The potatoes can be cooked ahead of time and reheated by tossing them into boiling water, reheating them in a steamer, or heating them in a 350-degree oven. Toss with the herbs at the last minute.

LEFTOVERS: Add to salads, omelets, or vegetable tarts.

PER PORTION

Calories	115	Protein	3 G
Fat	.26 G	Carbohydrate	26 G
Sodium	12 MG	Cholesterol	0

CHAPTER FIVE

IMPROMPTU ENTERTAINING:
Dishes from the Pantry

I have long had a fantasy of making meals day after day using only the ingredients I had on hand—grains, beans, pasta, canned tomatoes and tuna from my pantry, the olives, anchovies, and capers I always have in my refrigerator, the herbs growing on my terrace. I've never really done it (I would have to have salad), but the idea is part of the inspiration for this chapter.

The other half of the inspiration comes from my experience of living in a city where shopping was difficult. Because we often invited friends over for dinner on the spur of the moment, it was essential for me to have good staples on hand that could make a meal, an hors d'oeuvre, or a main dish. I was also under deadline pressure and didn't have time to devote entire days to small weeknight dinner parties, despite my inclination. I had to discipline myself *not* to spend too much time in the kitchen; it was either that or not invite friends for dinner. And we wanted to see our friends.

These dishes, then, can be created from ingredients that are easy to keep in the pantry and refrigerator, and they are tasty and attractive enough to serve to guests. In some of the recipes, like the Quick White Bean and Sorrel Soup or the Lentil Soup with Cilantro, an extra fresh green or herb is included, but if you're in a pinch, and you want to make the soups, make simpler versions without the sorrel or herbs. I've included other fresh vegetables and herbs in some of the recipes, but if you can't get hold of them, omit them and substitute dried herbs such as thyme, rosemary, oregano, or basil.

STOCKING THE KITCHEN

What are the foods that we usually have on hand or that are easy to keep in the refrigerator or pantry? Eggs certainly, and milk; canned tomatoes and tuna; pasta, rice, beans, canned beans, and other grains; garlic, onions, olive oil. The other items I try never to be without are lemons, yogurt, and *fromage blanc* or cottage cheese, Parmesan cheese, good imported black olives, capers, anchovies, sun-dried tomatoes, dried imported mushrooms (*cèpes* or *porcini,* which are the same thing), and fresh parsley (which keeps for a week if stored properly). I also like to have chicken or vegetable stock in the freezer, but if I don't, garlic broth is easy to make and takes only an hour of simmering (see page 415).

As for desserts, besides serving fresh fruit, which can be embellished easily, you can come up with special desserts based on fruits that keep well—oranges, apples, grapefruit, bananas—and dried fruit compotes and soufflés. A custard sauce (crème Anglaise) will make even canned fruit into an event; look for some good-quality, either unsweetened or very slightly sweetened, preserved fruit in jars. Frozen strawberries and raspberries too are dessert possibilities that you can lay in. Raspberries take to freezing much better than strawberries.

SUGGESTIONS FOR IMPROMPTU DISHES DRAWN FROM OTHER CHAPTERS

Roasted Peppers with Tuna and Anchovies (page 280)
Hummus (page 39)
Tapenade (page 38)
Thyme Biscuits (page 79)
Whole Wheat Scones (page 394)
Dried *Porcini* Soup (page 88)
Warm Lentil Salad (page 348)
Wild Rice Pilaf (page 180)
Raspberries with *Fromage Blanc* (page 119)
Raspberries with Crème de Framboise Liqueur (page 196)

TOMATO SAUCE
USING CANNED TOMATOES

MAKES 1 CUP

When you can't get good fresh tomatoes, it's not worth making tomato sauce from anything other than canned, which are at least picked when ripe. The best are the Italian imported ones. I am never without them. This can be a chunky rustic sauce or put through a food mill for a smoother one. Cooked down, it becomes a *concassée*, or thick tomato sauce. This recipe is quite basic, embellished only with garlic, salt, and a little bit of sugar. The pinch of cinnamon is something my mother taught me; it brings out the sweetness of the tomatoes without adding a taste of cinnamon. From here you can go in many directions, adding dried herbs or fresh, chili peppers or cilantro, ad infinitum.

Note that the same amount of canned tomatoes makes (somehow) only half as much sauce as fresh tomatoes (see Fresh Tomato Concassée, page 423).

1 tablespoon olive oil

2 to 3 large garlic cloves to taste, minced or put through a press

1 28-ounce can tomatoes, drained, the tomatoes seeded and coarsely chopped

¼ teaspoon sugar, approximately

salt to taste

a tiny pinch of ground cinnamon (optional)

freshly ground pepper to taste (optional)

Heat the olive oil over low heat in a heavy-bottomed saucepan or frying pan. Add 1 clove of the garlic and sauté, stirring, just until it begins to color and give off a fragrant aroma. Add the tomatoes, remaining garlic, sugar, and salt and raise the heat to medium-low. Cook, uncovered, stirring from time to time, for 15 to 20 minutes. The tomatoes should bubble briskly, but not so fast that they stick to the bottom of the pan and scorch. At the end of the cooking, stir in the pinch of cinnamon and freshly ground pepper if you wish. Taste and adjust the seasonings.

If you want a thicker tomato mixture, continue to simmer over medium-low heat, stirring often, until the mixture reaches the desired consistency (for omelets and scrambled eggs on pages 305 and 306, for instance, it should be thick). Put through the medium blade of a Mouli food mill for a smoother consistency.

ADDITIONS: Flavor the sauce with any of the following if you wish:

- up to 1 teaspoon crumbled dried herbs (thyme, oregano, basil, rosemary, alone or in combination): stir in 5 minutes before the end of the cooking

- a pinch or 2 of cayenne pepper: add toward the end of the cooking

- 1/4 to 1/2 teaspoon hot red pepper flakes: add toward the end of the cooking

- 1 to 3 tablespoons slivered or chopped fresh basil or cilantro: add at the end of the cooking

- 1 small onion, chopped: sauté along with the garlic until it begins to color

- 1 small carrot, finely chopped: sauté along with the garlic and/or onion

- 1 celery rib, finely chopped: sauté along with the garlic and/or onion

ADVANCE PREPARATION: The sauce, without additional fresh herbs, will hold for 3 or 4 days in the refrigerator and can be frozen.

PER PORTION

Calories	74	Protein	2 G
Fat	4 G	Carbohydrate	10 G
Sodium	324 MG	Cholesterol	0

TOMATO SAUCE WITH . . .

Tomato sauce can transform so many foods into a "dish." Serve the preceding sauce with:

- Spaghetti or other pasta: One recipe of the sauce tossed with $1/2$ to $3/4$ pound spaghetti; this recipe makes a very light coating for $3/4$ pound pasta; double for a thicker topping.

- Fish fillets or steaks: One recipe of the sauce will be enough for four $1/4$-pound servings. You can bake the fish in the sauce or broil or steam the fish separately.

- Scrambled eggs: See recipe, page 305.

- Omelets: See recipe, page 306.

- *Bruschette:* Top grilled or toasted bread, which you have rubbed with a cut clove of garlic, with the sauce. Makes a delicious lunch or supper.

- Polenta: See recipe, page 307.

- Pizza: One recipe of the sauce is enough for one 12- to 15-inch pizza

- Kasha and other grains

SCRAMBLED EGGS À LA PROVENÇALE

SERVES 4

These salmon-colored scrambled eggs make a great impromptu late-night supper. Made with 1 part whole eggs and 2 parts egg whites, they are slightly runny, but that doesn't affect their marvelous flavor.

    8 medium eggs *or* 4 eggs and 8 egg whites
 1/4 cup thick tomato sauce (made from canned tomatoes, page 302,
        or fresh, page 423)
        salt and freshly ground pepper to taste
    1 tablespoon olive oil
    1 tablespoon chopped fresh basil or chives (optional)

Beat the eggs or eggs and egg whites together in a bowl. Stir in the tomato sauce, salt, and pepper. Heat the oil over low heat in a heavy-bottomed saucepan or a *bain-marie*. Add the eggs and cook slowly, over low heat, stirring constantly, until they are cooked through but still fairly runny. Stir in the basil or chives if desired. Serve at once, with toasted country bread.

ADVANCE PREPARATION: The tomato sauce will hold for a few days in the refrigerator.

PER PORTION

Calories	166	Protein	11 G
Fat	12 G	Carbohydrate	2 G
Sodium	131 MG	Cholesterol	374 MG

TOMATO OMELET

SERVES 4

This is yet another Provençal dish. All of my favorite omelets come from the south of France. This one is a rolled omelet.

8 medium eggs *or* 4 eggs and 8 egg whites

   salt and freshly ground pepper to taste

2 tablespoons olive oil, or 3 if cooking the omelets individually

¾ cup thick tomato sauce (made from fresh tomatoes, page 423, or canned, page 302), with or without herbs

¼ cup freshly grated Parmesan cheese (optional)

   Tomatoes Vinaigrette (page 424) for garnish (optional)

Depending on the size of your omelet pan, you can make 2 large omelets or 4 individual ones.

Beat together the eggs or eggs and egg whites. Add salt and pepper. Heat 1 tablespoon olive oil in a nonstick or well-seasoned omelet pan for large omelets or about 2½ teaspoons for individual omelets. When the oil is hot, add the eggs and cook, shaking the pan and gently lifting the sides of the omelet and tilting the pan so that the egg can run underneath. When it is just about cooked through, spread 3 tablespoons of the tomato sauce down the middle for individual omelets or half the tomato sauce for large omelets. Sprinkle with the Parmesan if desired. Fold in both sides of the omelet over the filling, slide out of the pan, and serve. Garnish with Tomatoes Vinaigrette if you wish.

ADVANCE PREPARATION: The tomato sauce will hold for a couple of days in the refrigerator.

PER PORTION

Calories	246	Protein	12 G
Fat	18 G	Carbohydrate	8 G
Sodium	354 MG	Cholesterol	374 MG

POLENTA WITH TOMATO SAUCE

SERVES 4

Cornmeal is a grain I always have on hand, and one of my favorite dishes is *polenta*. I'd make it for company anytime. It's great topped with a simple tomato sauce and Parmesan.

    olive or vegetable oil for the cutting board or platter
5   cups water, plus additional boiling water in a kettle
³/₄ teaspoon salt
¹/₂ pound (about 1¹/₃ cups) coarse stone-ground yellow cornmeal
1   recipe tomato sauce (from canned tomatoes, page 302, or fresh, page 423)
¹/₄ cup freshly grated Parmesan cheese

Brush a large clean cutting board or platter with olive or vegetable oil. Bring the 5 cups of water to a rolling boil in a deep, heavy pot. Have additional water simmering in a kettle. Add the salt and reduce the heat so the water is just boiling—a little higher than a simmer. Use a long-handled wooden spoon and stir the water constantly in one direction while you add the cornmeal in a very slow stream, so slow that you can see the individual grains. To do this, pick up the cornmeal by handfuls and let it run through your fingers. The mixture will become harder and harder to stir as you add all the cornmeal. Never stop stirring. If it seems extremely thick, add boiling water from the kettle, a little at a time. Once all the cornmeal has been added, continue to stir in the same direction for 20 minutes. The *polenta* should come away from the sides of the pan when it's done. It may seem done before the 20 minutes are up, but the cornmeal won't be properly cooked and won't have a creamy consistency. Keep adding small ladlefuls of boiling water as it becomes impossible to stir. When it is done, it will have the consistency of very thick cream of wheat, and a spoon should stand up when stuck into the middle.

Pour or scrape the *polenta* out of the pot onto the oiled cutting board or platter, smooth the top, top with the tomato sauce, sprinkle on the Parmesan, and serve hot. Or let the *polenta* cool and serve as described on the next page.

ADVANCE PREPARATION: The tomato sauce can be made up to a day or two ahead of time and refrigerated.

(continued)

LEFTOVERS: Slice up leftovers and either place in a lightly oiled baking dish or cut into little squares for hors d'oeuvres. Heat through in a medium-hot oven until the edges begin to crisp, or grill under the broiler or on an outdoor grill. Serve topped with the sauce of your choice.

PER PORTION

Calories	340	Protein	9 G
Fat	10 G	Carbohydrate	54 G
Sodium	851 MG	Cholesterol	5 MG

EGGS POACHED IN CURRIED TOMATO SAUCE

SERVES 4 GENEROUSLY

This dish, reminiscent of *huevos rancheros,* is adapted from a recipe in Susan Campbell and Caroline Conran's *Poor Cook.* It can be more or less spicy, according to taste. You make a piquant tomato sauce and poach the eggs in it, then spoon the sauce and poached eggs over rice or grains. The eggs cool the heat of the sauce. The dish is great for supper, lunch, or brunch. The tamarind, which you can find in stores that sell Indian ingredients, adds a nice tart flavor. But lemon juice is a suitable substitute (and as we are being impromptu, you will probably be more likely to have it around; however, tamarind keeps for months).

1 tablespoon tamarind paste *or* a 1-inch ball of tamarind pulp (1/2 ounce) plus 1/2 cup warm water *or* juice of 1/2 lemon

1 tablespoon sunflower or safflower oil

1 onion, chopped

2 or 3 large garlic cloves to taste, minced or put through a press

1 or 2 hot chili peppers to taste, seeded and minced, *or* 1 or 2 teaspoons hot chili powder

3/4 to 1 teaspoon ground cumin to taste

1/2 teaspoon ground coriander

1 teaspoon curry powder (optional)

²/₃ cup water

2 pounds fresh or canned tomatoes, peeled, seeded, and chopped

   salt and freshly ground pepper to taste

   pinch of cayenne pepper (optional)

4 to 8 medium eggs to taste

2 to 3 tablespoons chopped cilantro to taste (optional)

1 recipe basmati rice (page 116) or other grains

If you are using tamarind, soak it in ¹/₂ cup warm water for 10 minutes, strain, and reserve the water.

Heat the oil over medium heat in a wide heavy-bottomed saucepan that will accommodate all the eggs. Add the onion and sauté until it is softened and beginning to color. Add the garlic and chili peppers and continue to sauté for a few minutes until the garlic begins to color. Add the spices and 2 tablespoons of the water (*not* the tamarind water) and stir together for a minute. Add the tomatoes, remaining water, and salt and pepper. Bring to a simmer and simmer over medium-low heat for 15 minutes, stirring often. Stir in the tamarind soaking water or lemon juice, taste, and adjust the seasonings. Add the cayenne if you want this more *picante*.

Gently break the eggs into the simmering sauce. Poach them in the simmering sauce for 5 minutes or until set. Sprinkle with the cilantro if desired. Remove from the heat and serve at once, over hot rice or other grains.

ADVANCE PREPARATION: The sauce can be made hours in advance and held on top of the stove until you are ready to eat. You may have to thin it out with a little water if it seems too thick for you to properly poach the eggs in. Reheat to a simmer and break in the eggs.

PER PORTION

Calories	521	Protein	17 G
Fat	11 G	Carbohydrate	87 G
Sodium	106 MG	Cholesterol	281 MG

BRUSCHETTE WITH VERACRUZANA SAUCE

SERVES 2

This is a recipe I made up because I had leftover Veracruzana Sauce in my refrigerator after a cooking class. Exhausted and hungry one night, I made dinner with the ingredients I had on hand, and it was so good that I've been serving it to guests ever since. This makes a delicious starter or a great lunch dish.

2 thick slices of country bread, such as the sourdough country breads on pages 380–83

1 teaspoon olive oil

½ cup Veracruzana Sauce (page 101)

1 garlic clove, halved

4 teaspoons freshly grated Parmesan cheese (optional)

Preheat the oven to 450 degrees. Brush the bread with olive oil and toast in the oven until it begins to brown. Meanwhile, heat the Veracruzana Sauce in a small saucepan.

Remove the toasted bread from the oven, rub with the garlic, and top with the sauce. If you are adding the Parmesan, sprinkle the bread with the cheese and heat through in the oven or under the broiler until the cheese begins to melt. Serve hot.

ADVANCE PREPARATION: The sauce will keep for several days in the refrigerator. The bread should be toasted just before being served.

PER PORTION

Calories	243	Protein	7 G
Fat	5 G	Carbohydrate	44 G
Sodium	491 MG	Cholesterol	0

BRUSCHETTE WITH WHITE BEANS

SERVES 2

I was once at a very fancy hotel in Scotland, Inverlochy Castle, and I interviewed the maître d', who told me how accommodating the chef was. People tended to stay at this beautiful hotel for a week or so at a time, and they often tired of eating rich, starred meals every night. "If people want to eat beans and toast, he will make them beans and toast." This was the first time I'd ever really considered beans and toast as a meal—something that is a common enough repast in the UK. I figured the chef must serve a pretty good version of it at Inverlochy Castle, and I set about to put together a nice version myself. It's best if you have fresh herbs, but I've given a version with dried herbs as well. This dish, which has a more Italian than British nature, makes a delicious starter or a late supper with a nice green salad.

2 thick slices of country bread, such as the sourdough country breads on pages 380–83 (or 4 slices if the bread is not very wide)

2 to 3 garlic cloves to taste, 1 cut in half, the other 2 minced or put through a press

1 tablespoon olive oil

1 15-ounce can white beans, borlotti beans, or kidney beans, with about half their liquid

2 tablespoons fresh lemon juice or more to taste

1/4 cup chopped fresh herbs, such as parsley, basil, tarragon, sage, thyme, rosemary, marjoram, or 1 to 2 teaspoons crumbled dried thyme and rosemary, mixed, to taste plus 1/2 teaspoon crumbled dried tarragon

freshly ground pepper to taste

2 tablespoons freshly grated Parmesan or Gruyère cheese

Toast the bread until crisp on the outside but still slightly soft on the inside. Rub with a cut clove of garlic and brush with olive oil. If the slices are very long, cut them in half.

Mix together the beans, remaining garlic, lemon juice, herbs, and lots of freshly ground pepper. Heat through in a saucepan and pile onto the bread. Sprinkle on the cheese and serve.

(continued)

ADVANCE PREPARATION: The beans can be tossed with everything except the herbs hours before serving.

PER PORTION

Calories	530	Protein	24 G
Fat	10 G	Carbohydrate	88 G
Sodium	473 MG	Cholesterol	5 MG

SPOON BREAD

SERVES 4

I'm always rediscovering spoon bread. I'll go for quite a while without making it, then remember how good it is. It's like a light, savory cornmeal pudding and makes an easy supper, accompanied by a big salad and bright green vegetables. I've given mine a slightly Mediterranean flavor by substituting olive oil for the traditional butter. Made this way, the flavor reminds me of some of the Basque corn breads that contain olive oil. This recipe is definitely worth remembering when all you have on hand is eggs, milk, and cornmeal.

$1^{1}/_{2}$ cups water

$^{3}/_{4}$ teaspoon salt plus additional to taste

1   cup stone-ground yellow cornmeal

$1^{1}/_{2}$ cups skim milk

1   tablespoon olive oil

    freshly ground pepper to taste

2   medium egg yolks

4   medium egg whites

    pinch of cream of tartar

Preheat the oven to 350 degrees. Butter a 2-quart straight-sided soufflé dish or a gratin dish.

      Bring the water to a boil in a heavy-bottomed saucepan and add the $^{3}/_{4}$ teaspoon salt. Slowly add the cornmeal, stirring all the while with a wooden spoon. The mixture will be quite thick. Now stir in the milk, stirring all the while with either a whisk or a wooden spoon. Cook the mixture over medium-low heat for about 10 minutes. It should be thick and fairly smooth. Taste and correct salt.

Remove the cornmeal mixture from the heat and stir in the olive oil, pepper, and egg yolks.

Beat the egg whites until stiff, adding a pinch of cream of tartar at the beginning. Stir one quarter of the egg whites into the cornmeal mixture, then fold the cornmeal mixture into the egg whites. The mixture should be thoroughly amalgamated. It isn't going to be a soufflé, so you don't have to worry if you fold longer than you do for a soufflé. The important thing is to achieve an even consistency.

Turn the mixture into the prepared baking dish. Bake for 30 minutes or until puffed and beginning to brown on the top. Serve at once. (You spoon it from the dish; that's why it's spoon bread.)

VARIATION:

Cumin Spoon Bread: Add 2 teaspoons cumin seeds to the cornmeal mixture when you stir in the olive oil and the egg yolks.

<table>
<tr><td colspan="6" align="center">PER PORTION</td></tr>
<tr><td>Calories</td><td>230</td><td>Protein</td><td>10 G</td></tr>
<tr><td>Fat</td><td>6 G</td><td>Carbohydrate</td><td>32 G</td></tr>
<tr><td>Sodium</td><td>511 MG</td><td>Cholesterol</td><td>98 MG</td></tr>
</table>

TUNA RISOTTO

SERVES 6 AS A MAIN DISH

No, this is not an authentic Venetian seafood *risotto,* but I wouldn't say it's not fancy. The generous *risotto,* with its fragrant aroma and brilliant saffron hue, specked with chopped parsley and bits of tomato, is no plain dish. Anchovies add sharp flavor, an ample amount of tuna is stirred in at the last minute, and you might just fool your guests into thinking there's a fishmonger around the corner.

2 6½-ounce cans water-packed tuna

7 cups garlic broth (page 415), vegetable stock (page 414), or Mild Fish *Fumet* (page 416)

4 garlic cloves, minced or put through a press

   a large handful of minced fresh parsley

   pinch of crumbled dried thyme

   juice of ½ lemon

   freshly ground pepper to taste

   pinch of hot red pepper flakes or cayenne pepper

1 tablespoon olive oil

1 small onion *or* 2 shallots, minced

3 or 4 anchovy fillets to taste, rinsed and chopped (optional)

1 pound fresh or canned tomatoes, peeled, seeded, and chopped

   salt to taste

2 cups Arborio rice

½ cup dry white wine

   heaped ¼ teaspoon powdered saffron

Drain the tuna over a bowl and add the brine from 1 can only to the stock. Break up the tuna with a fork in a bowl and mix in 1 garlic clove, the parsley, thyme, lemon juice, pepper, and hot red pepper flakes or cayenne.

Have the stock simmering in a saucepan.

Heat the oil over medium-low heat in a wide heavy frying pan and sauté the onion or shallot and the remaining garlic until the onion begins to color. Add the anchovies and tomatoes, some salt (taste first—the anchovies may provide enough salt), and pepper and continue to sauté, stirring often, for about 5 minutes or a little longer. Add the rice and stir to coat with the mixture. Cook, stirring, for a minute or 2. Add the white wine and cook over medium heat until it has just about evaporated.

Now begin adding the simmering stock, a ladleful or 2 at a time, and cook, stirring until each ladleful is just about absorbed. The stock should just cover the rice and should be bubbling but not boiling too quickly. Continue adding stock and cooking until the rice is cooked al dente, which will take about 25 minutes or so. When the rice is just about al dente, stir the saffron into the stock and continue adding ladlefuls of the stock to the rice as above. When the rice is al dente, add a final ladleful of stock, stir in the tuna mixture, stir together for a minute, and adjust the seasonings. Serve at once.

ADVANCE PREPARATION: You can mix together the tuna with the garlic, parsley, thyme etc. hours ahead of making this.

LEFTOVERS: Use leftover *risotto* as the basis for a flat omelet. Mix with beaten eggs and cook in a nonstick pan as for the flat omelets on pages 30–34.

PER PORTION

Calories	376	Protein	21 G
Fat	5 G	Carbohydrate	62 G
Sodium	990 MG	Cholesterol	30 MG

TUNA AND BEAN SALAD

SERVES 4

There are many versions of this salad, two of which are in my book *Mediterranean Light*. This one is pared down to the essentials, but it's still lovely enough to serve to guests. The salad is equally suitable as a starter, lunch dish, or light supper.

- 2 6½-ounce cans water-packed tuna, drained
- 1 15-ounce can white beans, borlotti beans, or chick-peas
- 1 garlic clove, minced or put through a press
- 1 small red onion, chopped (optional)
- 3 to 4 tablespoons chopped fresh parsley to taste
- 1 recipe Low-Fat Yogurt Vinaigrette (page 433)

   salt and freshly ground pepper to taste

   romaine or leaf lettuce for serving (optional)

   sliced lemon and imported black olives for garnish

Place the tuna in a bowl and break up with a fork. Add the beans, garlic, onion if desired, and parsley and toss together. Toss with the vinaigrette and add salt and pepper. Serve over lettuce leaves if you wish, divided among 4 salad plates, with sliced lemon and black olives on the side.

ADVANCE PREPARATION: The tuna and bean mixture will hold for a day in the refrigerator, but it's best to toss the parsley with the mixture just before serving.

PER PORTION

Calories	266	Protein	35 G
Fat	.95 G	Carbohydrate	29 G
Sodium	407 MG	Cholesterol	35 MG

PITA PIZZAS

Slice a pita bread in half so you have 2 circles, top them with tomato sauce, a little cheese, herbs, whatever strikes your fancy, toast them in the oven, and you have an instant pizzalike meal. The pita gets crispy on the edges and just short of crisp on the bottom. This is a dinner I've whipped up upon returning home from vacation, with nothing fresh on hand and pitas in the freezer.

The nutritional data given include all of the topping options, when in fact you'll be choosing just one or two of them, so your actual numbers will be lower.

    2 fairly large pita breads, split in half (I prefer whole wheat)
    1 cup Fresh Tomato Concassée (page 423) or Tomato Sauce Using Canned Tomatoes (page 302)

FOR THE TOPPING

        sliced onion

        slivered garlic

        fresh or dried herbs

        freshly grated Parmesan or Gruyère cheese, about 1 tablespoon per pita half

        roasted or sautéed green, red, or yellow bell peppers

        steamed or baked eggplant, chopped or sliced

        tuna (1 6½-ounce can is enough for 4 pita halves)

        capers and imported black olives (1 tablespoon drained capers and about 6 olives per pita half)

        anchovy fillets

Preheat the oven to 400 degrees. Top the pita halves with tomato sauce and other toppings of your choice. Place on a baking sheet or right on a heated baking stone and bake for 10 to 15 minutes, until the topping is bubbly and the pitas are crisp around the edges.

ADVANCE PREPARATION: The tomato sauce can be made a day or 2 ahead of time and held in the refrigerator.

PER PORTION

Calories	209	Protein	7 G
Fat	6 G	Carbohydrate	33 G
Sodium	344 MG	Cholesterol	4 MG

PIZZA WITH TOMATO SAUCE, TUNA, AND CAPERS

SERVES 4 AS A MAIN DISH, 8 AS AN HORS D'OEUVRE

Pizza topped with tomato sauce and tuna is a common dish in pizzerias on the Côte d'Azur. It couldn't be easier. I've added a few more touches here, and it's one of our favorites.

enough pizza dough for a 14- or 15-inch pizza pan (pages 390–91) *or* 2 pita breads, split in half into 2 thin rounds

2 tablespoons olive oil

2 large garlic cloves, minced or put through a press

1 28-ounce can tomatoes, drained, the tomatoes seeded and chopped

salt to taste

pinch of sugar

1/2 to 1 teaspoon crumbled dried thyme and rosemary to taste, mixed, or *herbes de Provence*

freshly ground pepper to taste

half of a 6½-ounce can water-packed tuna, drained

1 tablespoon drained capers, rinsed

a sprinkling of hot red pepper flakes (optional)

additional *herbes de Provence* or crumbled dried thyme (optional)

Preheat the oven to 500 degrees. Press out the pizza dough to fit the pan, pinching an attractive lip around the edge.

Heat 1 tablespoon of the oil in a heavy-bottomed saucepan and sauté the minced garlic over medium heat until it begins to color. Add the tomatoes, salt, and sugar. Cook, stirring often, over moderate heat, for 15 to 20 minutes. Stir in the herbs and pepper. Adjust the seasonings and remove from the heat.

Spread the tomato sauce over the pizza dough. Break up the tuna with a fork and sprinkle over the tomato sauce. Scatter on the capers and olives and sprinkle with hot pepper flakes and additional dried thyme or *herbes de Provence* if you wish. Drizzle the remaining tablespoon of oil over the pizza.

Bake for 15 minutes, until the dough is crisp and brown. Serve hot.

ADVANCE PREPARATION: The dough can be prepared hours ahead of time and refrigerated or frozen until about an hour before baking. The tomato sauce will hold for a day. The pizza should be assembled shortly before being baked.

NOTE: If you're using pita bread, preheat the oven to 400 degrees and bake for 10 to 15 minutes.

PER PORTION

Calories	427	Protein	19 G
Fat	10 G	Carbohydrate	69 G
Sodium	1,006 MG	Cholesterol	9 MG

HARD-BOILED EGGS WITH AILLADE
(Eggs with Garlic, Capers, and Anchovies)

SERVES 6

Here's another recipe from Provence. This region of France makes such good use of its anchovies and capers. The garlic is cooked with the egg, giving it a sweet, mild flavor. This easy combination makes a fine hors d'oeuvre, first course, or light lunch or supper.

- 6 medium eggs
- 10 large garlic cloves, peeled
- 6 anchovy fillets, soaked in water for 10 minutes
- 1 tablespoon drained capers, rinsed
- 1 teaspoon red wine vinegar
- 1 tablespoon fresh lemon juice
- 3 tablespoons olive oil
- salt if necessary and freshly ground black pepper to taste
- 2 tablespoons chopped fresh parsley, tarragon, or basil or a combination
- 1 or 2 fresh garlic cloves to taste, minced or put through a press (optional)
- 1 small shallot, minced (optional)
- a light sprinkling of cayenne pepper

Combine the eggs and whole garlic cloves in a saucepan and bring to a boil. Boil for 10 minutes over low heat. Drain, set the garlic cloves aside, run the eggs under cold water, and peel.

Cut the eggs in half lengthwise. Remove the yolks.

Combine the garlic, anchovy fillets, egg yolks, and capers in a mortar and pestle or in a food processor fitted with the steel blade and pound or process to a paste. Add the vinegar and lemon juice and slowly drizzle in the oil. Add salt if necessary and freshly ground pepper to taste. Stir in the fresh herbs. If you wish, add some minced garlic and minced shallot.

Fill the egg whites with the *aillade* and sprinkle a little cayenne pepper over the tops. Arrange on a platter and serve.

ADVANCE PREPARATION: These eggs will hold for several hours in the refrigerator.

PER PORTION

Calories	79	Protein	2 G
Fat	7 G	Carbohydrate	2 G
Sodium	185 MG	Cholesterol	2 MG

WHOLE WHEAT SPAGHETTI WITH COTTAGE CHEESE, GARLIC, AND HERBS

SERVES 4 GENEROUSLY

This pasta dish should be made with a variety of vivid-tasting fresh herbs, but if you have only parsley on hand it will still be good. And if you don't even have parsley, stir dried thyme and rosemary into the whipped cottage cheese and you'll have an earthy dish with Provençal flavors. Although you could use other pasta for this dish, spaghetti is particularly nice with the creamy sauce, and whole wheat spaghetti is the tastiest.

1½ cups low-fat cottage cheese

⅓ cup skim milk

1 to 2 garlic cloves to taste, minced or put through a press

¼ cup chopped fresh herbs, such as parsley, basil, chervil, chives, thyme, dill, rosemary, marjoram, *or* 1 teaspoon each crumbled dried thyme and rosemary

salt and freshly ground pepper to taste

¾ pound whole wheat spaghetti or other pasta

¼ cup freshly grated Parmesan cheese

Whip together the cottage cheese and milk in a food processor fitted with the steel blade or put the cottage cheese through a fine sieve and whisk together with the milk. Add the garlic (this can be done in the food processor) and stir in the herbs. Don't use the food processor to add the herbs unless you want a green sauce. Add salt and pepper.

Bring a large pot of water to a boil. Add a teaspoon or so of salt and the pasta. Cook until al dente. Drain and toss with the cottage cheese mixture. Serve at once and pass the Parmesan on the side.

ADVANCE PREPARATION: The cottage cheese mixture will hold for a day in the refrigerator.

PER PORTION

Calories	395	Protein	26 G
Fat	4 G	Carbohydrate	68 G
Sodium	477 MG	Cholesterol	9 MG

FUSILLI WITH TOMATO SAUCE, BEANS, AND BASIL

SERVES 4 GENEROUSLY

This is a very simple version of *pasta e fagioli*. It's a dish I often serve if I've invited people over for dinner on a Monday, that being the day in Paris when markets are closed.

1 recipe tomato sauce (page 302 for canned, page 423 for fresh)

1 15-ounce can white beans (Great Northern or Navy), drained

1 to 2 garlic cloves to taste, minced or put through a press (optional)

1/4 to 1/2 teaspoon hot red pepper flakes to taste, *or* a pinch of cayenne pepper (optional)

    freshly ground pepper to taste

3 or 4 tablespoons slivered fresh basil leaves to taste

1 teaspoon salt, approximately

3/4 pound fusilli

1/3 cup freshly grated Parmesan cheese

Put the tomato sauce in a saucepan and stir in the beans, garlic, red pepper or cayenne, freshly ground pepper, and basil. Keep warm while you cook the pasta.

Meanwhile, bring a large pot of water to a boil. Add about a teaspoon of salt and the pasta. Cook until al dente, drain, and toss with the sauce and about half the Parmesan. Serve, passing the remaining Parmesan at the table.

ADVANCE PREPARATION: The sauce, without the basil, will keep for a day or 2 in the refrigerator. Add the basil when you heat the sauce through before serving.

PER PORTION

Calories	554	Protein	24 G
Fat	8 G	Carbohydrate	97 G
Sodium	486 MG	Cholesterol	6 MG

PASTA, TUNA, AND . . .

All of the recipes that follow are unadorned, down-to-earth, tasty combinations of pasta, tuna, and 1 or 2 other ingredients. They aren't meant to be fancy; on the other hand, I wouldn't think twice about serving these dishes to an unexpected guest. Each dish has its own twist, but the basic combination is the same. However, the variations aren't meant to follow each other night after night.

If you find that some of the tuna and pasta dishes are a bit dry, add a tablespoon or two of olive oil or some extra *fromage blanc* (page 417).

FUSILLI OR PENNE WITH TUNA, PEAS, AND BROCCOLI

SERVES 2 TO 3

This is a perfect Saturday night supper. If you have no broccoli on hand, you can use the peas only, which was my original intention when I was developing the recipe. I just happened to have a big stalk of broccoli in the refrigerator that needed to be eaten, and it was a nice addition to the dish. The fusilli is a nice shape here, because the little bits of tuna get lodged between its ridges. Penne would also be good.

1   6½-ounce can water-packed tuna, drained

2   large garlic cloves, minced or put through a press

½   cup *fromage blanc* (page 417) or plain nonfat yogurt
      lots of freshly ground pepper

1   teaspoon salt

6   ounces fusilli or penne

1   cup shelled fresh or thawed frozen peas

1   to 1½ cups broccoli florets (or use all frozen peas)

¼   cup chopped fresh parsley

1   tablespoon olive oil

¼   cup freshly grated Parmesan cheese

Bring a large pot of water to a boil. Meanwhile, mash the tuna in a bowl with the garlic. Mix in the *fromage blanc* or yogurt and grind in some black pepper.

When the water reaches a rolling boil, add the salt and pasta. Cook until the pasta is almost al dente, 7 to 10 minutes, and throw the peas and broccoli into the water. By the time the pasta is cooked, the vegetables will be done too but still crisp to the bite.

Drain the pasta and vegetables and toss in a warm dish with the tuna, parsley, and olive oil. Serve at once with Parmesan on the side.

ADVANCE PREPARATION: You could have all the ingredients ready to go hours ahead of time—the vegetables prepped, the tuna mixed with the garlic and *fromage blanc* or yogurt, the parsley chopped, and the Parmesan grated.

PER PORTION

Calories	449	Protein	36 G
Fat	9 G	Carbohydrate	56 G
Sodium	855 MG	Cholesterol	31 MG

PASTA, TUNA, ANCHOVIES, AND CAPERS

SERVES 2 TO 3

This pungent combination can be put together in minutes. It's easy to have all the ingredients on hand.

1 6¹/₂-ounce can water-packed tuna, drained

3 large garlic cloves, minced or put through a press
  juice of ¹/₂ large lemon

¹/₂ cup *fromage blanc* (page 417) or plain nonfat yogurt
  lots of freshly ground pepper

4 anchovy fillets, rinsed and chopped

1 tablespoon capers, rinsed and drained

2 to 3 tablespoons chopped fresh parsley to taste

1 teaspoon salt

PASTA WITH DRIED MUSHROOMS

SERVES 4 GENEROUSLY

Dried mushrooms can spruce up any dish. They aren't cheap, but you don't need much for this terrific combination, bathed in a strong mushroom broth.

1 ounce (1 cup) dried mushrooms, preferably *porcini* (*cèpes*) or *girolles,* or a combination

2 cups boiling water

1 tablespoon olive oil

3 large garlic cloves, minced or put through a press

1 tablespoon soy sauce

2 tablespoons dry red or white wine

½ teaspoon crumbled dried thyme *or* 1 teaspoon chopped fresh

¼ to ½ teaspoon crumbled dried rosemary to taste *or* 1 teaspoon chopped fresh

salt and freshly ground pepper to taste

½ cup *fromage blanc* (optional; page 417)

3 tablespoons chopped fresh parsley (optional)

¾ pound fusilli or fettuccine

¼ cup freshly grated Parmesan cheese

Place the dried mushrooms in a bowl and pour on the boiling water. Let sit for 20 to 30 minutes. Line a strainer with cheesecloth and drain the mushrooms over a bowl. Squeeze the mushrooms over the strainer to extract all the soaking liquid. Rinse the mushrooms thoroughly and drain on paper towels. Reserve the soaking liquid.

Heat the olive oil in a heavy-bottomed saucepan or frying pan and add the garlic. Sauté over medium-low heat just until it begins to color and add the mushrooms. Sauté for a minute to coat with olive oil, stirring, and add the soy sauce, wine, thyme, and rosemary. Add the soaking liquid from the mushrooms and bring to a boil over medium heat. Reduce the liquid by half. Taste and add salt and freshly ground pepper to taste. Add more garlic if you wish and stir in the *fromage blanc* and the parsley if you're using them.

(continued)

Meanwhile, bring a large pot of water to a boil. Add about a teaspoon of salt and the pasta. Cook the pasta until al dente, drain, and toss with the mushroom mixture and Parmesan.

ADVANCE PREPARATION: The mushroom sauce will last for a day in the refrigerator without the addition of the parsley.

PER PORTION

Calories	421	Protein	18 G
Fat	7 G	Carbohydrate	71 G
Sodium	472 MG	Cholesterol	6 MG

RISOTTO WITH DRIED MUSHROOMS AND PEAS

SERVES 6 AS A MAIN DISH

This delicious rich, chewy *risotto* is a little like the traditional Italian Risi e Bisi (page 330), *risotto* with peas, but the dried mushrooms give it a "meatier" character.

1 ounce (1 cup) dried mushrooms, preferably *porcini* (*cèpes*) or *girolles,* or a combination

2 cups boiling water

6 cups vegetable stock (page 414), garlic broth (page 415), or chicken stock (page 413)

salt to taste

2 tablespoons olive oil

½ small onion

3 large garlic cloves, minced or put through a press

2 teaspoons soy sauce

2 cups Arborio rice, washed

½ cup dry white wine

½ teaspoon crumbled dried thyme *or* 1 teaspoon fresh leaves

$^{1}/_{4}$ to $^{1}/_{2}$ teaspoon crumbled dried rosemary to taste, *or* 1 teaspoon chopped fresh

1$^{1}/_{2}$ cups shelled fresh or thawed frozen peas

    lots of freshly ground pepper

$^{1}/_{4}$ cup chopped fresh parsley

$^{1}/_{4}$ cup freshly grated Parmesan cheese

Place the dried mushrooms in a bowl and pour on the boiling water. Let sit for 20 to 30 minutes. Line a strainer with cheesecloth and drain the mushrooms over a bowl. Squeeze the mushrooms over the strainer to extract all the soaking liquid. Rinse the mushrooms thoroughly and drain on paper towels. Add the strained soaking liquid to the stock. Adjust the salt and bring the stock to a simmer in a saucepan.

Heat the olive oil in a heavy-bottomed frying pan and add the onion and $^{1}/_{3}$ of the minced garlic. Sauté over medium-low heat just until the mixture begins to color and add the mushrooms and remaining garlic. Sauté for a minute or two, stirring, and add the soy sauce. Stir together and add the rice. Cook, stirring, over medium heat for about a minute. Stir in the white wine, thyme, and rosemary. Cook over medium heat, stirring all the while. The wine should bubble, but not too quickly. You want some of the flavor to cook into the rice before it evaporates.

When the wine has just about evaporated, stir in a ladleful of the simmering stock. It should just cover the rice and should bubble slowly like the wine. Cook, stirring constantly, until it is just about absorbed. Add another ladleful of the stock and continue to cook in this fashion, not too quickly but not too slowly, adding more broth when the rice is almost dry. After 20 minutes, add the peas and continue to add stock as above. After 25 to 35 minutes the rice should be cooked al dente, firm to the bite. Add lots of freshly ground pepper.

Add another ladleful of stock and stir in the parsley and Parmesan. Taste and adjust seasonings, stir for a few seconds, then serve at once.

ADVANCE PREPARATION: The mushrooms can be soaked and rinsed hours ahead of time, and fresh peas can be shelled hours ahead of time.

LEFTOVERS: Use leftover *risotto* as the basis for a flat omelet. Mix with beaten eggs and cook in a nonstick pan as for the flat omelets on pages 30–34. Or stuff mushrooms with it and serve as an hors d'oeuvre (page 66).

PER PORTION

Calories	358	Protein	9 G
Fat	6 G	Carbohydrate	65 G
Sodium	241 MG	Cholesterol	3 MG

RISI E BISI

SERVES 6 AS A MAIN COURSE

There is no reason why you can't make this classic Venetian *risotto* with frozen peas. I always cook my peas less than they do in traditional Italian recipes, and here I add the thawed frozen peas to the *risotto* at the end of the cooking. This is much like the other *risotti* in this book, very pretty, fragrant, and filling.

7   cups vegetable stock (page 414), garlic broth (page 415), or chicken stock (page 413)

1   tablespoon olive oil

1   small onion, minced

2   or 3 large garlic cloves to taste, minced or put through a press

2   cups Arborio rice, washed

1/2 cup dry white wine

    salt to taste

2   cups thawed frozen petite peas or shelled fresh peas

1   medium egg, beaten

1/2 cup chopped fresh parsley

1/4 cup freshly grated Parmesan cheese or to taste

    freshly ground pepper to taste

Have the stock simmering in a saucepan.

Heat the oil in a wide heavy-bottomed frying pan and sauté the onion and garlic over medium-low heat until the onion is golden. Add the rice and continue to sauté, stirring, until all the grains are separate and coated with oil.

Stir in the white wine and salt to taste and cook over medium heat, stirring all the while. The wine should bubble, but not too quickly. You want some of the flavor to cook into the rice before it evaporates.

When the wine has just about evaporated, stir in a ladleful or 2 of the stock. It should just cover the rice and should bubble slowly like the wine. Cook, stirring constantly, until it is just about absorbed. Continue to add stock a little at a time and to cook in this fashion, not too quickly but not too slowly, adding more broth when the rice is almost dry. Add the peas after 20 minutes or when the rice is just short of being cooked al dente and continue as above. After 25 to 35 minutes the rice should be cooked al dente (you might have stock left over; that's fine).

Beat together the egg, parsley, and Parmesan and stir in a ladleful of the stock. Stir this mixture into the rice off the heat. Taste and adjust seasonings, adding salt and freshly ground pepper to taste. Return to the heat and stir for a few seconds, then serve at once.

ADVANCE PREPARATION: If you're using fresh peas, you can shell them hours ahead of time.

LEFTOVERS: Use leftover *risotto* as the basis for a flat omelet. Mix with beaten eggs and cook in a nonstick pan as for the flat omelets on pages 30–34. Or stuff mushrooms with it and serve as an hors d'oeuvre (page 66).

PER PORTION

Calories	360	Protein	10 G
Fat	5 G	Carbohydrate	65 G
Sodium	149 MG	Cholesterol	34 MG

QUICK WHITE BEAN
AND SORREL SOUP

SERVES 4

This is a quick, lightened-up version of a traditional French soup. It can be quite thick if you want it that way, or you can thin it out with milk.

1 tablespoon olive oil

2 garlic cloves, minced or put through a press

¼ pound sorrel, washed

6 lettuce leaves, washed and broken into smaller pieces

1½ to 2 cups garlic broth (page 415) or chicken stock (page 413), as needed

2 15-ounce cans white beans (Great Northern or Navy), with their liquid

 salt and freshly ground pepper to taste

½ cup skim milk or as needed

 fresh lemon juice to taste

 chopped fresh parsley and garlic croutons (page 392) for garnish

Heat the olive oil in a soup pot over low heat and sauté the garlic just until it begins to color. Add the sorrel and lettuce leaves and let them wilt in the water left on the leaves. Add 1½ cups of the stock and the beans with their liquid, bring to a simmer, cover, and simmer for 10 minutes. Put through a food mill or puree in a blender. Return to the pot and season to taste with salt and pepper. Thin to the desired consistency with the milk. Add the extra ½ cup of stock if it's still too thick. Heat through and serve, sprinkled with a little lemon juice and garnished with chopped fresh parsley and garlic croutons.

ADVANCE PREPARATION: This soup will hold for a few hours on top of the stove. The sorrel and lettuce can be washed hours ahead of time as well.

PER PORTION

Calories	311	Protein	18 G
Fat	4 G	Carbohydrate	52 G
Sodium	270 MG	Cholesterol	1 MG

LENTIL SOUP WITH CILANTRO

SERVES 4

This is a thick, coarse puree of lentils, with lots of pungent cilantro stirred in at the last minute. Preparing the ingredients is quick work, and the soup cooks in about 40 minutes.

1   cup green or brown lentils, washed and picked over

1   small onion

2   garlic cloves, minced or put through a press

1   bay leaf

6½   cups water

1   teaspoon salt plus additional to taste

    freshly ground pepper to taste

1   bunch of cilantro, chopped

¼   cup plain nonfat yogurt for garnish

Combine the lentils, onion, garlic, bay leaf, and water in a soup pot. Bring to a boil, reduce the heat, and simmer for 40 minutes. Add the salt toward the end of the cooking time. Remove from the heat. Discard the onion and bay leaf. Put the soup through a Mouli food mill or puree half of it in a blender. Heat through, add salt and pepper to taste, stir in the cilantro, and serve, topping each bowl with a dollop of plain nonfat yogurt.

ADVANCE PREPARATION: The soup can be made, without the cilantro, a day ahead of time. The cilantro is added just before serving.

PER PORTION

Calories	177	Protein	15 G
Fat	.75 G	Carbohydrate	30 G
Sodium	17 MG	Cholesterol	0

TOMATO GARLIC SOUP

SERVES 6

This is a variation on a Provençal garlic soup, but it's thicker because of the tomatoes. It's a comforting, easy-to-make *potage*, good at any time of year.

1½   28-ounce cans of tomatoes, with their liquid

7   large garlic cloves, minced or put through a press

1   bay leaf

salt to taste

½   teaspoon crumbled dried thyme *or* up to 1 teaspoon fresh leaves to taste

freshly ground pepper to taste

4   medium eggs (optional)

3   tablespoons chopped fresh basil or parsley to taste

3   tablespoons freshly grated Parmesan or Gruyère cheese

garlic croutons (page 392) for garnish

Drain the liquid from the canned tomatoes into a measuring cup. Seed and chop the tomatoes or puree in a food processor fitted with the steel blade or a blender. Place in a soup pot or saucepan. Add water to the tomato liquid to measure 5 cups total. Combine with the tomatoes and bring to a boil. Add the garlic, bay leaf, salt (1 teaspoon to start), and thyme and simmer for 10 to 15 minutes. Add pepper and adjust the salt.

Just before serving, beat the eggs if you're using them and stir in the herbs and cheese. Stir a ladleful of the hot soup into the egg, turn off the heat, and stir the egg mixture into the soup. If you're not using the eggs, serve the soup and top each bowlful with 1½ teaspoons of herbs and 1½ teaspoons of Parmesan. Add the croutons and serve.

OTHER ENRICHMENTS:

- Pasta (fusilli, orecchiette, broken spaghetti, vermicelli): Add a couple of handfuls (about 2 ounces) to the soup shortly before serving and let simmer until the pasta is cooked al dente. Serve at once, as above.

- Rice (about ⅓ cup): Add to the soup and cook until just tender. Serve as above.

- Potatoes: Add ¾ pound new potatoes, scrubbed and sliced, to the soup mixture at the beginning and simmer until tender. Proceed with the recipe.

- Beans: Add 1½ cups cooked beans to the soup, heat through, and serve as above.

ADVANCE PREPARATION: The soup can be taken off the heat before you beat in the eggs and allowed to sit for several hours, covered.

PER PORTION

Calories	70	Protein	4 G
Fat	2 G	Carbohydrate	11 G
Sodium	411 MG	Cholesterol	4 MG

POTATO GARLIC SOUP

SERVES 4

I don't know anyone who doesn't like potato soup, and this one is particularly tasty with its earthy, savory broth. It goes together in just a few minutes.

6 cups water

1 pound potatoes, peeled if old or scrubbed and sliced ¼ inch thick

1 bay leaf

1 teaspoon salt or to taste

6 garlic cloves, minced or put through a press

¼ to ½ teaspoon crumbled dried thyme

freshly ground pepper to taste

1 or 2 medium eggs to taste, beaten

3 tablespoons freshly grated Parmesan or Gruyère cheese

2 or 3 tablespoons chopped fresh parsley to taste

Combine the water, potatoes, bay leaf, and salt in a soup pot and bring to a simmer. Add the garlic and thyme, cover, and simmer for 15 to 20 minutes, until the potatoes are tender. Add pepper.

Beat the eggs in a bowl and stir in the cheese and parsley. Ladle some soup into the eggs and stir together. Turn off the heat under the soup and stir the egg mixture into the soup pot. Adjust salt and serve.

ADVANCE PREPARATION: The potatoes can be scrubbed and peeled hours ahead of time. Hold in a bowl of cold water. The soup can be taken off the heat before you beat in the eggs and allowed to sit for several hours, covered.

PER PORTION

Calories	144	Protein	7 G
Fat	3 G	Carbohydrate	23 G
Sodium	665 MG	Cholesterol	74 MG

PRUNE SOUFFLÉ

SERVES 6

All you need for this dessert is prunes, egg whites, an orange to zest, a little bit of honey, and *eau-de-vie*. It's light and rich-tasting, but there are no egg yolks. You need time for soaking the prunes, but the rest goes quickly.

1   pound prunes

2   cups boiling water or enough to cover the prunes

1   to 2 tablespoons mild-flavored honey to taste (optional)

1   teaspoon vanilla extract

2   tablespoons prune *eau-de-vie* or kirsch

1   tablespoon crème fraîche (optional)

1   tablespoon finely grated orange zest

8   medium egg whites

    pinch of salt

    pinch of cream of tartar (optional)

Put the prunes in a bowl and pour on the boiling water. Let soak for 2 hours.

Preheat the oven to 400 degrees. Butter a 2-quart soufflé dish. Drain the prunes, reserving the soaking water, and pit them. Puree the prunes with their soaking water in a food processor fitted with the steel blade and add the honey, vanilla, and eau-de-vie. Mix together until smooth. Stir in the crème fraîche if you're using it and the orange zest.

Beat the egg whites until stiff but not dry, adding a pinch of salt and a pinch of cream of tartar if desired when they begin to foam. Stir one quarter of the egg whites into the prune puree and gently fold in the rest. Turn into the prepared soufflé dish. Bake for 25 to 35 minutes, until browned on the top and puffed. It should be runny in the middle. Serve at once.

ADVANCE PREPARATION: The prunes can be soaked a day ahead of time, and the prune puree will hold for a day in the refrigerator. The soufflé mixture can sit for several hours before the egg whites are added.

PER PORTION

Calories	210	Protein	6 G
Fat	.39 G	Carbohydrate	50 G
Sodium	88 MG	Cholesterol	0

DRIED APRICOT SOUFFLÉ

SERVES 6

Dried apricots have such an intense good flavor, and this soufflé is ambrosial. Like the prune soufflé on the preceding page, it consists of little more than the fruit and egg whites; the yolks are left out (use them for a crème Anglaise for another meal). The almondy amaretto is a particularly nice touch.

1 pound dried apricots

2 cups boiling water or enough to cover the apricots

1 or 2 tablespoons mild-flavored honey to taste (optional)

2 tablespoons fresh lemon juice

2 to 3 tablespoons amaretto to taste

8 medium egg whites

pinch of salt

pinch of cream of tartar (optional)

Put the apricots in a bowl and pour on the boiling water. Let soak for 2 hours.

Preheat the oven to 400 degrees. Butter a 2-quart soufflé dish. Drain the apricots, reserving the soaking water. Puree the apricots in a food processor fitted with the steel blade along with the soaking liquid and add the honey, lemon juice, and amaretto. Mix together until smooth.

Beat the egg whites until stiff but not dry, adding a pinch of salt and a pinch of cream of tartar if you wish when they begin to foam. Stir one quarter of the egg whites into the apricot puree and gently fold in the rest. Turn into the prepared soufflé dish. Bake for 25 to 35 minutes, until browned on the top and puffed. It should still be runny in the middle. Serve at once.

ADVANCE PREPARATION: The apricots can be soaked a day ahead of time, and the apricot puree will hold for a day in the refrigerator. The soufflé mixture can sit for several hours before the egg whites are added.

PER PORTION

Calories	208	Protein	7 G
Fat	.34 G	Carbohydrate	49 G
Sodium	93 MG	Cholesterol	0

DRIED FRUIT AND APPLE COMPOTE

SERVES 6

Sweet and tart, this is a nice winter compote. The leftovers are great with yogurt for breakfast. It makes a nice brunch dish as well.

       juice of 1 lemon
2   cups apple juice
4   fairly large tart apples, peeled, cored, and coarsely chopped
1/2   pound mixed dried fruit, such as raisins, pitted prunes, currants, figs, apricots
1   3-inch cinnamon stick, broken up, *or* 1 teaspoon ground
1/2   teaspoon freshly grated nutmeg
2   tablespoons Calvados (optional)

Combine the lemon juice and apple juice in a saucepan large enough to hold the apples and dried fruit. Add the remaining ingredients and bring to a simmer. Simmer, uncovered, for 40 minutes or until thick. Serve warm or at room temperature.

ADVANCE PREPARATION: This compote will hold for hours, in or out of the refrigerator, and will keep for a couple of days in the refrigerator.

PER PORTION

Calories	190	Protein	1 G
Fat	.65 G	Carbohydrate	49 G
Sodium	9 MG	Cholesterol	0

INDIAN PUDDING WITH A HINT OF MAPLE SYRUP

SERVES 6 TO 8

I forgot all about Indian pudding when I moved to France. Then, on a trip to Boston, I ordered it at a famous Boston restaurant. But I found the Indian pudding I was served there altogether too cloying and rich. This is such a good idea for a dessert, and you can keep it fairly light.

- 1 quart skim milk
- 6 tablespoons stone-ground yellow cornmeal
- 1/3 cup blackstrap or plain molasses
- 3 tablespoons maple syrup
- 2 medium eggs, beaten
- 3/4 to 1 teaspoon salt to taste
- 1 teaspoon ground ginger
- 2 tablespoons whiskey
- 1 tablespoon unsalted butter or margarine
- 1/2 cup dark or golden raisins

Preheat the oven to 325 degrees. Butter a 2-quart soufflé dish or casserole.

Bring the milk to a boil in a 3-quart heavy-bottomed saucepan and slowly add the cornmeal in a very thin stream, stirring all the time with a wooden spoon or whisk, as if you were making *polenta* (page 307). Simmer, stirring all the while, over low heat for 15 minutes or until the mixture has the consistency of runny cream of wheat. Add the molasses and maple syrup, stir for a couple of minutes longer, and remove from the heat.

Stir for a minute off the heat and add the remaining ingredients. Combine well and pour into the baking dish. Bake for 1 to 1½ hours, until a knife inserted in the center comes out almost clean and the top is beginning to brown. The consistency should be that of a slightly cakey pudding. Serve warm, with plain low-fat yogurt on the side. For a splurge you can serve the pudding with cream or whipped cream, sweetened with maple syrup.

PER PORTION

Calories	180	Protein	6 G
Fat	3 G	Carbohydrate	31 G
Sodium	335 MG	Cholesterol	53 MG

OEUFS À LA NEIGE
(A Light Version of Floating Island)

SERVES 6

My friend Christine Picasso serves this often for dessert. Hers is much lighter than classic *oeufs à la neige*, because she adds only a tablespoon or so of vanilla sugar to her egg whites (Escoffier recommends a pound of sugar for 8 egg whites). Mine is even lighter than Christine's because I use skim milk for the crème Anglaise. I give the option here of honey or sugar for the crème Anglaise. I prefer the flavor of the honey version, provided the honey used is mild (clover, acacia, or lavender). The dessert should be made a couple of hours before serving to allow for chilling, as it should be served cold. It's one of my favorites (I have a weakness for crème Anglaise).

FOR THE CRÈME ANGLAISE

- ½ teaspoon vanilla extract *or* 1 vanilla bean, split in half
- 3 cups skim milk
- 8 medium egg yolks
- ½ cup mild-flavored honey *or* ⅔ cup sugar

FOR THE EGG WHITES

- 8 medium egg whites
  pinch of salt
- ¼ teaspoon cream of tartar (optional)
- 1 tablespoon vanilla sugar (page 412)
  a large pot of boiling water

First make the crème Anglaise. If you are using the vanilla bean, scrape the insides into the milk. Add the bean pod. Bring to a bare simmer in a heavy-bottomed saucepan and simmer for 8 or 10 minutes, being careful not to boil. Remove the bean pod from the milk. Beat the egg yolks and honey or sugar together until very thick and lemon-colored. Being careful that the milk is not boiling, beat into the egg yolks. Return this mixture to the saucepan and heat over medium-low heat, stirring constantly with a wooden spoon. Do not allow the mixture to boil. The crème Anglaise is ready when it reaches the consistency of thick cream and coats both sides of your spoon evenly. Remove from the heat and strain into a large bowl. Whisk in the vanilla now if you are using vanilla extract instead of a vanilla bean. Allow to cool.

(continued)

Beat the egg whites until they begin to foam and add the salt and cream of tartar if you're using it. Continue beating until thick and add the vanilla sugar. Beat until stiff. Meanwhile, bring a large pot of water to a boil.

Reduce the heat under the pot of boiling water so that it simmers. Using a large soupspoon or serving spoon, take up a spoonful of the beaten egg whites. Take another spoon and round off the top of the mound so that the egg whites are shaped like an egg. Gently slide off the spoon (you can use a spatula to help unmold) into the simmering water. Cook for 15 seconds and flip over. Cook for another 15 seconds and remove from the water with a slotted spoon. Don't cook too long or the mixture will harden. Drain on a kitchen towel, then float on the crème Anglaise. Continue with the remaining egg whites. Refrigerate and serve cold.

ADVANCE PREPARATION: The crème Anglaise can be made a day ahead of time, and the finished dessert will keep for a day in the refrigerator.

PER PORTION

Calories	229	Protein	12 G
Fat	6 G	Carbohydrate	32 G
Sodium	159 MG	Cholesterol	259 MG

BAKED APPLES WITH
WHISKEY AND HONEY

SERVES 4

These apples become tart and slightly caramelized on the outside as they bake. Whiskey and honey go together nicely to add even more tang to the dish. This dessert is incredibly simple and can be assembled hours ahead of time.

4   tart baking apples

     juice of ¹/₂ lemon

     ground cinnamon

2   teaspoons mild-flavored honey

¹/₄   cup single-malt whiskey

2   tablespoons raisins

Preheat the oven to 375 degrees and brush a baking dish with butter.

Cut a cone out of the top of each apple (you don't need to core them). Spoon some lemon juice into each cavity and sprinkle with cinnamon. Add ¹/₂ teaspoon honey to each apple, spoon in a tablespoon of whiskey, and stuff with raisins.

Bake for about 40 minutes or until the skins have split and the apples are softened. Serve hot, warm, or at room temperature.

ADVANCE PREPARATION: The apples can be assembled hours ahead of time and baked hours ahead of time if you are serving them at room temperature.

PER PORTION

Calories	127	Protein	0
Fat	.64 G	Carbohydrate	33 G
Sodium	1 MG	Cholesterol	0

GOUÈRE AUX POMMES

SERVES 6

This recipe is adapted from one of Elizabeth David's. It is almost like an apple clafouti, but a little cakier; it's a bit like a coffee cake. Apples are incorporated into a batter, which is turned into a baking dish and baked.

        juice of ½ lemon
    2   tablespoons brandy, Calvados, or whiskey
    2   tablespoons raw brown (turbinado) sugar or mild-flavored honey
    1   pound (about 3 medium) tart apples
    2   medium eggs
    2   tablespoons granulated sugar
    ¾   cup skim milk
    1   teaspoon vanilla extract
        pinch of salt
    1½ cups unbleached white flour or whole wheat pastry flour

Preheat the oven to 350 degrees. Butter a 2-quart baking dish or a 10-inch pie pan or ceramic tart pan.

Combine the lemon juice, brandy, and brown sugar or honey in a bowl. Peel, core, and slice the apples into the bowl. The slices should be fairly thick.

Beat together the eggs, sugar, milk, vanilla, and salt. Sift the flour and stir in. Combine well. Fold in the apple mixture. Turn into the prepared baking dish.

Bake for 45 minutes, until puffed and browned and a tester inserted in the center comes out clean. Serve warm or cooled.

ADVANCE PREPARATION: This dessert can also be frozen. Thaw at room temperature and reheat, if you wish, in a 350-degree oven.

PER PORTION

Calories	219	Protein	6 G
Fat	2 G	Carbohydrate	44 G
Sodium	58 MG	Cholesterol	63 MG

CHAPTER SIX

COME OVER, I'LL MAKE A SALAD

"Why don't you come over?"

"I don't want you to go to any trouble."

"It's no trouble; I'll just make a big salad."

How often have I said this? An informal visit with a friend often means a nice salad, good bread and wine, maybe some cheese and fruit. For one thing, salads are what my husband and I most often eat for supper and what I most often eat for lunch (usually, when I'm alone, leftovers from last night's dinner). I use the term *salad* loosely; vegetables of one kind or another always go into it, it is always dressed with some kind of vinaigrette (see the recipes on pages 426–35), and there are usually fresh or dried herbs. From there you can go in a lot of directions: pasta, grains, beans, fish, chicken, rabbit, cheese, nuts . . . and one of my most frequent ingredients, stale bread or croutons. Salads are great vehicles for leftovers. They can be like soups, changing daily with new ingredients. Some are protein-rich; others are more vegetable-oriented. But all of the salads in this chapter are substantial enough to serve as a light meal.

GIANT WHITE BEANS WITH SAGE, LEMON, AND OLIVE OIL

SERVES 4 TO 6

Giant white beans—fava beans—go beautifully with fresh sage. I had a huge crop of sage in one of my window boxes one summer and used it with everything. This is one of my favorite results. It's good warm or chilled.

    2 cups dried giant white beans, washed and picked over

    6 cups water

    1 medium onion stuck with 6 cloves

    2 garlic cloves, plus 1 additional (optional), minced or put through a press

    1 bay leaf

    1 to 2 teaspoons salt to taste

    1/4 cup fresh lemon juice

2 to 3 teaspoons red wine vinegar to taste

3 tablespoons olive oil

salt and freshly ground pepper to taste

15 to 20 fresh sage leaves to taste, cut or torn into thin slivers

Soak the beans in water to cover for 6 hours or overnight. Drain. The skins will billow out from the beans, but don't remove them (I am always tempted to), because the beans will fall apart during cooking without their skins.

Combine the beans and water in a large soup pot and bring to a boil. Skim off any gray foam that rises and add the onion, 2 garlic cloves, and bay leaf. Reduce the heat and cover. Simmer for 1 hour and add salt. Simmer for another ½ to 1 hour, until the beans are soft but not mushy. Cooking these beans is a bit tricky because they make the transition between being done and being mushy very quickly. When they get too well done, they fall apart easily.

Remove the beans from the heat and drain, reserving some of the cooking water (or all of it; it makes a good stock). Transfer the beans to a bowl and toss with the lemon juice, vinegar, additional garlic clove if desired, olive oil, 3 tablespoons of the bean cooking liquid, and salt and pepper. If you're serving the beans warm, add the fresh sage and serve. If you're serving the beans cold, refrigerate and add the sage about 1 hour before serving. Serve from an attractive bowl or platter and accompany with sliced tomatoes and cucumbers and good country bread.

VARIATION: Add one 6½-ounce can drained water-packed tuna and toss with the salad.

SERVING SUGGESTION: Serve on roasted red pepper halves (page 419) for a beautiful lunch or light supper.

ADVANCE PREPARATION: The salad will keep well for a couple of days in the refrigerator, although it's best to add fresh sage shortly before serving.

LEFTOVERS: As the salad keeps so well, you can continue to serve it as a starter for another few days. The beans also make a fine hors d'oeuvre, served with toothpicks (page 50).

PER PORTION

Calories	296	Protein	16 G
Fat	7 G	Carbohydrate	44 G
Sodium	561 MG	Cholesterol	0

WARM LENTIL SALAD

SERVES 6

I love lentil salads, and this one, tangy with mustard, is especially good. It's partially based on a recipe in Patricia Wells's *Bistro Cooking* (Workman Publishing, 1989), with my own additions. Try to find the little green Le Puy French lentils for this—they have a marvelous peppery flavor. Use brown lentils if you can't find green ones. The addition of a teaspoon of red wine vinegar to the lentil cooking water is, according to Ms. Wells, recommended by a French grandmother for a really fragrant pot of lentils.

1 pound (about 2½ cups) green or brown lentils, washed and picked over

1 medium onion

2 cloves

2 garlic cloves, plus 1 additional large clove (optional), minced or put through a press

1 bay leaf

¼ cup plus 1 teaspoon red wine vinegar

1 heaped tablespoon Dijon mustard

salt and freshly ground pepper to taste

2 tablespoons olive oil or plain nonfat yogurt (optional)

2 to 4 tablespoons finely chopped fresh parsley to taste

6 tablespoons Goat Cheese Spread (optional; page 35) for topping

Place the lentils in a heavy-bottomed saucepan or casserole. Cover with water by 1 inch.

Cut the onion in half and stick a clove into each half. Add to the lentils and water along with 2 garlic cloves, the bay leaf, and 1 teaspoon red wine vinegar. Bring to a gentle boil, reduce the heat, cover, and simmer gently for 25 to 35 minutes, until the lentils are tender but intact. Check the lentils a few times during the cooking, and if the water has evaporated, add about ¼ cup (not more). By the time the lentils are tender, most of the liquid should be absorbed. If the lentils are still swimming in broth, pour off some of it (you can reserve it for soups, sauces, and dressings if you wish). Add salt and pepper at the end of the cooking time. Discard the onion and bay leaf.

Mix together the ¼ cup vinegar, mustard, salt and pepper to taste, and oil or yogurt. Stir into the lentils. Add 1 additional garlic clove if you wish and taste and adjust salt and pepper. Serve warm, sprinkled with parsley and topped with a spoonful of the Goat Cheese Spread if desired.

ADVANCE PREPARATION: The salad, without the parsley, will keep for a day in the refrigerator. Reheat gently in a saucepan to serve warm.

PER PORTION

Calories	269	Protein	21 G
Fat	I G	Carbohydrate	46 G
Sodium	121 MG	Cholesterol	0

TUNA CARPACCIO WITH HORSERADISH SAUCE

SERVES 4

This sauce is based on a Michel Guérard recipe. He uses beef for his *carpaccio*, and it's so light and low in calories that you could really use beef here with very little difference in the nutritional values. My version uses thinly sliced raw tuna; the horseradish sauce is a perfect accompaniment. It has the lovely taste of horseradish without the nose-burning pungency.

½ pound center-cut very fresh tuna fillet, dark meat and connective tissue trimmed away

FOR THE HORSERADISH SAUCE

1 tablespoon plus 1 teaspoon finely grated fresh horseradish

1 tablespoon sherry vinegar or red wine vinegar

½ teaspoon tamari soy sauce

1 tablespoon plus 1 teaspoon whipping cream or *fromage blanc* (page 417)

1 tablespoon olive oil

1 tablespoon water

salt and freshly ground pepper to taste

FOR THE VINAIGRETTE

2 tablespoons sherry vinegar

2 tablespoons olive oil

3 tablespoons plain nonfat yogurt

salt and freshly ground pepper to taste

FOR THE SALAD GARNISH

1 small head of frisée (curly endive) or a mixture of lettuces, washed, dried, and torn into small pieces

a handful of chopped fresh herbs, such as chervil, tarragon, basil, parsley, chives, plus some whole sprigs

Wrap the tuna in plastic wrap and place it in the freezer for 10 minutes, then slice it as thin as possible (about 1/4 inch) and place on plates. Cover and refrigerate.

Combine all the ingredients for the horseradish sauce and blend until smooth in a blender or just whisk together in a bowl or shake together in a jar. Set aside.

Make a vinaigrette for the salad: Whisk together the sherry vinegar, olive oil, and plain nonfat yogurt. Add salt and pepper to taste.

Just before serving, toss the lettuce and herbs with the vinaigrette. Using a small kitchen brush or a clean paintbrush, coat the tuna with the horseradish sauce. Place a small mound of salad in the middle and decorate with sprigs of fresh herbs. Serve at once.

ADVANCE PREPARATION: The tuna can be arranged on the plates, covered tightly with plastic wrap, and refrigerated hours before serving. The sauce will also hold for several hours in the refrigerator. You can wash and dry the lettuce leaves and wrap them in a towel, then seal in a plastic bag and refrigerate for several hours or overnight.

PER PORTION

Calories	208	Protein	15 G
Fat	15 G	Carbohydrate	4 G
Sodium	79 MG	Cholesterol	29 MG

TUNA CEVICHE

SERVES 6 AS A STARTER, 4 AS A MAIN DISH

This beautiful ceviche, with its play of pale greens and pinkish-gray fish, makes a perfect starter for a Mexican dinner, but it also goes well with main dishes that are not Mexican or Tex-Mex. The ceviche is also great as a main dish on a hot summer night or as a luncheon dish. It looks beautiful on a buffet. Unlike ceviches made with white-fleshed fish or scallops, the tuna ceviche is not marinated for very long. If the tuna is "cooked" by the lime juice, it will lose its nice pink color.

3 very fresh tuna steaks, about ½ inch thick (about 1½ pounds meat in all)

1¼ cups fresh lime juice (from 8 or 9 medium limes)

juice of ½ orange

1 small red onion, very thinly sliced

2 garlic cloves, minced or put through a press

1 or 2 fresh or pickled jalapeño or serrano chilies, seeded and thinly sliced

1 tablespoon capers, rinsed and drained

1 medium or small avocado, peeled, pitted, and diced

salt and freshly ground pepper to taste

2 tablespoons olive oil

¼ cup chopped fresh cilantro

leaf or Boston lettuce leaves

FOR GARNISH (ANY OR ALL)

lime wedges

cooked corn on the cob, broken into pieces

cilantro sprigs

radish roses

Cut the tuna into small dice, about ½ to ⅝ inch thick. Toss with the lime juice in a bowl, cover, and refrigerate for about 2 hours, but not significantly longer, stirring from time to time to redistribute the lime juice. The fish is done when it's opaque on the outside but still pink in the center.

Rinse the chicken breasts and pat dry. Lightly butter or oil the bottom of a wide saucepan and pour in the wine. Place the chicken breasts in the saucepan in a single layer and add water to cover. Add the bay leaf, garlic, and about $1/2$ teaspoon salt. Bring to a simmer and skim off any foam that rises to the surface. Poach for about 10 minutes, until the chicken breasts are cooked through and firm. Remove from the heat and drain, reserving the stock for another use (such as a sauce or a soup). Allow to cool.

Cut the chicken into $1/2$-inch cubes. Toss with the cucumber, walnuts, scallions, and herbs.

Make the dressing. Mix together the lemon juice, vinegar, mustard, garlic, salt and pepper, and the yogurt. Combine well and whisk in the oil. Adjust the seasonings.

Toss the salad with the dressing. Line a platter or individual plates with the lettuce or endive leaves. Top with the salad. Sprinkle on additional herbs and serve.

NOTE: Turkey breasts or leftover turkey can be substituted for the chicken.

ADVANCE PREPARATION: This salad will hold for a day in the refrigerator. Herbs should be added close to serving time. You can wash and dry the lettuce leaves and wrap them in a towel, then seal in a plastic bag and refrigerate for several hours or overnight.

LEFTOVERS: The salad makes a nice hors d'oeuvre, served in Belgian endive leaves. Chop up the leftovers a little smaller for this.

PER PORTION

Calories	313	Protein	31 G
Fat	17 G	Carbohydrate	10 G
Sodium	299 MG	Cholesterol	66 MG

ORIENTAL CHICKEN SALAD

SERVES 4

This chicken salad is pungent with ginger and crunchy with cucumber and bean sprouts.

FOR THE SALAD

4 boneless, skinless chicken breasts (about 1 pound)

1/2 cup dry white wine

1 bay leaf

1 garlic clove, crushed

1/2 teaspoon salt, approximately

1 cup peeled, seeded, and julienned cucumber

4 water chestnuts, sliced

1 medium red bell pepper, cut into thin 1-inch strips

a handful of mung bean or soybean sprouts, cut into 1-inch lengths if very long

4 scallions, both white and green parts, thinly sliced

1/4 cup chopped cilantro

1 small head of leaf or romaine lettuce or Chinese cabbage, leaves separated, washed, and dried

FOR THE DRESSING

1 tablespoon fresh lemon juice

2 tablespoons vinegar: rice wine, balsamic, champagne, cider, or sherry *or* omit the lemon juice and use 3 tablespoons vinegar

1 garlic clove, minced or put through a press

2 to 3 teaspoons finely minced fresh ginger to taste

salt and freshly ground pepper to taste

3 tablespoons Chinese or dark sesame oil or walnut oil

1 tablespoon soy sauce

1/2 teaspoon hot chili oil or sauce (optional)

1 tablespoon sesame tahini

1/2 cup chicken stock from the poaching

additional cilantro for garnish

Rinse the chicken breasts and pat dry. Lightly butter or oil the bottom of a wide saucepan and pour in the wine. Place the chicken breasts in the saucepan in a single layer and add water to cover. Add the bay leaf, garlic, and about 1/2 teaspoon salt. Bring to a simmer and skim off any foam that rises to the surface. Poach for about 10 minutes, until the chicken breasts are cooked through and firm. Remove from the heat and drain 1/2 cup of the stock for the dressing. Allow to cool.

Cut the chicken into 1/2-inch cubes. Toss with the remaining salad ingredients except the lettuce.

Make the dressing. Combine all the ingredients except the stock in a blender or a jar and blend or shake until smooth. Slowly add the stock. Adjust the seasonings.

Toss the salad with the dressing. Line a platter or individual plates with lettuce or cabbage leaves. Top with the salad. Sprinkle on additional cilantro and serve.

ADVANCE PREPARATION: This salad will hold for a day in the refrigerator. Cilantro should be added close to serving time. You can wash and dry the lettuce or cabbage leaves and wrap them in a towel, then seal in a plastic bag and refrigerate for several hours or overnight.

LEFTOVERS: The salad makes a nice hors d'oeuvre, served in Belgian endive leaves. Chop up the leftovers a little smaller for this.

PER PORTION

Calories	283	Protein	29 G
Fat	14 G	Carbohydrate	11 G
Sodium	347 MG	Cholesterol	66 MG

TOFU AND VEGETABLE SALAD

SERVES 4

Tofu, doused with soy sauce and tossed with vegetables in a creamy vinaigrette, is a good high-protein ingredient for a salad.

³/₄ pound very fresh tofu, diced

2 to 3 teaspoons soy sauce to taste

1 red bell pepper, roasted (page 419) and cut into thin strips

1 cup peeled (if waxy), seeded and diced cucumber in ¹/₄-inch cubes

2 ounces (2 generous handfuls) arugula, washed, dried, and stems removed, *or* 2 ounces radicchio, leaves broken up, washed, and dried

1 cup lentil or mung bean sprouts (optional)

a handful of chopped fresh herbs, such as chervil, basil, tarragon, parsley

1 tablespoon sesame seeds

1 recipe Lemon-Yogurt Vinaigrette (page 434)

Toss the tofu with the soy sauce, then with the vegetables, herbs, and sesame seeds. Just before serving, toss with the Lemon-Yogurt Vinaigrette.

ADVANCE PREPARATION: The ingredients for the salad can all be prepared up to a day ahead of time. Toss with the dressing just before serving.

PER PORTION			
Calories	146	Protein	11 G
Fat	8 G	Carbohydrate	11 G
Sodium	339 MG	Cholesterol	1 MG

FUSILLI OR PENNE (OR BOTH) WITH TOMATOES, BALSAMIC VINEGAR, AND MOZZARELLA

SERVES 6

This salad requires the ripest, sweetest tomatoes you can find. It makes a great summer dinner. I don't seed the tomatoes, because their juice contributes to the sauce for the pasta.

2 pounds ripe sweet tomatoes, peeled and cut into wedges

salt and freshly ground pepper to taste

1 or 2 garlic cloves to taste, minced or put through a press

3 tablespoons balsamic vinegar

3 tablespoons olive oil

1/2 cup tightly packed basil leaves, torn or cut up with scissors

10 ounces fusilli or penne or a combination

1/4 pound fresh mozzarella cheese, thinly sliced

Toss the tomatoes, salt and pepper, and garlic together in a bowl with the balsamic vinegar and olive oil. Add the basil.

Cook the pasta until al dente in a large pot of boiling water. Drain and toss with the tomato mixture and mozzarella. Adjust the seasonings and serve or refrigerate until shortly before serving.

ADVANCE PREPARATION: This salad will hold for a couple of hours in the refrigerator, but the basil should be added 30 minutes or less before serving.

PER PORTION

Calories	325	Protein	11 G
Fat	12 G	Carbohydrate	44 G
Sodium	30 MG	Cholesterol	13 MG

BUCKWHEAT NOODLE SALAD

SERVES 4

Buckwheat noodles (soba) are one of my great weaknesses. They have a distinctive, earthy flavor and go well with a number of vegetables. In the winter you can make this salad with broccoli, in the spring and summer with asparagus and sweet peas. The dressing is a tangy Oriental one, fragrant with ginger and pungent with chili.

FOR THE SALAD

salt to taste

1/2 pound buckwheat noodles (can be found in Oriental stores and health-food stores)

2 tablespoons Chinese or dark sesame oil

1 pound broccoli, broken into florets, stems set aside for another use, *or* 1/2 pound asparagus, trimmed and cut into 1-inch pieces, steamed until crisp-tender, and refreshed under cold water

1 cup shelled fresh peas, steamed until crisp-tender, *or* 1 cup thawed frozen peas

a handful of mung or soy bean sprouts

5 scallions, both white and green parts, thinly sliced

2 tablespoons sesame seeds

1 red bell pepper, seeded and cut into thin strips (optional)

1/4 cup chopped cilantro

FOR THE DRESSING

1 tablespoon fresh lemon or lime juice

2 tablespoons vinegar: rice wine, balsamic, champagne, cider, or sherry (or omit the lemon juice and use 3 tablespoons vinegar)

1 garlic clove, minced or put through a press

2 to 3 teaspoons finely minced fresh ginger to taste

salt and freshly ground pepper to taste

3 tablespoons Chinese or dark sesame oil *or* walnut oil (optional)

1 tablespoon soy sauce

$^1/_2$ teaspoon hot chili oil or sauce *or* a couple of dashes of cayenne pepper (optional)

1 tablespoon sesame tahini

$^1/_2$ cup plain nonfat yogurt

additional cilantro for garnish

Bring a large pot of water to a boil, add salt and the noodles, and cook until al dente. Drain and toss with the sesame oil and remaining salad ingredients.

Make the dressing. Combine all the ingredients in a jar or a blender and shake together or blend well.

Toss the salad with the dressing shortly before serving. Garnish with additional cilantro.

ADVANCE PREPARATION: The cooked noodles can be tossed with the sesame oil and vegetables hours before serving. Hold in a covered bowl in the refrigerator. Just before serving toss with the dressing and cilantro.

PER PORTION

Calories	382	Protein	16 G
Fat	12 G	Carbohydrate	59 G
Sodium	642 MG	Cholesterol	1 MG

WARM BROCCOLI SALAD
WITH CHICK-PEAS

SERVES 4

This is one of my favorite winter salads and one I serve quite often. It's very quick to make.

    1   bunch (1½ to 2 pounds) broccoli, broken into florets, stems
        peeled and sliced
 1½   cups cooked chick-peas (canned are okay, but drain them)
    1   to 2 ounces Parmesan cheese to taste, slivered
    1   small red bell pepper, thinly sliced (optional)
    2   tablespoons chopped fresh chives
    1   recipe Lemon-Yogurt Vinaigrette (page 434)

Steam the broccoli until tender, about 5 to 8 minutes. Drain, refresh under cold water, shake dry, and toss with the remaining ingredients. Serve warm.

ADVANCE PREPARATION: All the ingredients can be prepped for this salad hours ahead of serving.

PER PORTION

Calories	204	Protein	15 G
Fat	5 G	Carbohydrate	28 G
Sodium	310 MG	Cholesterol	8 MG

TOMATILLO DRESSING

MAKES 1¹/₃ CUPS, TO SERVE 5

The idea for this dressing came from the Green Tomatillo Mole on page 156. It has a delightful tangy flavor and is especially good with grain and corn salads. It's also perfect for chicken and rabbit and can stand alone as a dip.

¹/₂ pound (5 medium) tomatillos, husked and washed, *or* 1 13-ounce can, drained

1 or 2 fresh or pickled hot green chilies (jalapeño or serrano) to taste, stems, seeds, and membranes removed

2 tablespoons fresh lime juice or cider vinegar

¹/₄ medium onion, roughly chopped

1 to 2 garlic cloves, to taste, roughly chopped

6 cilantro sprigs or more to taste

¹/₄ teaspoon ground cumin (optional)

1 tablespoon olive oil

salt to taste

If you're using fresh tomatillos, simmer in water to cover with the chili peppers for 10 to 15 minutes. Drain and place in the blender jar. If you're using canned tomatillos, place them in the blender jar along with the remaining ingredients. Blend all the ingredients together until the mixture is smooth.

ADVANCE PREPARATION: This dressing will hold for several hours, in or out of the refrigerator.

PER PORTION

Calories	40.33	Protein	.79 G
Fat	3 G	Carbohydrate	3.29 G
Sodium	.66 MG	Cholesterol	0

QUINOA SALAD WITH TOMATILLO DRESSING

SERVES 4 GENEROUSLY AS A MAIN DISH SALAD

Quinoa is a high-protein grain native to Peru. It has been a staple there for centuries, but for some reason the conquistadores did not bring quinoa back to Europe, as they did the potato, when they discovered Peru in the 16th century. In recent years, however, the delicate grain has caught on in North America.

1 cup quinoa

2 cups water

¼ teaspoon salt or to taste

2 tablespoons toasted pine nuts, hulled pumpkin seeds, or hulled sunflower seeds

1 cup diced cucumber *or* 1 green bell pepper, diced

1 red bell pepper, diced

4 radishes, thinly sliced

1 to 2 tablespoons chopped chives to taste

½ cup chopped cilantro leaves

2 ounces mozzarella or white Cheddar cheese, diced

1 recipe Tomatillo Dressing (page 363)

1 tablespoon olive oil or quinoa cooking water

salt and freshly ground pepper to taste

lettuce leaves for serving

radish roses for garnish

cilantro sprigs for garnish

Soak the quinoa in a bowl of cold water for 5 minutes. Drain through a strainer and run under cold water for another few minutes to remove all bitter-tasting impurities.

Place the water in a medium saucepan and bring to a boil. Add the salt and stir in the quinoa. Reduce to a simmer, cover, and cook for 15 to 20 minutes. The quinoa should be just cooked through, al dente. Drain through a strainer set over a bowl.

Toss the cooked quinoa with the nuts, vegetables, herbs, cheese, dressing, and olive oil or cooking water. Add salt and pepper to taste.

The salad is good warm or cooled. Line plates or a platter with the lettuce leaves and top with the quinoa salad. Garnish with radish roses and cilantro sprigs.

ADVANCE PREPARATION: This salad will hold for a few hours in the refrigerator.

LEFTOVERS: This makes a great filling for vine leaves, endive leaves, lettuce leaves, or chard.

PER PORTION

Calories	312	Protein	11 G
Fat	15 G	Carbohydrate	36 G
Sodium	219 MG	Cholesterol	11 MG

MEXICAN CORN SALAD WITH TOMATILLO DRESSING

SERVES 6 AS A STARTER OR 4 AS A MAIN DISH SALAD

This is a colorful, crunchy salad. Make sure your corn is really sweet. The sweet kernels are wonderfully complemented by the tangy dressing.

3/4 pound corn kernels (from 4 ears of corn, or use frozen), steamed or boiled until just tender (about 6 minutes)

1 green bell pepper, finely diced

1 red bell pepper, finely diced

1 small red onion, chopped

1 or 2 jalapeño or serrano chilies to taste, seeded and chopped

4 or 5 radishes to taste, sliced

3 ounces slightly dry goat cheese, crumbled, *or* 1/4 pound tofu, crumbled

1/4 cup chopped cilantro

salt and freshly ground pepper to taste

1 recipe Tomatillo Dressing (page 363)

lettuce leaves for serving

radish roses for garnish

cilantro sprigs for garnish

Toss together the corn, bell peppers, onion, chili pepper, radishes, goat cheese, and cilantro. Add a little salt and pepper and toss with the dressing. Line salad plates, a platter, or a bowl with lettuce leaves and top with the salad. Garnish with radish roses and sprigs of cilantro and serve.

ADVANCE PREPARATION: The salad will hold in the refrigerator for several hours.

LEFTOVERS: Use this salad, chopped up smaller, to fill potatoes, like the potatoes filled with corn and sage on page 54.

PER PORTION

Calories	174	Protein	7 G
Fat	9 G	Carbohydrate	20 G
Sodium	119 MG	Cholesterol	16 MG

EGG SALAD WITH HERBS

SERVES 4

Removing some of the yolks and filling out this salad with lots of vivid-tasting fresh herbs makes it quite different from the egg salad most of us grew up with. You'll find none of the mayonnaise we usually associate with egg salad; instead I use a tangy low-fat yogurt vinaigrette.

8 medium eggs

1 cup chopped fresh parsley

3 tablespoons chopped fresh tarragon

2 tablespoons chopped fresh chives

2 tablespoons chopped fresh basil or chervil

1 small red onion, finely chopped (optional)

1 red bell pepper, finely chopped

2 celery ribs, finely chopped

1 recipe Lemon-Yogurt Vinaigrette (page 434)

1 to 3 teaspoons Dijon mustard to taste

  salt and freshly ground pepper to taste

2 teaspoons balsamic vinegar

2 tablespoons olive oil

1/4 pound arugula (4 generous handfuls), washed and stemmed

Hard-cook the eggs according to the instructions for Deviled Eggs on page 58. Peel, cut in half, and remove 4 of the yolks.

Chop the remaining eggs and egg whites and toss with the remaining ingredients except the arugula, vinegar, and olive oil. Adjust the seasonings.

Mix together the balsamic vinegar and olive oil and toss with the arugula. Line plates with this mixture, top with the egg salad, and serve.

ADVANCE PREPARATION: The salad will hold for several hours in the refrigerator, but toss the arugula at the last minute.

(continued)

LEFTOVERS: This is terrific on canapés, as a filling for potatoes, or with blinis or crêpes (pages 74 and 399).

PER PORTION

Calories	195	Protein	13 G
Fat	12 G	Carbohydrate	10 G
Sodium	322 MG	Cholesterol	188 MG

A SALAD OF ARUGULA, CORN, HERBS, AND PARMESAN

SERVES 4 AS A MAIN DISH SALAD, 6 AS A SIDE DISH OR STARTER

This colorful salad is full of surprising, pleasing flavors. The dressing is very mild; it shouldn't compete with the pungent arugula or the herbs.

        1 ear of corn
        1 red bell pepper, roasted (see page 419)
    1/2 pound arugula, stemmed, washed, and dried
        6 large basil leaves, cut into large pieces
        6 fresh sage leaves, slivered
        1 ounce Parmesan cheese, cut into very thin slivers
        1 tablespoon balsamic vinegar
    1/4 cup olive oil
    1/2 teaspoon Dijon mustard
           salt and freshly ground pepper to taste

Steam the corn until tender, 5 to 10 minutes. When it is cool enough to handle, cut the kernels from the cob.

   If you wish, toss the red pepper with garlic and a little vinegar and olive oil (see recipe on page 419).

   Combine the arugula, corn, basil, sage, and Parmesan in a salad bowl. Mix together the vinegar, olive oil, mustard, and salt and pepper. Toss with the salad. Scatter the peppers over the top and serve.

ADVANCE PREPARATION: All of the separate ingredients for the salad can be prepped hours ahead of serving and refrigerated. The pepper can be roasted several days ahead of time and tossed with vinegar and olive oil or just olive oil.

PER PORTION

Calories	217	Protein	5 G
Fat	18 G	Carbohydrate	11 G
Sodium	163 MG	Cholesterol	5 MG

A SALAD OF POTATOES, DANDELION GREENS, AND BEETS

SERVES 4

The idea for this salad comes from Elizabeth David. It's a wonderful combination. It reminds me a bit of one of my husband's favorite salads, which we used to eat at the Paris restaurant Le Boeuf sur le Toit, until they stopped serving it. That was a salad of lamb's lettuce and beets. The dandelion greens are more pungent than lamb's lettuce. This salad can be served with the beets and potatoes warm or at room temperature.

1 pound new potatoes, scrubbed

$1/2$ pound fresh beets, peeled and quartered

1 tablespoon red wine or sherry vinegar

1 tablespoon fresh lemon juice

1 teaspoon Dijon mustard

1 small garlic clove, minced or put through a press (optional)

$1/4$ cup olive oil

1 tablespoon plain nonfat yogurt

salt and freshly ground pepper to taste

$1/4$ pound (4 handfuls) dandelion greens, trimmed, washed, and dried

1 or 2 tablespoons chopped fresh herbs, such as tarragon, parsley, thyme to taste

(continued)

Steam the potatoes and beets until tender (the potatoes will be done first, after 10 or 15 minutes; the beets will take 20 to 30 minutes). Meanwhile, mix together the vinegar, lemon juice, mustard, garlic if desired, olive oil, and yogurt. When the potatoes are done, remove them from the heat and slice about ½ inch thick, cutting them in half if they are very wide. When the beets are done, remove from the heat and, when cool enough to handle, cut in julienne, about ¼ inch thick and ½ to ¾ inch long. Toss them with the potatoes, salt and pepper lightly, and toss with the dressing.

Just before serving, toss the potatoes and beets with the dandelion greens and fresh herbs.

ADVANCE PREPARATION: The vegetables can be prepped hours ahead of serving, but don't toss the potatoes and beets together too far ahead of time or the potatoes will be too pink. You can toss the potatoes with some of the dressing if you cook them ahead of time.

PER PORTION

Calories	245	Protein	4 G
Fat	14 G	Carbohydrate	28 G
Sodium	98 MG	Cholesterol	0

CÉLERI RÉMOULADE
(Celery Root in Mustard Sauce)

SERVES 4

This is one of my favorite French salads, although I prefer my low-fat version to the rich French rémoulade, which is dressed with a mustardy mayonnaise and can be very heavy. But I always love the flavor of the celeriac, or celery root, a vegetable that is underappreciated in America. I get cravings for this salad; the celery root must be very high in minerals or vitamins (or both).

2 tablespoons fresh lemon juice

1 to 2 heaped tablespoons Dijon mustard to taste

   salt and freshly ground pepper to taste

1 cup *fromage blanc* (page 417) or plain nonfat yogurt

1 pound celeriac (1 large celery root)

Combine the lemon juice, mustard, and salt and pepper to taste. Whisk in the *fromage blanc* or yogurt.

   Peel the celeriac and grate in a food processor fitted with the grating disk or through a Mouli food mill. Toss immediately with the dressing (or the celeriac will discolor).

ADVANCE PREPARATION: Once the dressing and celeriac are tossed together, the salad will keep for up to a day in the refrigerator.

PER PORTION

Calories	85	Protein	8 G
Fat	1 G	Carbohydrate	13 G
Sodium	449 MG	Cholesterol	2 MG

A SALAD OF FRISÉE, MUSHROOMS, PINE NUTS, CHERVIL, AND GOAT CHEESE

SERVES 6 AS A SIDE DISH, 4 AS A MAIN DISH

This salad is always a hit. It can be a starter or a main dish salad, depending on how hungry you are. Take it to the table before you toss it; it's too pretty for your guests to miss.

3 tablespoons olive oil

12 thin rounds (6 ounces) of a not-too-salty goat cheese, such as Ste.-Maure

$\frac{1}{2}$ teaspoon crumbled dried thyme *or* 1 fresh sprig

$\frac{1}{2}$ teaspoon crumbled dried rosemary *or* 1 fresh sprig

freshly ground pepper

1 small *or* $\frac{1}{2}$ large head of frisée (curly endive—about $\frac{3}{4}$ pound), leaves separated, washed thoroughly, and dried

8 medium mushrooms, trimmed, cleaned, and thinly sliced

juice of $\frac{1}{2}$ lemon

1 medium red bell pepper, seeded and thinly sliced

2 tablespoons pine nuts

a handful of fresh chervil leaves, washed and dried

Low-Fat Yogurt Vinaigrette (page 433)

Pour the olive oil into a small baking dish that will accommodate the twelve rounds of goat cheese and place the goat cheese rounds in the olive oil. Turn them over and sprinkle with the herbs and black pepper. Let marinate while you prepare the remaining ingredients.

Break up the lettuce leaves and place in an attractive salad bowl or place them in the bowl and cut into smaller pieces with scissors.

Toss the sliced mushrooms with the lemon juice and add to the lettuce. Add the red pepper.

Toast the pine nuts for 3 to 5 minutes in a dry pan over medium-high heat or in a 350-degree oven until they are just beginning to brown. Add them to the salad and throw in the chervil.

Preheat the oven to 425 degrees. Five to 10 minutes before you wish to serve, place the baking dish with the cheese in the preheated oven. Roast the cheese until it begins to bubble. Remove from the heat and, with the aid of a flat spatula, transfer the rounds of cheese to the salad. Take the salad to the table and toss with the dressing. Serve at once.

ADVANCE PREPARATION: All of the ingredients for the salad can be prepared hours ahead of time and refrigerated until shortly before assembling the salad. The cheese can marinate for a day. The only last-minute thing is the roasting of the cheese. The salad dressing should be made fairly close to serving time.

PER PORTION

Calories	224	Protein	8 G
Fat	19 G	Carbohydrate	7 G
Sodium	207 MG	Cholesterol	26 MG

POTATO AND ARUGULA SALAD

SERVES 4 TO 6

Arugula is one of my favorite foods. I can eat it by the handful, standing by the sink, with nothing on it. It goes nicely with potatoes here. It should not be dressed with too much vinegar, which fights with its already acidic taste.

1   pound new potatoes, scrubbed and peeled if desired

    salt and freshly ground pepper to taste

1   tablespoon sherry vinegar

1   tablespoon plain nonfat yogurt

4   tablespoons olive oil

1   small garlic clove, minced or put through a press (optional)

3   cups (about ¼ pound or 1 large bunch) approximately, arugula, trimmed, washed, and rinsed

1   tablespoon chopped fresh tarragon (optional)

Steam or boil the potatoes in salted water until tender. Drain and slice about ½ inch thick. Salt and pepper lightly. Mix together the vinegar, yogurt, olive oil, and the garlic if you're using it and toss with the potatoes while they are still hot. Allow to cool if not serving right away.

Toss the arugula with the potatoes and tarragon if you're using it and serve.

NOTE: This salad is good whether the potatoes are warm or cold.

ADVANCE PREPARATION: The arugula can be trimmed, washed, and dried hours before being served and stored in a plastic bag in the refrigerator. The potatoes can be scrubbed hours ahead of cooking.

PER PORTION

Calories	217	Protein	3 G
Fat	14 G	Carbohydrate	21 G
Sodium	23 MG	Cholesterol	0

POTATO AND SPINACH SALAD

SERVES 4 TO 6

This salad is best if the potatoes are slightly warm. They are sweet and earthy against the slightly sweet, richly flavored spinach.

- 1 pound waxy potatoes, scrubbed
- 1 or 2 tablespoons chopped fresh herbs such as tarragon, parsley, thyme to taste

  salt and freshly ground pepper to taste
- 1/2 pound fresh spinach, stemmed, washed, and dried

FOR THE DRESSING

- 1 tablespoon white wine vinegar or sherry vinegar
- 2 tablespoons fresh lemon juice
- 1 teaspoon Dijon mustard
- 1 small garlic clove, minced or put through a press (optional)
- 1/4 cup olive oil
- 1/4 cup plain nonfat yogurt

Steam or boil the potatoes until tender, about 15 minutes. Meanwhile, mix together all the dressing ingredients. When the potatoes are done, remove them from the heat and slice about 1/2 inch thick, cutting them in half if they are very wide. Toss with the herbs, salt and pepper, and half the dressing.

Break the spinach leaves into smaller pieces. Just before serving, toss the potatoes with the spinach and remaining dressing.

PER PORTION

Calories	232	Protein	4 G
Fat	14 G	Carbohydrate	24 G
Sodium	90 MG	Cholesterol	0

CHAPTER SEVEN

BREADS, SAUCES, STOCKS, AND OTHER BASIC RECIPES

In this chapter I've grouped together breads and breadlike foods like crêpes, pastry dough, and pizza dough, basic recipes that come up several times in the preceding menus. I do realize that most people *don't* make their own bread, and happily, good bakeries are beginning to flourish in many American cities. On the other hand, guests absolutely adore homemade bread, which can be made at your leisure and frozen. Find the best possible bread you can, be it French baguette, sourdough, rye, or whole wheat. For croutons, use either sourdough bread or baguettes.

In addition to breads, you'll find recipes here for some basic cookies that keep well for weeks in a tin or jar. I always like to serve cookies with simple fruit desserts or sorbets; they dress up a meal.

Here too is where you'll find stocks for soups, sauces like pesto, tomato, salsa, and crème Anglaise, fresh pasta, basic green salad, a wide selection of vinaigrettes, roasted red peppers, and *fromage blanc*.

CHEF: FRENCH SOURDOUGH STARTER

This is the starter I've been using over the years for my sourdough breads. It is based on Patricia Wells's version of the starter, or *chef*, used by the famous French baker Lionel Poilâne. Unlike most sourdough starters, the *chef* isn't runny but is more like a spongy dough. You keep it going by saving about 1 cup of dough every time you make sourdough bread. Mine is always changing, because I tend to vary the flours I use in my breads.

THE FIRST DAY

- $1/3$ cup water
- $1/4$ pound (1 cup less 2 tablespoons) unbleached white or whole wheat flour or a combination

AFTER 72 HOURS

- $1/2$ cup lukewarm water
- 6 ounces ($1^1/3$ cups) whole wheat flour or unbleached white flour or a combination

On the first day, stir together the water and flour until smooth. Cover with a damp towel and let sit at room temperature for 72 hours (3 days). The dough will form a crust on the top and turn a grayish color, which is normal. Keep wetting the towel to reduce the drying. The dough will rise slightly and take on an acidic aroma.

After 72 hours, add the water to the starter and blend together. If the dough has formed a crust on the top like cardboard, peel it off and discard it. I find that this happens if the flour I work with is very coarse, but with finer whole wheat flour or unbleached white it doesn't happen. Add the flour and stir to blend. Transfer to a floured work surface and knead into a smooth ball.

Return the starter to the bowl, cover with a damp towel, and let sit in a warm place for 24 to 48 hours. Again, a crust may form on the top. If it is hard, like cardboard or wood, peel off and discard before proceeding with a bread recipe.

STORING AND FREEZING: Store the *chef* in a covered bowl or jar in the refrigerator. It will keep for weeks, but it's best if you use it at least once a week and replenish it with dough from the bread you're making. If you know that you won't be using it for several weeks, the starter can be frozen. Always allow it to come to room temperature before you use it.

FRENCH SOURDOUGH COUNTRY BREAD

*MAKES 1 LARGE LOAF (2 POUNDS, 6 OUNCES) OR 2 SMALL LOAVES,
SERVING 16 GENEROUSLY*

This is very close to a really traditional French *pain de campagne*. Bakers in
France are required by law to use 5 percent rye flour in their country breads. I
use a tiny bit more than 5 percent rye flour and sometimes add a small amount of
semolina, but this is optional. This very sticky dough yields a chewy, resilient,
slightly sour loaf with a thick, hard crust.

When you're making sourdough country bread it helps to have a *banneton*
for the second rising, after you've shaped the dough. A *banneton* is a basket that
is lined with fabric. You dust the inside of the *banneton* generously with flour,
place the shaped dough in it upside down, and it rises without losing its shape.
When you are ready to bake the bread, you simply reverse the risen loaf from the
basket onto a baking stone or sheet. You can make your own *banneton* by lining a
bowl with a kitchen towel that you have dusted with flour.

2½ teaspoons (1 envelope) active dry yeast

2 cups lukewarm water

½ pound (about 1 cup) sourdough starter (page 379), or use all if
you are using fresh starter for the first time

2 ounces (scant ½ cup) rye flour

2 ounces (½ cup) semolina (optional; replace with 2 ounces
unbleached white flour)

1¼ pounds (4⅜ cups) unbleached white flour, as needed

2½ teaspoons salt

Dissolve the yeast in the water in a large bowl or in the bowl of your electric
mixer and let sit for 10 minutes. Stir in the sourdough starter. Mix together
well.

To knead the dough by hand: Stir the rye flour and the semolina into the liquids.
Combine 1 pound (3½ cups) of the unbleached white flour and the salt.
Gradually fold into the liquids. By the time you have added 1 pound, you should
be able to knead. Flour your work surface and scrape out the dough. Using a
pastry scraper to help fold the dough, knead for 10 to 15 minutes, adding flour
to the surface and to your hands as necessary. The dough will be very sticky.
Shape into a ball.

To knead in an electric mixer: Add the rye flour and the semolina to the liquids.
Combine the unbleached white flour and the salt. Add all at once to the liquid

mixture. Mix together briefly using the paddle, until everything is amalgamated. Then scrape the dough off the paddle and replace it with the dough hook. Knead at low speed for 2 minutes, then at medium speed for 8 minutes. Turn out onto a floured surface, knead a few times, and shape into a ball.

RISING, FORMING THE LOAF: Clean the bowl, oil it if desired, return the dough to it, and cover with plastic wrap and a towel. Let rise in a warm spot for 1½ to 2 hours, until doubled in bulk.

Flour your hands and wrists and punch down the dough. Knead for 2 or 3 minutes on a lightly floured surface, using a pastry scraper to make it easier to manipulate the sticky dough. Remove a cup (about ½ pound) of the starter and place in a bowl to use for your next loaf of bread. Cover the starter and refrigerate after a few hours if you're not going to use it again within a day. Shape the dough into a ball or into 2 balls.

To form the loaf using a banneton: Dust a clean dry towel very generously with flour and line a bowl or basket. Or oil a 2-quart bowl very generously and dust with cornmeal. Form the dough into a ball, dust the surface with flour, and place in the towel-lined *banneton,* rounded side down. Cover with a towel and let rise in a warm spot for 1 to 1½ hours, until doubled in bulk. You can also let the dough rise in the refrigerator for several hours or overnight. Turn out the dough onto an unoiled baking sheet dusted with cornmeal, or preferably a baking stone dusted with cornmeal, peel off the towel, and slash with a sharp knife or a razor.

To form the loaf without a banneton: Form the dough into a ball, dust the surface, and let rise in an oiled bowl for about 1½ hours, until doubled in bulk. Reshape the dough gently and place on a baking sheet that has been oiled and sprinkled with cornmeal. Let rise for about 15 minutes while you preheat the oven. Slash with a razor blade or sharp knife just before baking.

BAKING: Preheat the oven to 400 degrees. Spray the loaf with water, and place in the oven. Spray the oven twice more during the first 10 minutes of baking. Bake for 45 minutes, until brown; the loaf should respond to tapping with a hollow thumping sound when it's done. Remove from the heat and cool on a rack.

NOTE: You can achieve an even crustier loaf if you place an empty pan on the bottom shelf of the oven while reheating the oven. When the oven is preheated, pour 2 cups water into the pan; the steam will help give the bread a thick, hard crust.

STORING AND FREEZING: This bread will keep for 4 days, in a cool, dry place. Do not wrap in plastic. Cover the cut sides only with foil, or wrap in a dry kitchen towel. The bread freezes well, though the crust will not be as hard and crisp after freezing. Wrap tightly in foil, then seal in a plastic bag. You can thaw it in a 350-degree oven, wrapped in the foil, in 45 minutes to an hour. It will take 3 hours to thaw at room temperature.

(continued)

LEFTOVERS: Use for croutons, added to salads and soups.

PER PORTION

Calories	182	Protein	5 G
Fat	.50 G	Carbohydrate	38 G
Sodium	345 MG	Cholesterol	0

PARTIALLY WHOLE WHEAT
SOURDOUGH COUNTRY BREAD

MAKES 1 LARGE ROUND LOAF, SERVING 16 GENEROUSLY

This version has the same sour taste as the preceding recipe, but a grainier, denser texture. The dough is somewhat sticky.

   2 teaspoons active dry yeast
   2 cups lukewarm water
  ½ pound (about 1 cup) sourdough starter (page 379)
   1 pound (3½ cups) whole wheat flour
2½ teaspoons salt
      up to ½ pound (1¾ cups) unbleached white flour, as needed

Dissolve the yeast in the water in a large bowl or in the bowl of an electric mixer and let sit for 10 minutes. Stir in the starter and combine thoroughly.

To knead the dough by hand: Combine the whole wheat flour and salt and gradually fold into the liquid mixture. By the time you have added all of it, you should be able to knead. Add a generous amount of unbleached flour to your work surface and scrape out the dough. Using a pastry scraper to help fold the dough, knead for 10 to 15 minutes, adding unbleached white flour as necessary. Shape into a ball.

To use an electric mixer: Combine the whole wheat flour, unbleached white flour, and salt and add to the liquids. Mix together briefly using the mixing attachment, until everything is amalgamated. Then scrape off the mixing attachment and replace it with the dough hook. Knead at low speed for 2 minutes, then at medium speed for 6 to 8 minutes. The dough will be sticky. Scrape out of the bowl onto a floured work surface, knead a few times, and shape into a ball.

RISING AND FORMING THE LOAF: Clean the bowl, oil if desired, and return the dough to it. Cover with plastic wrap and a towel and let rise in a warm spot for 1½ to 2 hours, until doubled in bulk.

Flour your hands and wrists and punch down the dough. Knead for 2 or 3 minutes on a lightly floured surface, using a pastry scraper to make it easier. Remove a cup (about ½ pound) of the starter and place in a bowl to use for your next loaf of bread. Cover the starter and refrigerate after a few hours if you're not going to use it again within a day.

To form the loaf using a banneton: Dust a clean dry towel with flour and line a bowl or basket. Form the dough into a ball, dust the surface with flour, and place it in the *banneton*, rounded side down. Cover with a towel and let rise in a warm spot for 1½ to 2 hours, until almost doubled in bulk. You can also let the dough rise in the refrigerator for several hours or overnight.

To form the loaf without a banneton: Form the dough into a ball and let rise in an oiled bowl for about 1½ hours, until doubled in bulk. Reshape the dough gently and place on a baking sheet that has been oiled and sprinkled with cornmeal. Let rise for about 20 minutes while you preheat the oven. Slash with a razor blade or sharp knife just before baking.

BAKING: Preheat the oven to 400 degrees. Place an empty pan on the bottom shelf of the oven. When the oven is preheated, pour 2 cups water into the pan; the steam will help give the bread a thick, hard crust. If you're using a *banneton*, turn out the dough onto an unoiled baking sheet, or preferably a baking stone dusted with cornmeal, peel off the towel, and slash with a sharp knife or a razor. Spray the loaf, whether using a *banneton* or not, with water, and bake for 45 minutes, until brown; it will respond to tapping with a hollow thumping sound when it's done. Remove from the heat and cool on a rack.

STORING AND FREEZING: This bread will keep for up to a week in a cool, dry place. Do not wrap in plastic. Cover the cut sides only with foil, or wrap in a dry kitchen towel. The bread freezes well, though the crust will not be as hard and crisp after freezing. Wrap tightly in foil, then seal in a plastic bag. You can thaw it in a 350-degree oven, wrapped in the foil, in 45 minutes to an hour. It will take 3 or 4 hours to thaw at room temperature.

LEFTOVERS: Use for croutons, added to salads and soups.

PER PORTION

Calories	175	Protein	6 G
Fat	.72 G	Carbohydrate	37 G
Sodium	311 MG	Cholesterol	0

BLACK BREAD

2 16-INCH LONG OR 8- TO 10-INCH ROUND LOAVES, SERVING 20

This is a lovely, slightly sweet dark loaf with a close crumb, compact and easy to slice. I often make it for parties and catering, because it slices very nicely and you can get a lot of thin slices out of a long loaf. It goes very well with savory dips and smoked salmon.

The dough is wet and soft but stiffens up as you knead. The surface will remain tacky.

FOR THE SPONGE

- 1 tablespoon active dry yeast
- 1½ cups lukewarm water
- ½ cup strong brewed black coffee (can be instant), cooled to lukewarm
- 3 tablespoons blackstrap molasses
- ½ teaspoon ground ginger
- ¼ pound (1 scant cup) fresh whole wheat bread crumbs
- ½ pound (1¾ cups) unbleached white flour

FOR THE DOUGH

- ¾ pound (2⅔ cups) rye flour
- 2 teaspoons salt
- 2 tablespoons safflower or sunflower oil
- ¼ pound (1 cup less 2 tablespoons) whole wheat flour

  up to ¼ pound (1 scant cup) unbleached white flour for kneading

FOR THE TOPPING

- ½ teaspoon instant coffee granules
- ¼ cup hot water
- 1 medium egg

  sesame seeds or poppy seeds (optional)

Dissolve the yeast in the water and let sit for 5 minutes. Stir in the coffee and molasses. Add the ginger and bread crumbs and mix well. Stir in the white flour, a cup at a time, and mix well. Stir about 100 times and cover with plastic wrap and a towel. Set in a warm place to rise for 50 to 60 minutes.

RISING, FORMING THE LOAVES, AND BAKING: Rinse out the bowl, dry it, and oil it. Place the dough in the bowl, seam side up first, then seam side down. Cover with plastic wrap and a kitchen towel and set in a warm place to rise for 1½ hours or until the dough has doubled in size.

Punch down the dough and let rise again until doubled in bulk, about 1 hour. Meanwhile, butter or oil a baking sheet or baguette pans and sprinkle with cornmeal.

Lightly flour your work surface and turn out the dough. It will be soft and sticky. Keep your hands and board lightly floured and work quickly.

Divide the dough into 4 equal pieces and shape them into balls. Cover the ones you're not working with lightly with plastic wrap so they don't dry out. Shape into baguettes. To do this, flatten out each piece of dough, one at a time, into a rectangle, then fold lengthwise like a letter, pinch the seam, then fold in half lengthwise again, and roll the dough on the table like a sausage, moving your hands from the center to the ends, until the loaf is long and slender, about 2 inches in diameter. Place the loaves in the baguette pan or on baking sheets. Brush with the egg wash if you're using it.

Cover the loaves with a dry towel and let rise for 20 to 30 minutes. Meanwhile, preheat the oven to 400 degrees. Place an empty pan on the bottom shelf of your oven, and when the oven is preheated, fill it with water.

Slash 3 or 4 times across the top of the loaves with a sharp knife or a razor. Spray the loaves with water and spray the inside of the oven. Place the loaves in the oven, spray a couple more times during the first 10 minutes, and bake for 35 to 45 minutes, until golden brown; the loaves will respond to tapping with a hollow sound when they're done. For extra-shiny loaves, brush several times during the baking with the egg wash. Remove from the heat, unmold if you're using baguette pans, and cool on a rack.

STORING AND FREEZING: These loaves keep for 2 to 3 days in a cool, dry place. Do not wrap in plastic. Cover the cut end with foil or wrap in a kitchen towel. The bread can also be frozen (but the crust will lose its crispness). Wrap tightly in foil and seal in plastic bags.

LEFTOVERS: This bread makes good bread crumbs.

PER PORTION

Calories	120	Protein	4 G
Fat	1 G	Carbohydrate	23 G
Sodium	61 MG	Cholesterol	6 MG

CALZONE POCKET BREAD

MAKES 2 6- BY 9-INCH FLAT LOAVES, SERVING 8

A little Paris restaurant called Cosi serves up calzone-like sandwiches with a variety of fillings, while operas play in the background. At Cosi they make a chewy, rich-tasting flat white bread in a wood-fired stone oven that goes all day long. The fragrant bread is split down the middle, brushed with olive oil, and reheated in the oven, then stuffed like a pita with the filling of your choice, salad bar style. What makes these sandwiches really work is the bread, which is fantastic. I often eat it plain, brushed with olive oil and heated through in the oven, or even better, lightly toasted in a toaster.

I don't have a wood-fired oven, so my "Cosi bread" doesn't have the same smoky flavor as the restaurant's. But I do have a baking stone, which helps, and I recommend one for this bread. It is a very satisfying bread, sort of like pita bread but more substantial. Depending on the filling, you could heat it with or without the filling in it or eat it simply with olive oil brushed on the surface. Timing here is essential: the bread shouldn't get stiff as it bakes but should just begin to brown.

$1^{1}/_{2}$ teaspoons active dry yeast

$1^{1}/_{2}$ cups lukewarm water

$^{1}/_{4}$ pound (1 scant cup) whole wheat flour

1 pound ($3^{1}/_{2}$ cups) unbleached white flour

2 teaspoons salt

2 tablespoons olive oil, approximately, for brushing the bread before baking

Dissolve the yeast in the water in a large bowl or in the bowl of an electric mixer and let sit for 10 minutes.

To knead the dough by hand: Combine the whole wheat flour, $^{1}/_{2}$ pound ($1^{3}/_{4}$ cups) of the unbleached white flour, and the salt. Gradually fold into the liquids. When the dough is stiff enough to scrape out of the bowl, flour your work surface and scrape out the dough. Using a pastry scraper to help fold the dough, knead for 10 to 15 minutes, adding flour to the surface and to your hands as necessary. Shape into a ball.

To use an electric mixer: Combine the whole wheat flour, unbleached white flour, and salt. Add all at once to the liquid mixture. Mix together briefly using the paddle, until everything is amalgamated. Then scrape the dough off the paddle and replace it with the dough hook. Knead at low speed for 2 minutes, then at medium speed for 8 minutes. Turn out onto a floured surface, knead a few times, and shape into a ball.

RISING, FORMING THE LOAVES, AND BAKING: Clean the bowl and oil it. Place the dough in it, rounded side down first, then rounded side up, and cover with plastic wrap and a towel. Let rise in a warm spot for about 2½ hours, until doubled in bulk.

Flour your hands and punch down the dough. Knead for a minute on a lightly floured surface, using a pastry scraper to make it easier to manipulate the dough if necessary.

Preheat the oven to 475 degrees, preferably with a baking stone in it.

Divide the dough in half and shape each half into a ball. Let the balls rest, covered with plastic wrap, for about 10 minutes. Roll out each half on a well-floured surface into an oblong, about 9 inches long, 6 inches wide, and ½ inch thick. If you have a baking stone, place these oblongs on well-floured boards or peels. If you do not have a baking stone, place the dough on unoiled nonstick baking sheets that have been dusted lightly with cornmeal. Brush the tops of the dough with olive oil, about a tablespoon for each.

If you are using a baking stone, slide or flip the flat bread dough from the peel or board onto the stone. Place in the middle of the oven and bake for 10 minutes, or until the bread is just beginning to brown and has baked through. It should not puff up too much or stiffen all the way through. The outside should be slightly crusty and the inside soft. Remove from the heat and cool on a rack while you repeat with the second piece of dough.

To serve, cut the breads into quarters or sixths. Run a serrated knife across the middle of the bread to open it up like a pita bread. Heat and fill with the filling of your choice or just brush with olive oil and reheat slightly before serving.

NOTE: These make nice hors d'oeuvres, cut into small pieces, brushed with olive oil, and heated or lightly toasted in a toaster or warming oven, then brushed with olive oil and sprinkled with herbs.

LEFTOVERS: The bread can be split and toasted.

PER PORTION

Calories	183	Protein	5 G
Fat	.50 G	Carbohydrate	38 G
Sodium	345 MG	Cholesterol	0

SOURDOUGH PIZZA CRUST

MAKES 2 15-INCH PIZZA CRUSTS

One day it occurred to me that a pizza dough made with the sourdough starter that I always have on hand in my refrigerator might be a very nice thing and also a nice variation from the breads that I make every week to keep my sourdough alive. This makes an earthy, slightly acidic crust.

 $^{1}/_{2}$ **pound (1 cup) sourdough starter (page 379)**

 1 **teaspoon active dry yeast**

 $1^{1}/_{2}$ **cups lukewarm water**

 1 **tablespoon olive oil**

 1 **pound ($3^{1}/_{2}$ cups) whole wheat flour or unbleached white flour**

 2 **teaspoons salt**

 2 **to 3 ounces ($^{1}/_{2}$ to $^{2}/_{3}$ cup) additional unbleached white flour, as needed, for kneading**

Bring the sourdough starter to room temperature.

Dissolve the yeast in the water in a large bowl or in the bowl of an electric mixer. Let sit for 10 minutes. Stir in the *chef* and the olive oil.

Combine the flour and salt.

To knead the dough by hand: Gradually fold the flour into the liquids. By the time you have added about three quarters of it, you should be able to knead. Flour your work surface and scrape out the dough. Using a pastry scraper to help fold the dough, knead for 10 to 15 minutes, adding flour to your work surface and to your hands as necessary. Shape the dough into a ball.

To use an electric mixer: Add the flour and salt all at once to the liquids. Mix together briefly using the paddle, until everything is amalgamated, then scrape the dough off the paddle and change to the dough hook. Knead at low speed for 2 minutes, then at medium speed for 8 to 10 minutes, adding unbleached white flour if the dough seems very liquid (it will be sticky). Scrape the dough out of the bowl and knead for a minute or so. Shape into a ball.

RISING, FORMING THE LOAVES, AND BAKING: Clean and oil the bowl and place the dough in it. Cover with plastic wrap and a towel and set in a warm place to rise for 2 hours or longer, until doubled in bulk.

Punch down the dough and remove a cupful of the dough to use as starter for a future loaf. Place the starter in a bowl and cover. Refrigerate after an hour or so if you're not going to use it again that day.

Divide the dough in 2 and shape into balls. Press out to fit 15-inch pizza pans, pressing the dough very thin (about ¼ to ⅛ inch) and folding an attractive lip around the edge of the pan. Let sit for 30 minutes to an hour before baking. You can also refrigerate the dough for a longer time at this point.

Preheat the oven to 500 degrees. Top with the topping of your choice and bake for 15 minutes, until brown and crisp. Serve hot.

ADVANCE PREPARATION: The dough can be refrigerated after being rolled out, for several hours. It can be frozen before or after being rolled out. Allow frozen dough to come to room temperature before baking.

PER PORTION

Calories	195	Protein	7 G
Fat	2 G	Carbohydrate	39 G
Sodium	369 MG	Cholesterol	0

GARLIC CROUTONS
(Crostini)

———

These *crostini* are great with spreads like tapenade (page 38), with melted goat cheese in a salad (see recipe, page 373), or cut into cubes and added to a salad or soup.

>   thin slices of country bread, such as those on pages 380–83, or *baguette*
> 1 or 2 garlic cloves to taste, cut in half lengthwise
>   olive oil (optional)

Toast the bread in a toaster or under a broiler until lightly browned. Remove from the heat and immediately rub 1 or both sides (depending on your taste for garlic) with the cut side of a garlic clove. Brush lightly with olive oil if you wish. If you are working with long slices from a round loaf, cut in half or into thirds so that your croutons are 2 to 2½ inches long.

For spreads, leave whole. For soups and salads you might want to cut these into smaller cubes.

ADVANCE PREPARATION: Croutons can be made several hours before serving and wrapped in foil.

		PER PORTION	
Calories	43	Protein	1.5 G
Fat	.11 G	Carbohydrate	9 G
Sodium	81 MG	Cholesterol	0

CORN BREAD

SERVES 8 TO 10

This recipe is to my mind a perfect corn bread. Very easy to make, it never fails to please everyone, and I never change the recipe. It multiplies very easily.

    1 cup stone-ground yellow cornmeal
  1/2 cup whole wheat flour
  3/4 teaspoon salt
    1 tablespoon baking powder
  1/2 teaspoon baking soda
    1 cup plain nonfat yogurt or buttermilk
  1/2 cup milk
    1 tablespoon mild-flavored honey
    2 medium eggs
    3 tablespoons unsalted butter

Preheat the oven to 450 degrees.

Sift the cornmeal, flour, salt, baking powder, and baking soda into a large bowl. Beat together the yogurt, milk, honey, and eggs in another bowl.

Place the butter in a 9-inch square baking pan or a 9-inch cast-iron skillet and place the pan in the oven for about 3 or 4 minutes, until the butter melts. Remove from the heat, brush the butter over the sides and bottom of the pan, and pour the remaining melted butter into the yogurt and egg mixture. Stir the liquids together well, then fold into the dry mixture. Do this quickly, with just a few strokes of a wooden spoon or plastic spatula. Don't worry about lumps. You don't want to overwork the batter.

Pour the batter into the warm greased pan and bake for 30 to 40 minutes, until the top is golden brown and a toothpick inserted in the center comes out clean. Let cool in the pan or serve hot.

STORING AND FREEZING: Store the corn bread in a cool, dry place, wrapped in foil or plastic wrap. It will keep for 3 days but is best eaten on the day it's made. It does not freeze well.

PER PORTION

Calories	139	Protein	5 G
Fat	5 G	Carbohydrate	19 G
Sodium	369 MG	Cholesterol	47 MG

WHOLE WHEAT SCONES

MAKES 12 SCONES

Scones are one of my great weaknesses, especially whole wheat scones with currants in them. They're very easy to make and are terrific with tea in the morning or afternoon.

¼ pound (1 scant cup) unbleached white flour

¼ pound (1 scant cup) whole wheat flour or whole wheat pastry flour *or* use ½ pound (1¾ cups) whole wheat flour and omit the unbleached white flour

½ teaspoon salt

2 teaspoons baking powder

½ teaspoon baking soda

1 tablespoon unrefined brown sugar (turbinado sugar)

5 tablespoons cold unsalted butter, cut into pieces

1 tablespoon mild-flavored honey

½ cup sour skim milk, buttermilk, or plain low-fat yogurt or 1 or 2 tablespoons more, as needed

½ cup dried currants

Preheat the oven to 450 degrees. Butter a baking sheet.

Sift the flours, salt, baking powder, and baking soda into a bowl. Stir in the sugar. Cut in the butter, then take up the flour and roll briskly between the palms of your hands so the mixture has the consistency of coarse cornmeal. This can also be done in a food processor fitted with the steel blade, using the pulse action.

Mix together the honey and milk and stir into the flour mixture along with the currants (this too can be done in a food processor). If the mixture seems dry, add a tablespoon more of sour skim milk, buttermilk, or yogurt. Gather up the dough and gently knead it, not working the dough like bread but just pressing it together so that it comes together in a cohesive lump. It should be slightly sticky, so lightly flour your hands. The less you work the dough, the lighter your scones will be. Roll out to a thickness of about ¾ inch and cut into squares, triangles, or rounds.

Place on the prepared baking sheet and bake for 12 to 15 minutes, until beginning to brown. Serve warm.

ADVANCE PREPARATION: These scones are best when freshly baked, but they can be stored in a cool, dry place, wrapped in foil or plastic wrap, for a couple of days. They can be frozen; wrap in foil, then seal in plastic bags. They can be thawed in 35 minutes in a 350-degree oven.

PER PORTION

Calories	140	Protein	3 G
Fat	5 G	Carbohydrate	22 G
Sodium	209 MG	Cholesterol	13 MG

YEASTED OLIVE OIL PASTRY

MAKES ENOUGH FOR 2 12-INCH CRUSTS, A 14-INCH CRUST, OR A 10- TO 12-INCH DOUBLE CRUST, SERVING 8

This is a light, crunchy pastry, very easy to work with and extremely low in fat as pastries go. I use it for my quiches and other savory tarts. This is the perfect answer for a relatively low-fat and low-cholesterol tart.

1 teaspoon active dry yeast

¼ cup lukewarm water

1 medium egg, at room temperature

¼ cup olive oil

¼ pound (scant cup) whole wheat pastry flour

¼ pound (scant cup) unbleached white flour

½ to ¾ teaspoon salt to taste

Dissolve the yeast in the water and let sit 5 to 10 minutes. Beat in the egg and olive oil. Combine the flours and salt and stir in (this can be done in an electric mixer; combine the ingredients using the paddle, then switch to the dough hook). Work the dough only until it comes together in a coherent mass, then shape it into a ball. Place in a lightly oiled bowl, cover with plastic wrap, and let rise in a warm spot for 2 hours or a little longer. It will not rise too much, but it will expand and soften.

When the pastry has risen and softened, punch it down gently and divide into 2 unequal pieces for a torte, with 1 piece just slightly smaller than the other, or 1 piece for a 14-inch tart (you'll have excess dough for this; you can cut away leftovers and roll them out and use for hors d'oeuvres—see pages 21, 23, and 25), or 2 pieces for 2 10- or 12-inch tarts. Shape into a ball or balls, cover with plastic wrap, and let rest for 10 minutes. Butter a 10- to 12-inch tart pan for a torte, a 12- to 14-inch pan for a tart, and roll out the dough to fit the dish. The dough should be easy to handle. Roll it very thin, about 1/8 inch thick or thinner, and line the dish. Pinch an attractive lip around the edge of the dish. (At this point the dough can be frozen.) Cover loosely with a kitchen towel and let rest for 20 to 30 minutes. If you are making a torte, don't roll out the top piece of dough until you have filled the torte.

Prebake the dough according to the recipe. Fill with the filling of your choice. Roll out the top piece of dough for a torte and place over the filling. Join the edges. Bake at 375 to 400 degrees, following specific recipe instructions for timing.

ADVANCE PREPARATION: These crusts freeze well. Prebake for 9 to 10 minutes instead of 7 minutes before filling, or bake according to the specific recipe. The dough can also be held for a day in the refrigerator, before or after being rolled out.

PER PORTION

Calories	169	Protein	4 G
Fat	8 G	Carbohydrate	21 G
Sodium	181 MG	Cholesterol	23 MG

SWEET ALMOND PIECRUST

MAKES 1 12- TO 14-INCH CRUST

This is one of two dessert crusts made with partially whole wheat pastry flour. Both are crumbly and rich, and because they're made with whole wheat flour and honey, they're not as easy to roll out as traditional *pâte brisée*. But their flavor is so good that the extra effort is worth it. It helps to roll out the pastry between sheets of wax paper. Also, be sure to brush the crusts with egg before prebaking, to prevent sogginess.

    1 cup whole wheat pastry flour

   1/2 cup unbleached white flour

   1/2 cup finely ground almonds

   1/4 teaspoon salt

   1/2 cup (1/4 pound) unsalted butter

   1/2 teaspoon almond extract (optional)

    1 tablespoon mild-flavored honey

    1 to 2 tablespoons ice-cold water, as needed

Mix together the flours, ground almonds, and salt in a bowl. Cut in the butter until it's well incorporated and the dough is like coarse meal. Mix in the almond extract if desired and the honey. If the dough is moist and comes together easily, gather it into a ball. If it is dry, add a tablespoon or 2 of ice-cold water, as needed. Gather the dough into a ball and wrap in plastic wrap. Refrigerate for several hours or overnight.

Remove the dough from the refrigerator. Pound with a rolling pin to flatten, then roll out between sheets of wax paper. Butter a 12- to 14-inch tart pan and line with the dough. Do not be dismayed if the dough breaks up as you handle it (this is inevitable). Just patch the dough together in the pan. Pinch an attractive lip around the edge and proceed with the recipe.

ADVANCE PREPARATION: This dough freezes well and can be transferred directly from the freezer to the preheated oven for prebaking.

PER PORTION			
Calories	224	Protein	4 G
Fat	15 G	Carbohydrate	20 G
Sodium	71 MG	Cholesterol	31 MG

SWEET DESSERT CRUST

MAKES 1 12- TO 14-INCH CRUST

See the preceding recipe for information on making this rich crust.

 1 cup whole wheat pastry flour
 1 cup unbleached white flour
 1/4 teaspoon salt
 1/2 cup (1/4 pound) unsalted butter
 1 to 2 tablespoons mild-flavored honey to taste
 1 tablespoon ice-cold water if needed

Mix together the flours and salt. Cut in the butter until the butter is incorporated and the dough has the texture of coarse meal. Mix in the honey. If the dough comes together, gather it into a ball. Otherwise, add a tablespoon of ice-cold water and gather into a ball. Wrap in plastic wrap and refrigerate for several hours or overnight.

Remove the dough from the refrigerator. Pound with a rolling pin to flatten, then roll out between sheets of wax paper. Butter a 12- to 14-inch tart pan and line with the dough. Do not be dismayed if the dough breaks up as you handle it (this is inevitable). Just patch the dough together in the pan. Pinch an attractive lip around the edge and proceed with the recipe.

ADVANCE PREPARATION: This dough freezes well and can be transferred directly from the freezer to the preheated oven for prebaking.

PER PORTION

Calories	221	Protein	4 G
Fat	12 G	Carbohydrate	26 G
Sodium	70 MG	Cholesterol	31 MG

CRÊPES

MAKES 12 TO 14 CRÊPES

These are delicious whether made with whole wheat or unbleached white flour. You can wrap them around any number of fillings—a great way to transform leftovers into a new dish. Crêpes store easily.

To make crêpes you should have a well-seasoned 6- or 7-inch crêpe pan that you never wash and use only for crêpes. If you don't have one of these, a nonstick omelet pan will work, but not quite as well.

 2 large eggs

 ³/₄ cup skim milk

 ¹/₂ cup water

 3 tablespoons unsalted butter, melted

 ¹/₂ teaspoon salt

 ¹/₄ pound (1 scant cup) flour: either sifted whole wheat pastry flour, half whole wheat pastry flour and half unbleached white, or all unbleached white flour

 unsalted butter for cooking the crêpes

Put the eggs, milk, water, melted butter, and salt in a blender or a food processor fitted with the steel blade (a blender is preferable). Turn it on and slowly add the flour. Whirl at high speed for 1 minute.

If you don't have a blender or food processor, sift together the flour and salt. Beat the eggs and stir in the flour. Gradually add the milk, water, and butter, beating vigorously with a whisk. Strain through a sieve.

Refrigerate the batter for 1 to 2 hours. This allows the flour particles to swell and soften so the crêpes will be light.

Have the batter ready in a bowl, with a whisk on hand for stirring, as the flour tends to settle and the batter will need to be stirred every once in a while, especially if you're using whole wheat flour. Also have a ladle and a plate on which to put the finished crêpes.

Place the pan over moderately high heat and brush the bottom with butter. When the pan just begins to smoke, remove from the heat and ladle about 3 tablespoons of batter (a standard ladle filled about ³/₄ full). Immediately tilt the pan from side to side or swirl to distribute the batter evenly. Return the pan to the heat and cook for about 1 minute. Loosen the edges gently with a spatula or a butter knife and, if the crêpe comes up from the pan easily, turn and cook for about 30 seconds on the other side. If the crêpe sticks, wait another 30 seconds, then turn. (Don't panic if the first few stick; the pan will eventually become well seasoned and they will come away easily.) Turn the crêpe from the pan onto a plate, with the first side down (the darker, prettier side). When you fill the crêpes, place the filling on the less cooked side.

Brush the pan again with butter and continue with the remainder of the batter. After the first 3 or 4 crêpes you won't have to brush the pan each time, but only after every 3 or 4 crêpes.

VARIATIONS:

Dessert Crêpes: Using the recipe above, replace ¼ cup of the water with ¼ cup of Grand Marnier or orange juice. Proceed as above.

Herb Crêpes: Add 3 tablespoons finely chopped fresh herbs, such as chives, parsley, basil, tarragon, dill, to the batter just before you make the crêpes.

ADVANCE PREPARATION: You can keep these in the refrigerator for a couple of days or freeze them. Stack them between pieces of wax paper or parchment and seal them in a plastic bag or foil. They take 2 hours to thaw at room temperature.

PER CRÊPE

Calories	80	Protein	2 G
Fat	5 G	Carbohydrate	7 G
Sodium	135 MG	Cholesterol	38 MG

DESSERT CRÊPES PER CRÊPE

Calories	91	Protein	2 G
Fat	5 G	Carbohydrate	8 G
Sodium	135 MG	Cholesterol	38 MG

HERB CRÊPES PER CRÊPE

Calories	80	Protein	2 G
Fat	5 G	Carbohydrate	7 G
Sodium	135 MG	Cholesterol	38 MG

BUCKWHEAT CRÊPES

MAKES ABOUT 15 6- OR 7-INCH CRÊPES

Buckwheat crêpes are my favorite French "fast food." They are made in little stands and in small restaurants called *crêperies* in Paris and all over Brittany, where they originated, and are topped with a number of nutritious items—cheese, egg, spinach, smoked salmon, tomatoes, ham, and others. The French call them *galettes au sarrasin* or *au blé noir*. These crêpes rank among the world's greatest street food, made right in front of you on large round griddles. The vendor pours some of the batter, which he has mixed up in a huge bowl, onto the middle of the griddle, then with a flat spatula he spreads it over the surface. It is so thin that it needs to be cooked only on one side. If you have ordered an *oeuf/fromage*, the crêpe maker will fry the egg right on top of the crêpe, sprinkle on the cheese, fold the crêpe in half, then in half again, and wrap it like a cone in a piece of wax paper. He hands it to you, hot and buttery, and voilà!—a nutritious and mouth-watering quick lunch.

I make my own buckwheat crêpes like ordinary crêpes in a well-seasoned crêpe pan. They are good to have on hand and freeze well.

1 cup skim milk

1/3 cup water

1/2 teaspoon salt

2 large eggs

3/4 cup buckwheat flour

1/4 cup unbleached white flour

2 tablespoons unsalted butter, melted

unsalted butter for the pan

Place the milk, water, salt, and eggs in a blender and turn on. Add the flours, then the melted butter, and blend at high speed for 1 minute. Refrigerate for 1 to 2 hours before making the crêpes.

To make the crêpes, use a 6- to 7-inch crêpe pan (or larger for a more authentic crêpe) or a cast-iron or nonstick skillet. Place the pan over moderate heat and brush the bottom with butter. When the pan just begins to smoke, remove from the heat and pour in or ladle in the batter, about 3 tablespoons per crêpe. Immediately tilt or twist the pan to distribute the batter evenly and return to the heat. Cook the crêpe for about 1 minute and gently loosen the edges by running a butter knife or thin spatula around the edge. If the crêpe comes up from the pan easily and is nicely browned, turn it and cook for 30 seconds on the other side. If it sticks, wait another 30 seconds, then turn. Turn the crêpe onto a plate and continue cooking them in this way until all the batter is used up.

ADVANCE PREPARATION: Crêpes freeze well. Stack them between pieces of wax paper or parchment and seal in plastic bags. They take 2 hours to thaw at room temperature.

PER CRÊPE

Calories	42	Protein	2 G
Fat	I G	Carbohydrate	7 G
Sodium	92 MG	Cholesterol	3 MG

WHITE AND GREEN PASTA MADE WITH EGG WHITES ONLY

———

EACH PASTA RECIPE SERVES 2 AS A MAIN DISH, 3 AS A SIDE DISH

The idea for this very light, low-cholesterol pasta comes from Michel Guérard. In some ways I like it even better than homemade pasta made with whole eggs; it's easier to cook it al dente. You can make all white pasta or all green by simply doubling the proportions. The dough for the white pasta is slightly moist, and the green pasta dough is a little dry, so add flour and/or water as needed.

FOR THE WHITE PASTA

5 ounces (1 cup plus 2 tablespoons) unbleached white flour plus additional as needed

pinch of salt

2 medium egg whites (¹/₄ cup)

FOR THE GREEN PASTA

¹/₄ pound (1 cup less 2 tablespoons) unbleached white flour

1 medium egg white (2 tablespoons)

pinch of salt

¹/₂ cup tightly packed fresh parsley leaves, very finely chopped after measuring

1 tablespoon water or more as needed

First make the white pasta dough, then the green; it's easiest to use a food processor.

To make the dough in a food processor: Place the flour and salt in the food processor, turn on, and add the egg white or the egg white and parsley. The white pasta may be sticky, in which case add a tablespoon more flour to the batter. The green pasta, on the other hand, may be dry and need the tablespoon of water. Process until the dough comes together in a ball.

Now remove from the food processor and knead the dough for 5 to 10 minutes, until stiff. You can knead it like bread, folding it over and leaning into it on a very lightly floured surface, or you can squeeze the dough from one end to the other, back and forth, or you can slam it down on the work surface, pick it up, and slam it down again. Do whatever seems easiest. The dough is stiff and will be much more difficult to knead than bread. Wrap it in plastic and allow it

403

to rest for 30 minutes before rolling out. Or refrigerate for up to 2 days, wrapped in plastic. The dough can also be frozen.

To make the dough by hand: Sift together the flour and salt and place on a large work surface or in a large bowl, in a mound. Make a depression in the center of the mound and pour the egg whites into this well. Using a fork, gently beat the egg whites together. When they are lightly beaten, begin brushing flour in from the top of the "walls" of the well and incorporating it into the egg whites with your fork. Use your free hand to keep the walls of the well intact while you brush in flour a little at a time. Don't worry if the egg white breaks through the sides of the well; just push the mixture back into the middle, incorporating flour as you do. As soon as it becomes impossible to incorporate flour into the mixture with your fork, brush in the remaining flour and incorporate as much as you can with your hands. Now brush away any hard bits of egg white and flour that haven't been amalgamated and gather the mixture into a ball. Knead and let rest as above.

ROLLING OUT THE DOUGH: I use a hand pasta machine to roll out my dough. It's a very satisfying, simple gadget. First cut the dough into quarters to facilitate rolling. Flatten it down a little and, with the roller set on 1, roll it through. The edges will be very jagged. Fold these jagged edges in toward each other, press down, and roll the dough again through the first setting. Repeat this process at each setting, dusting with a little unbleached white flour if it seems damp. If you can roll the dough through at 5 without tearing it, by all means do so. Once you've rolled to the desired thickness, attach the noodle cutting attachment and cut thick or thin noodles.

Let the pasta dry for 15 to 30 minutes before cooking it.

At this point you can either cook the pasta or dry it by laying it out on dusted wax paper or over the back of a chair or dowel for 24 to 48 hours (it takes longer in a humid climate). Once dry, store in a tightly covered container. You can also freeze fresh pasta. Once you have rolled it out and cut noodles, dust with unbleached white flour, wrap in plastic, then freeze in a plastic bag. Fresh pasta will keep, well dusted and wrapped in plastic or sealed in a plastic bag, for a day in the refrigerator.

COOKING THE PASTA: Fresh pasta cooks, literally, in seconds. Bring a large pot of water to a rolling boil. Add a generous amount of salt and a tablespoon of cooking oil. Add the pasta. It will float to the surface at once. Remove immediately and toss with sauce. If you're serving it cold, rinse it with cold water. To cook frozen pasta, transfer it directly from the freezer to the boiling water.

WHITE PASTA SIDE DISH PER PORTION

Calories	182	Protein	7 G
Fat	.43 G	Carbohydrate	36 G
Sodium	76 MG	Cholesterol	0

GREEN PASTA SIDE DISH PER PORTION

Calories	146	Protein	6 G
Fat	.2 G	Carbohydrate	30 G
Sodium	20 MG	Cholesterol	0

HERB PASTA

SERVES 4 AS A MAIN DISH, 6 AS A SIDE DISH

Double the quantities for the white pasta made with egg whites only (page 403). Add 4 teaspoons finely chopped fresh herbs, such as parsley, tarragon, or basil, to the flours and salt before adding the egg whites. The pasta will be beautifully speckled.

PER PORTION

Calories	182	Protein	7 G
Fat	.46 G	Carbohydrate	36 G
Sodium	78 MG	Cholesterol	0

WATERCRESS PASTA

SERVES 4 AS A MAIN DISH, 6 AS A SIDE DISH

This idea comes from my friend and assistant, Anne Trager, who is a brilliant cook. She thought of using watercress for green pasta because cress has such a sharp flavor and sometimes you want more taste in the pasta itself. It works beautifully, and the pasta is a beautiful rich green color.

2 ounces (1½ cups tightly packed) fresh watercress leaves

2 large egg whites

3 tablespoons very finely chopped flat-leaf parsley *or* 3 additional tablespoons watercress

½ pound (about 1¾ cups) unbleached white flour or more as needed

¼ teaspoon salt

3 to 5 tablespoons water, as needed

Wash the watercress and dry thoroughly. Chop in a food processor fitted with the steel blade or by hand until very finely chopped, almost a puree. Measure out ½ cup or a little more for a sharper, greener pasta. Combine the egg whites, watercress, and parsley.

Follow the instructions for making and cooking pasta in the preceding recipe.

ADVANCE PREPARATION: All pasta dough can be mixed a day ahead of being rolled out and refrigerated, wrapped tightly in plastic wrap. It can also be frozen for weeks. It takes 2 or 3 hours to thaw at room temperature.

PER PORTION

Calories	146	Protein	5 G
Fat	.39 G	Carbohydrate	29 G
Sodium	117 MG	Cholesterol	0

ANISE SUGAR COOKIES

MAKES 3 DOZEN COOKIES

I make these cookies with unrefined sugar, and they're crunchy and not too sweet. If I'm serving a Tex-Mex dinner, I'll roll them out and cut them with my Texas-shaped cookie cutter. Otherwise I'll cut rounds.

6 ounces unsalted butter

5 ounces (²/₃ cup) unrefined brown sugar (turbinado sugar)

1 medium egg

2 tablespoons fresh lemon juice

1 teaspoon vanilla extract

2 teaspoons aniseeds, crushed in a mortar and pestle

10 ounces (2¼ cups) whole wheat pastry flour or a combination of whole wheat pastry flour and unbleached white flour

1 teaspoon baking powder

¹/₂ teaspoon salt

In a mixer or a food processor fitted with the steel blade, cream the butter and sugar. Beat in the egg, lemon juice, vanilla, and aniseeds.

Sift together the flour or flours, baking powder, and salt and add to the butter mixture. Beat together and gather into a ball. Wrap in plastic and place in the refrigerator overnight or in the freezer for 1 or 2 hours.

Preheat the oven to 350 degrees. Butter cookie sheets. Cut the dough into quarters and roll out each quarter on a lightly dusted board. Keep the remaining dough in the refrigerator or freezer. Cut into desired shapes.

Bake for 10 minutes, until lightly browned. Remove from the cookie sheets and cool on racks.

ADVANCE PREPARATION: These will keep for weeks in a well-sealed tin or jar. The dough can be refrigerated for up to 2 days before being rolled out and baked.

PER COOKIE

Calories	76	Protein	I G
Fat	4 G	Carbohydrate	9 G
Sodium	45 MG	Cholesterol	16 MG

GINGER AND HONEY REFRIGERATOR COOKIES

MAKES 4 DOZEN COOKIES

These refrigerator cookies have lots of pungent fresh ginger in them and are great for tea and as an accompaniment to fruit desserts. Four tablespoons of ginger gives you a pleasant mild ginger flavor, 6 tablespoons a more pronounced one. Try them both ways to see which you prefer.

- $3/4$ cup (6 ounces) unsalted butter
- $1/3$ cup mild-flavored honey
- 2 ounces ($1/4$ cup) unrefined brown sugar (turbinado sugar)
- 1 medium egg
- 4 to 6 tablespoons grated or finely chopped fresh ginger
- 1 teaspoon vanilla extract
- $3/4$ pound ($2^2/3$ cups) flour
- 1 teaspoon baking powder
- $1/4$ teaspoon salt

In a mixer or a food processor fitted with the steel blade, cream the butter, honey, and sugar. Beat in the egg, ginger, and vanilla.

Sift together the flour, baking powder, and salt and add to the butter mixture. Beat together. Divide the dough in 2 and place each half on a piece of plastic wrap or wax paper. The dough will be wet and sticky. Using a spatula, shape into logs, about 2 inches in diameter and 10 inches long. Wrap well and place in the refrigerator overnight or in the freezer for 1 or 2 hours.

Preheat the oven to 350 degrees. Butter cookie sheets. Slice the logs into very thin rounds and place on baking sheets. Work with only a piece of a log at a time and keep the remaining dough in the refrigerator or freezer. Bake for 10 minutes, until lightly browned. Remove from the cookie sheets and cool on racks.

ADVANCE PREPARATION: The cookies will keep for a week or two in a well-sealed tin or jar. The dough can be refrigerated for up to 2 days before being rolled out.

PER COOKIE

Calories	65	Protein	1 G
Fat	3 G	Carbohydrate	9 G
Sodium	22 MG	Cholesterol	12 MG

ORANGE BISCOTTI

MAKES ABOUT 70 COOKIES

These crisp almond cookies, delicately perfumed with orange juice and zest, are terrific to have on hand. Hard and crunchy, they are meant to be dipped into fruity syrups, wine, tea, or coffee. These aren't nearly as sweet as most traditional *biscotti*. I cut them extremely thin. With no butter at all, this makes a wonderful low-fat sweet. The dough can be sticky and not as easy to work with as other *biscotti* doughs. It helps to use a dough scraper.

$1/4$ pound ($3/4$ cup) unskinned shelled almonds

2 medium eggs

$1/4$ cup mild-flavored honey

$1/2$ cup fresh orange juice

2 heaped tablespoons finely chopped orange zest (from 1 large orange)

up to 4 cups unbleached white flour, as needed

$1/4$ teaspoon salt

$3/4$ teaspoon baking soda

1 medium egg white

Preheat the oven to 375 degrees. Place the almonds on a baking sheet and roast for about 10 minutes, until lightly golden and toasty-smelling. Remove from the heat. Grind one quarter of the almonds fine and chop the rest into coarse pieces. Set aside.

In a mixer or a large bowl, blend together the eggs and honey. Mix in the orange juice and zest. Mix in $3^{1}/2$ cups flour, the salt, and the baking soda. Mix in the chopped and ground almonds. When all the ingredients are mixed together, place a small amount of flour on a work surface, remove the dough from the bowl, and knead for 10 to 15 minutes, adding flour as necessary. This can also be done in an electric mixer with a dough hook.

Divide the dough in half and shape into 2 long logs, about 2 inches in diameter. Place them on a buttered and flour-dusted baking sheet, not too close to each other. Beat the egg white until foamy and brush it over the logs. Bake for 20 minutes, until golden brown and shiny. Remove from the oven and turn the oven heat down to 275 degrees.

(continued)

Cut the logs into thin slices, about ¼ to ½ inch thick, at a 45-degree angle. Use a bread knife or a sharp chef's knife. Place the cookies on baking sheets and bake again for about 30 to 40 minutes, until dry and hard. Remove from the heat and cool.

ADVANCE PREPARATION: The dough can be wrapped in plastic and refrigerated for a day before baking. The *biscotti* will keep for weeks in a covered jar.

PER COOKIE			
Calories	42	Protein	1 G
Fat	1 G	Carbohydrate	7 G
Sodium	19 MG	Cholesterol	5 MG

PECAN COOKIES

MAKES 3½ DOZEN COOKIES

These cookies are slightly crisp on the outside and chewy on the inside. They couldn't be easier to make; all you need are pecans, raw sugar, and egg whites. The cookies keep for a week or more in a sealed jar.

　2　cups pecan pieces

　⅔　cup (5 ounces) unrefined brown sugar (turbinado sugar)

　4　medium egg whites

　42　pecan halves

Preheat the oven to 375 degrees. Roast the pecan pieces on a baking sheet for 7 to 8 minutes, just until they begin to brown, and remove from the oven. Allow to cool.

　　Grind together the pecan pieces and 2 tablespoons of the sugar in a food processor fitted with the steel blade until the pecans are fairly fine, but don't process too long or the pecans will begin to turn to butter. Add the remaining sugar and continue to process until you have a fairly fine, uniform mixture. Add the egg whites and process until the mixture is well blended. Scrape the mixture into a bowl, cover, and refrigerate overnight.

　　Preheat the oven to 375 degrees. Butter 2 baking sheets. Transfer the batter to a pastry bag* fitted with a star-shaped nozzle and pipe the batter in ¾- to 1-inch stars onto your baking sheets. Place a pecan half in the middle of each cookie. Bake the cookies for 12 to 15 minutes or until lightly browned around the bottom edge. Cool on racks.

PER COOKIE

Calories	58	Protein	I G
Fat	4 G	Carbohydrate	5 G
Sodium	6 MG	Cholesterol	0

* If you don't have a pastry bag, use a freezer-weight plastic bag instead. Cut off a corner tip, pile the cookie batter inside the bag, and squeeze the cookies through the hole in the corner. If you have a star-shaped nozzle, fit it right into the corner and you'll get perfect stars.

VANILLA SUGAR

MAKES 2 CUPS

This vanilla-scented sugar is easy to make and is great to have on hand for many desserts. You just submerge vanilla bean pods in a jar of sugar, and after a few weeks the sugar becomes infused with a subtle vanilla flavor. In addition to the fresh vanilla beans, you can dry out and recycle vanilla beans you have used for crème Anglaise and other sauces for this.

2　vanilla beans, split in half lengthwise

2　cups sugar

Scrape the seeds from the vanilla beans and reserve for another use. Place the sugar in a jar and submerge the pods in it. Cover and let sit for a couple of weeks.

To make this with vanilla pods you have simmered, allow the pods to dry thoroughly and make as above.

ADVANCE PREPARATION: This sugar lasts indefinitely. Keep replenishing the sugar, and the vanilla beans will continue to infuse it. Whenever you use vanilla beans for a recipe, dry the pods and add to more sugar.

PER TABLESPOON

Calories	49	Protein	0
Fat	0	Carbohydrate	13 G
Sodium	0	Cholesterol	0

CHICKEN OR TURKEY STOCK

MAKES 2 QUARTS

You can make this chicken stock with a fresh uncooked carcass or with the remains of a cooked chicken or turkey. Make it in quantity and freeze in 1-quart containers. Remember to make it a day before you need it so that you can skim off the fat, which will congeal in the refrigerator.

> a fresh carcass and giblets of 1 chicken or turkey *or* the carcass of a cooked chicken or turkey plus 2 to 4 extra wings

- 1 carrot, sliced
- 1 onion, quartered
- 1 leek, white part and the tender part of the green, cleaned and sliced
- 5 or 6 garlic cloves, crushed
    > a bouquet garni made with 1 bay leaf, 2 fresh thyme sprigs, and 2 fresh parsley sprigs
- 2 celery ribs, sliced
- 2½ quarts water or more (enough to cover everything by an inch)
- ½ teaspoon peppercorns
    > salt to taste

If you're using a fresh carcass, crack the bones slightly with a hammer. Combine all of the ingredients in a soup pot. Bring to a boil and skim off any foam that rises. Reduce the heat, cover, and simmer over very low heat for 2 hours. Strain and remove pieces of chicken from the bones (you can use it for salads or enchiladas). Discard the bones, etc. Place the stock in a bowl, cover, and refrigerate overnight. The next day, remove the stock from the refrigerator and skim off any fat that has risen to the surface. Use in soups and sauces or as a cooking bouillon, or freeze.

ADVANCE PREPARATION: This stock keeps for 3 days in the refrigerator and several months in the freezer.

Calories	43	Protein	1 G
Fat	2 G	Carbohydrate	6 G
Sodium	5 MG	Cholesterol	0

VEGETABLE STOCK

MAKES 2 QUARTS

This is an easy, fragrant all-purpose stock.

2 quarts water

2 onions, quartered

6 garlic cloves, peeled

2 carrots, coarsely sliced

2 leeks, white part only, cleaned and coarsely sliced

2 large potatoes, scrubbed and quartered

2 celery ribs, sliced

2 fresh parsley sprigs

1 bay leaf

¼ teaspoon crumbled dried thyme

salt to taste

12 black peppercorns

Combine all the ingredients in a soup pot and bring to a simmer. Cover, reduce the heat, and simmer for 1 hour. Strain and discard the vegetables.

ADVANCE PREPARATION: This stock freezes well and will keep for several days in the refrigerator.

PER CUP			
Calories	13	Protein	0
Fat	.02 G	Carbohydrate	3 G
Sodium	5 MG	Cholesterol	0

GARLIC BROTH

MAKES 6 CUPS

Garlic broth can be substituted for chicken broth in many recipes. This simplifies my life all the time. If a recipe calls for chicken broth and I don't have it, this makes a fragrant, easy substitute, a much better one than bouillon cubes or canned stock. It's also great for vegetarians.

> 2 heads of garlic, cloves separated and peeled
>
> 6 cups water
>
> 1 bay leaf
>
> 2 fresh parsley sprigs
>
> 2 fresh thyme sprigs *or* 1/4 teaspoon crumbled dried
>
> 1 to 2 teaspoons salt to taste
>
> 1 teaspoon olive oil

Combine all the ingredients in a stockpot and bring to a boil. Reduce the heat, cover, and simmer for 1 to 2 hours. Strain.

ADVANCE PREPARATION: This broth keeps for 3 days in the refrigerator, and can be frozen.

PER CUP

Calories	22	Protein	1 G
Fat	.81 G	Carbohydrate	3 G
Sodium	551 MG	Cholesterol	0

MILD FISH FUMET

MAKES 1 QUART

This fish stock, based on a recipe by the French chef Michel Guérard, is much milder-tasting than those I've made in the past. It really does make a difference if you use flat fish fillets, such as sole.

2¼ pounds fish bones and heads (such as sole, whiting, brill; flat fish have the subtlest perfume; avoid fatty fish such as salmon and mackerel)

1 tablespoon unsalted butter

1 tablespoon peanut or sunflower oil

1 shallot, minced

1 medium onion, chopped

2 ounces mushrooms, cleaned and minced

½ cup dry white wine

6 cups water

salt to taste

a bouquet garni made with 1 bay leaf, 1 fresh thyme sprig, and several fresh parsley sprigs

Separate the fish heads from the skeletons. Soak the fish bones and heads in a bowl of cold water while you prepare the vegetables. Drain, pat dry, and crush the bones slightly with a rolling pin or place in a plastic bag and break the skeletons up with your hands.

Heat the butter and oil together in a large soup pot over low heat and add the fish bones, shallot, onion, and mushrooms. Sweat without browning for 5 minutes, stirring often. Add the white wine and bring to a boil.

When the wine has reduced by a little more than half, add the water, salt, and bouquet garni. Bring back to a boil, reduce the heat, and simmer, uncovered, for 20 minutes. Skim the gray foam that rises to the surface as the mixture cooks.

Strain the *fumet* into a bowl through a fine strainer or a strainer lined with cheesecloth, pressing the fish bones against the strainer with the back of a ladle or wooden spoon. Correct the seasoning. Refrigerate until ready to use.

ROASTED RED BELL PEPPERS

SERVES 4

I consider roasted peppers a necessary staple, and I like to have at least one red bell pepper in the refrigerator at all times. When I don't have any other plans for the pepper, I roast it and keep it on hand (it will keep for more than a week if covered with olive oil) to add to salads and pasta. Roasted red peppers are always pleasing as a first course or part of another course. The recipe below is for a starter course, but you can cut the recipe and roast just 1 or 2 peppers, to have on hand and use as you please.

4   medium red bell peppers

1   tablespoon red wine vinegar or more to taste (see note below)

1   or 2 large garlic cloves to taste, minced or put through a press

2   or 3 tablespoons olive oil (use the smaller amount if you are making these for a starter and more if storing in the refrigerator)

salt to taste

1   to 2 tablespoons fresh chopped basil, if available, to taste

There are several ways to roast the peppers. You can place them directly in a gas flame or below a broiler. Or you can place them in a dry skillet over an electric or gas burner or in a baking dish in a hot oven. You want all the skin to blister and blacken. Keep turning the peppers until they are uniformly charred, then place in a plastic bag or wrap in a kitchen towel until cool enough to handle.

Peel off the blackened skin, split in half, and remove the seeds and inner membranes. Rinse quickly under cool water and pat dry. Cut the halved peppers in half lengthwise or into wide strips if you're serving them as a starter. If you're serving them as a garnish, cut into thin strips. Place in a bowl or serving dish and toss with the vinegar (see note), garlic, olive oil, and salt to taste. Cover and refrigerate until ready to serve. Toss with the basil shortly before serving.

ADVANCE PREPARATION: Roasted red peppers will keep for at least a week in the refrigerator, as long as they're covered with oil.

(*continued*)

NOTE: If you are making the peppers just to have on hand and don't know exactly how you are going to use them, omit the vinegar (you might not want it, for instance, if you are going to add these to a pasta or use as a garnish).

PER 1 PEPPER PORTION

Calories	110	Protein	1 G
Fat	9 G	Carbohydrate	8 G
Sodium	4 MG	Cholesterol	0

SWEET RED PEPPER PUREE

MAKES ABOUT 1 TO 1½ CUPS, SERVING 4 TO 6

This puree, with its beautiful orange-red color, makes a great sauce for fish, crêpes, and pasta. You can stretch it as you like, with either olive oil or *fromage blanc*.

6 medium (about 2 pounds) red bell peppers

2 garlic cloves, minced or put through a press

up to 3 tablespoons olive oil or *fromage blanc* (page 417), as needed

salt and freshly ground pepper to taste

1 tablespoon red wine vinegar or balsamic vinegar (optional)

2 tablespoons chopped fresh basil, if available (optional)

Preheat the oven to 350 degrees. Brush a baking dish with olive oil and place the peppers in it. Cover with foil and bake for about 45 minutes or until the peppers are thoroughly softened. Turn off the oven, uncover the peppers, and allow to cool in the oven.

Remove the skins, seeds, and membranes from the peppers, but reserve the juice. Puree the peppers with their juice and the garlic in a food processor fitted with the steel blade or in a blender until thoroughly smooth. Press through a strainer. Whisk in the olive oil or *fromage blanc* and season with salt and pepper. For a tart sauce, stir in the vinegar. Add chopped fresh basil if desired.

ADVANCE PREPARATION: This keeps well in the refrigerator, for a few days at least, and longer if there's vinegar in it.

PER PORTION

Calories	72	Protein	I G
Fat	5 G	Carbohydrate	7 G
Sodium	4 MG	Cholesterol	0

PER PORTION WITHOUT OIL

Calories	38	Protein	2 G
Fat	.61 G	Carbohydrate	7 G
Sodium	27 MG	Cholesterol	0

TOMATO SALSA

MAKES A LITTLE UNDER 1 QUART

This vibrant fresh tomato salsa goes along with all of my Mexican and Tex-Mex meals, and also with some of my fish dishes.

    2   pounds ripe tomatoes, finely chopped
    1/2 small red onion, finely minced
    1   to 3 jalapeño or serrano peppers to taste, minced
    4   to 6 tablespoons chopped cilantro to taste
    1   tablespoon red wine vinegar or balsamic vinegar
        salt to taste

Combine all the ingredients in a bowl and chill until ready to serve.

ADVANCE PREPARATION: The salsa will hold for a few hours in the refrigerator.

PER 1/4 CUP PORTION

Calories	12	Protein	1 G
Fat	.11 G	Carbohydrate	3 G
Sodium	5 MG	Cholesterol	0

FRESH TOMATO CONCASSÉE

MAKES 2 CUPS, SERVING 8

This is vibrant when the tomatoes are good; if they aren't, use canned in the recipe on page 302. Fresh tomatoes go further than canned. The *concassée* makes a delicious topping for fish, pizza, or pasta and also makes a good side dish with savory crêpes and tarts.

- 1 tablespoon olive oil
- 4 to 6 garlic cloves to taste, minced or put through a press
- 2 pounds tomatoes, peeled, seeded, and finely chopped (about 3 cups)
- 1/4 teaspoon sugar, approximately
  salt and freshly ground pepper to taste

Heat the olive oil over low heat in a heavy-bottomed saucepan and add half the garlic. When it begins to color and smell fragrant, add the tomatoes and remaining garlic, the sugar, and salt to taste. Cook, uncovered, over medium-low heat for 15 to 20 minutes, stirring often. Add pepper, taste, and adjust the seasonings.

ADDITIONS: You can add dried herbs, such as thyme, oregano, rosemary, or basil, 5 to 10 minutes before the end of the cooking, or chopped fresh herbs like basil, parsley, or cilantro at the end of the cooking. For a slightly piquant flavor, sprinkle in a dash of cayenne or hot pepper flakes just at the end of the cooking.

ADVANCE PREPARATION: Without the addition of fresh herbs, this will keep for a couple of days in the refrigerator and can be frozen. But it's best at its freshest.

PER PORTION

Calories	43	Protein	1 G
Fat	2 G	Carbohydrate	6 G
Sodium	10 MG	Cholesterol	0

TOMATOES VINAIGRETTE

MAKES 3 CUPS, SERVING 4 TO 6 AS A PASTA SAUCE

This mouth-watering combination will work only with very sweet, ripe tomatoes. Then you can't go wrong. It's redolent with garlic and slightly sweet, because the balsamic vinegar brings out the sweetness of the tomatoes. I probably use Tomato Vinaigrette most often as a sauce for pasta. It's great with hot spaghetti or for cold pasta salads. But it goes equally well with fish, as a topping for *crostini* (page 392) or Toasted Pita Triangles (page 71), or by itself, as a garnish or side dish.

   2 pounds ripe sweet tomatoes, peeled, seeded, and finely chopped
     (about 3 cups)

   ¼ cup chopped fresh herbs, such as basil, tarragon, thyme, sage,
     parsley (basil is my first choice)

   1 to 2 garlic cloves to taste, minced or put through a press

   2 to 4 tablespoons balsamic vinegar or red wine vinegar to taste

   2 tablespoons olive oil

     salt and freshly ground pepper to taste

Combine all the ingredients and stir together well. Adjust the seasonings. Refrigerate or leave at room temperature.

NOTE: You might want to halve this recipe if you are making this as a topping for *crostini* or a sauce for fish. But for pasta I'd make a whole batch, and if you feel it's a bit much, keep some aside for salads and hors d'oeuvres later in the week.

ADVANCE PREPARATION: This will hold without the herbs for several hours and can even be made a day ahead of time. Add the herbs at the last minute.

PER PORTION

Calories	69	Protein	I G
Fat	5 G	Carbohydrate	7 G
Sodium	I2 MG	Cholesterol	0

TOSSED GREEN SALAD

SERVES 4 TO 6

I think the most important key to success with simple green salads, provided you've found good-quality lettuces, is to wash the greens *thoroughly*. Some of my old friends, who were around when I first started cooking, and my sister, all of whom have helped me in the kitchen in the past, will now do any other task for me besides washing the lettuce, so maniacal have I always been (also it's usually the first task delegated, and in the old days we didn't have salad spinners for drying, so that had to be done with kitchen towels). If you don't *look* at the lettuce leaves one by one, you'll miss the dirt. It usually sticks to the base of the leaves, on both sides; but sometimes it's all over the place. To wash lettuce efficiently the leaves need 2 soakings, and *each* leaf needs to be rinsed under running water, preferably twice.

HOW TO WASH SALAD GREENS: Fill half of a double sink, a large bowl, or the bottom part of your salad spinner with cold water. For lettuce, gently separate the leaves and run each one briefly under the tap, then place in the water to soak for a few minutes. For spinach and other greens, run each piece briefly under the faucet (tear off the stems of the spinach) if it is very sandy and then place in the water to soak; if it doesn't appear too sandy, place the leaves directly in the water. Swish the leaves around in the water, then pour off the soaking water.

Now take each leaf and run it under the faucet. Holding the base of the leaf between your thumb and forefinger, run under the faucet and briskly rub them with your thumb and forefinger on both sides to remove tenacious grit. Look closely to make sure all the dirt is removed.

Fill your basin with cold water again and place the leaves in it. Whirl them around in the water vigorously to remove any last bits of dirt. With spinach the dirt will often be caked on the leaves, so you have to rinse them more than once. Lift the leaves out of the water (don't just drain, because the dirt in the water will settle back on the leaves) and rinse once more. Now dry the leaves in batches in a salad spinner. Toss with the dressing just before serving.

If you're not using the lettuce right away, place it in a plastic bag or wrap in a clean kitchen towel, place in a plastic bag, and seal. Refrigerate until shortly before using.

AMOUNTS AND KINDS OF SALAD GREENS: Lettuces weigh varying amounts, but for most leafy lettuce (Boston or Bibb lettuce, red tip, oak leaf, curly endive, romaine, leaf lettuce) I would count on about ½ pound for 6 people as a salad course. If salad is to be the main feature of your meal, double that amount. Heads vary in size, but 1 medium head or 2 small heads of Boston or leaf lettuce, 1 medium head of red tip or oak leaf, or ½ head of romaine is usually the right amount. Always tear off and discard the tough outer leaves. Use about ½ cup oil-based dressing to dress ½ pound salad greens (you can use a few tablespoons more if you wish, but I find ½ cup sufficient if the salad greens are thoroughly tossed). Yogurt-based vinaigrettes coat leaves more thickly, so you might need more. Toss the greens over and over again in the dressing, turning them over themselves gently with salad spoons so that they are thoroughly coated.

There are lots of recipes in this book for special salads using arugula, endive, and spinach. When I call for a tossed green salad in my menus, I mean a simple green salad made with the lettuce or lettuces of your choice and tossed with a vinaigrette (see pages 426–35; sometimes you'll want a very mild one, other times a sharper vinaigrette; sometimes you'll want garlic, other times not). Generally, the more intense and complicated the flavors are in the meal, the milder you will want your vinaigrette to be. Add a handful of chopped fresh herbs if you like and perhaps some sliced fresh mushrooms (figure on 2 medium mushrooms, thinly sliced, per person) or a handful of broken walnuts. If you've got some great tomatoes on hand, cut a few into wedges and add (this salad in France is referred to as a mixed salad).

ADVANCE PREPARATION: Salad greens can be washed and sealed in plastic bags, as instructed above, a day before serving.

A FEW VINAIGRETTES

Here are recipes for both high-fat and low-fat vinaigrettes. The high-fat vinaigrettes are oil-based ones; the low-fat ones are yogurt-based. If you are eating a very low-fat meal, there's no reason why you can't go with the first recipes, but yogurt-based dressings will help fit crisp, nutritious salads into calorie- and fat-restricted meals. I find them creamy and delicious. You can still taste the oils— I use either walnut or olive oil—even though they're reduced to a minimum. You could even serve both, passing them so guests can choose.

Everyone has an opinion about what a vinaigrette should be. For some too much vinegar or mustard is anathema; others like it very sharp. The Italians toss their salads with nothing more than good vinegar and olive oil—and sometimes just olive oil—the French add mustard, sometimes lemon.

I'm in the sharp-vinaigrette club. Sometimes, with very tender lettuces, or if I am drinking an exceptionally good wine, I appreciate a mild one (recently, for example, at a fabulous restaurant in Paris called Au Trou Gascon, I enjoyed a salad tossed with nothing but walnut oil, maybe a soupçon of vinegar and a little mustard). I like lemony vinaigrettes too. Usually I use a 3-to-1 ratio of oil to vinegar (or oil and yogurt to vinegar), but sometimes I make it sharper—or milder—than that. There are lots of choices. I prefer olive oil to vegetable oil or sunflower oil (safflower is too strong, I find), but some people like a mix, and the French often use only sunflower oil or peanut oil. It depends on how strong your olive oil is, I suppose. If it's extremely dark and fruity, it will overpower the salad, but if it's light and fragrant it could be used by itself.

I hardly ever use salt in my salad dressings, although I am giving you the choice here. The reason is that I find mustard, which I almost always use, to be quite salty enough, and the sharp flavor of the vinegar is quite enough seasoning for the salad. Sometimes I have to send salads back in French restaurants, they're so salty. I can never understand why people think the dressings need so much salt. Anyway, let your palate be your guide.

Here, then, are a few vinaigrette choices. Try variations; it's the only way you'll know what you like. Vinaigrettes should not be made too far ahead of serving; they'll hold for a few hours, but after that they begin to taste a little acrid.

Oil and Vinegar

This recipe is as simple as you can get. Use 1 part red wine vinegar, 3 parts olive oil, and salt and pepper to taste. A salad for 6, with about ½ cup dressing, would take, maybe, 2 tablespoons vinegar and 6 tablespoons olive oil. Add the salt and pepper to the vinegar and mix or shake together (it won't dissolve in the oil), then add the oil and mix together with a fork or spoon or shake in a jar. If you want a very mild dressing, use as little as 1½ teaspoons vinegar. For a lovely nutty flavor, use 2 or 3 tablespoons walnut oil in place of the vegetable or olive oil.

PER TABLESPOON

Calories	90	Protein	0
Fat	10 G	Carbohydrate	0
Sodium	0	Cholesterol	0

Very Sharp Vinaigrette with Lemon, Vinegar, and Mustard

MAKES ¾ CUP, SERVING 6 TO 8

1 tablespoon fresh lemon juice

3 tablespoons vinegar: red wine, champagne, cider, or sherry

1 to 3 heaped teaspoons Dijon mustard or more to taste

1 small garlic clove, minced or put through a press (optional)

1 to 2 tablespoons chopped fresh herbs, such as tarragon, basil, parsley, chervil, chives, thyme, to taste, *or* ¼ teaspoon crumbled dried tarragon

salt and freshly ground pepper to taste

8 or 9 tablespoons olive oil to taste, or a combination of olive oil and sunflower oil

Combine everything but the oil and mix well with a fork, spoon, or whisk or shake in a jar. Add the oil and blend well.

PER TABLESPOON

Calories	86	Protein	0
Fat	10 G	Carbohydrate	0
Sodium	25 MG	Cholesterol	0

Milder Vinaigrette

MAKES 1 CUP

2 tablespoons fresh lemon juice (optional)

2 tablespoons vinegar: red wine, champagne, cider, or sherry

1 teaspoon Dijon mustard

1 small garlic clove, minced or put through a press (optional)

1 to 2 tablespoons chopped fresh herbs, such as tarragon, basil, parsley, chervil, chives, thyme, to taste, *or* ¼ teaspoon crumbled dried tarragon

   salt and freshly ground pepper to taste

¾ cup olive oil or a combination of olive oil and sunflower oil

Combine everything but the oil and mix well with a fork, spoon, or whisk or shake in a jar. Add the oil and blend well.

PER TABLESPOON

Calories	91	Protein	0
Fat	10 G	Carbohydrate	0
Sodium	9 MG	Cholesterol	0

Lemon Vinaigrette

MAKES ½ TO ¾ CUP

Try this with more or less lemon juice to see how sharp you like it.

- 2 to 3 tablespoons fresh lemon juice to taste
- 1 tablespoon vinegar: white or red wine, sherry, champagne, or cider
- 1 to 3 teaspoons Dijon mustard to taste
- salt and freshly ground pepper to taste
- 1 small garlic clove, minced or put through a press (optional)
- 1 to 2 tablespoons chopped fresh herbs, such as tarragon, basil, parsley, chervil, chives, thyme, to taste, *or* ¼ teaspoon crumbled dried tarragon
- 6 to 8 tablespoons olive oil to taste, or a combination of olive oil and sunflower oil

Combine everything but the oil and mix well with a fork, spoon, or whisk or shake in a jar. Add the oil and blend well.

PER TABLESPOON

Calories	78	Protein	0
Fat	9 G	Carbohydrate	0
Sodium	20 MG	Cholesterol	0

Walnut Vinaigrette

MAKES ¾ CUP

This dressing is very nice with endive salads and with salads calling for other bitter greens like chicory and radicchio. The amount of mustard and oil you use depends on how sharp you want the dressing to be.

1   tablespoon fresh lemon juice

2   tablespoons vinegar: red wine, champagne, cider, or sherry (or omit the lemon juice and use 3 tablespoons vinegar)

1   to 3 heaped teaspoons Dijon mustard or more to taste

1   to 2 tablespoons chopped fresh herbs, such as tarragon, basil, parsley, chervil, chives, thyme, to taste, *or* ¼ teaspoon crumbled dried tarragon (omit if unavailable)

   salt and freshly ground pepper to taste

¼   cup walnut oil

3   to 5 tablespoons olive or sunflower oil to taste, or a combination

Combine everything but the oils and mix well with a fork, spoon or whisk, or shake in a jar. Add the oils and blend well.

PER TABLESPOON

Calories	83	Protein	0
Fat	9 G	Carbohydrate	0
Sodium	38 MG	Cholesterol	0

Garlicky Vinaigrette

MAKES ¾ CUP

This dressing is nice with tomatoes and with the broccoli and endive salad on page 199. It's a standard vinaigrette with an extra-large clove of garlic.

1 to 2 tablespoons fresh lemon juice

2 tablespoons red wine vinegar

1 teaspoon Dijon mustard or more to taste

1 very large garlic clove, minced or put through a press

¼ teaspoon crumbled dried tarragon

1 tablespoon chopped fresh herbs, if available, such as tarragon, basil, chervil, parsley, thyme (optional)

½ cup olive oil or a combination of olive oil and sunflower or safflower oil (more to taste)

salt and freshly ground pepper to taste

Mix together the lemon juice, vinegar, mustard, garlic, and herbs. Combine well and whisk in the oil or oils. Add salt and pepper. Set aside and toss with the salad of your choice just before serving.

PER TABLESPOON

Calories	82	Protein	0
Fat	9 G	Carbohydrate	0
Sodium	13 MG	Cholesterol	0

Low-Fat Yogurt Vinaigrettes

Substitute plain nonfat yogurt for all but a tablespoon or two of the oil or oils in the preceding recipes.

LOW-FAT MILD
PER TABLESPOON

Calories	28	Protein	1 G
Fat	2 G	Carbohydrate	1 G
Sodium	22 MG	Cholesterol	0

LOW-FAT GARLICKY
PER TABLESPOON

Calories	26	Protein	.42 G
Fat	2 G	Carbohydrate	1 G
Sodium	18 MG	Cholesterol	.14 MG

Lemon-Yogurt Vinaigrette

MAKES 1¼ CUPS

This is especially nice with bean salads.

- ¼ cup fresh lemon juice
- 1 to 2 tablespoons vinegar: red wine, champagne, cider, or sherry to taste
- 1 small garlic clove, minced or put through a press
  salt and freshly ground pepper to taste
- 2 teaspoons Dijon mustard
- ¾ cup plain nonfat yogurt

Mix together everything but the yogurt. Whisk in the yogurt.

PER PORTION

Calories	21	Protein	2 G
Fat	.16 G	Carbohydrate	3 G
Sodium	72 MG	Cholesterol	1 MG

Low-Fat Walnut Vinaigrette

MAKES ⅔ CUP, SERVING 6

Walnut oil has such a distinctive flavor that even as little as 2 tablespoons comes through in this dressing. This vinaigrette is especially suitable for salads made with bitter lettuces like endive and chicory.

1 tablespoon fresh lemon juice

2 tablespoons vinegar: red wine, champagne, cider, or sherry *or* omit the lemon juice and use 3 tablespoons vinegar

1 to 3 heaped teaspoons Dijon mustard to taste

⅓ to ½ cup plain nonfat yogurt to taste

  salt and freshly ground pepper to taste

2 tablespoons walnut oil

Combine everything but the oil and mix well with a fork, spoon, or whisk or shake in a jar. Add the oil and blend well.

PER PORTION

Calories	53	Protein	1 G
Fat	5 G	Carbohydrate	2 G
Sodium	80 MG	Cholesterol	0

CRÈME ANGLAISE

MAKES ABOUT 2 CUPS, SERVING 8

If you can make a good crème Anglaise, you have a quick answer to the "What will I serve for dessert?" question. This will add a special touch to all sorts of simple fruit dishes. I once cooked on a sailboat for a week and had very few fresh ingredients. There was lots of canned fruit, however, and I would impress the crew by making crème Anglaise (the boat *was* fitted out with eggs, sugar, and milk) and serving it over the fruit.

Crème Anglaise is a custard sauce made with sweetened egg yolks and milk. It can be seasoned with vanilla or with spices like cinnamon or ginger. Mine is not traditional. I usually use honey (as long as it's a mild-flavored honey) rather than sugar, and I use low-fat or skim milk. So it's thinner—and lighter—than most; but you can get it to be thicker if you wish, by cooking it for a while (be sure, though, that you don't let it come to a boil or it will curdle).

The main thing to be careful about when you're making this is not ever to let the mixture reach the boiling point. If you think it's getting too hot, lift the pot from the heat and stir for a minute. Use a thick pot, such as Le Creuset or a copper saucepan, or if you don't have a thick pot, set your pot on a Flame Tamer.

As long as you stir constantly and watch closely, you'll succeed with this sauce, which should become a dessert staple in your house.

  4 medium egg yolks
 ⅓ cup mild-flavored honey *or* ½ cup sugar
1¼ cups skim milk (add an extra ¼ cup if using sugar)
  1 vanilla bean, split in half, *or* ½ teaspoon vanilla extract

Beat the egg yolks and honey or sugar together until very thick and lemon-colored. Meanwhile, if you're using a whole vanilla bean, scrape the inside of the bean into the milk. Add the pod to the milk and heat together in a heavy-bottomed saucepan to the simmering point. Remove the vanilla bean. Being careful that the milk is not boiling, beat into the egg mixture. Return this mixture to the saucepan and heat over medium-low heat, stirring constantly with a wooden spoon. Do not allow the mixture to boil. The crème Anglaise is ready when it reaches the consistency of thick cream and coats both sides of your spoon evenly. Remove from the heat and strain into a bowl. Whisk in the vanilla now if you are using vanilla extract instead of a vanilla bean. Set aside. Serve with fruit crisps or crumbles, with baked fruit, or with fruit compotes.

The crème Anglaise can be served warm, at room temperature, or chilled. Allow to cool before refrigerating.

ADVANCE PREPARATION: The sauce will keep for a couple of days in the refrigerator.

PER PORTION

Calories	84	Protein	3 G
Fat	2 G	Carbohydrate	14 G
Sodium	24 MG	Cholesterol	97 MG

CHAPTER EIGHT

CHOOSING WINES

You'll have seen, reading through the introductions to the menus in this book, that wine is one of my great passions. Indeed, some of my menus were designed to accompany particular wines.

Because my food is light (even the substantial dishes like *risotti* are low in fat and don't have intense meat flavors) and its flavors can be complex and robust, garlicky and Mediterranean; and because my "cellar" (it is a closet) is small and not too cold, and my pockets are not deep, I have very particular wine requirements. The wines that meet these requirements will be useful for you to learn about. You will not be advised to buy red Bordeaux and Burgundies, Italian Barolos, or powerful California cabernet sauvignons here, because most do not match my foods: they are too austere and tannic and have to be laid down for too long before they're ready to drink. Also, frankly, they're too expensive. I like lighter reds, young ones from the Loire, the Beaujolais, and southern France. The spicy, "bigger" reds, from the Rhône, Bandol, Spain, and Italy, as well as some California zinfandels and Australian Shiraz, match my dishes with big Mediterranean or Mexican flavors.

As for white wines, I usually shy away from big, oaky, buttery New World Chardonnays, because I find their flavors often become tedious over the course of a meal and they can be too domineering. I love crisp, flinty, and floral whites from the Loire and complex, fruity, or floral whites from Alsace; uncomplicated dry whites from Provence and fumé blancs (which are sauvignons) from California. I also love rosés, not the sweet ones, but dry, fruity rosés, like the elegant yet friendly Domaine Tempier rosé from Bandol. Often nothing matches my food better. And rosés make terrific aperitifs.

You can learn a lot about what wines should taste like by reading wine importer Kermit Lynch's *Adventures on the Wine Route* and by looking out for the wines he imports; his name is on the labels. Lynch's standards are the highest; many of the wines he imports are made by little-known small producers who make beautifully balanced, honest, not-too-expensive wines.

The best guide for buying wines is Robert Parker's *Wine Buyer's Guide*; Parker writes beautifully about wine and is a good teacher. His palate is remarkable, and he's a genius at choosing words that precisely describe a wine. If you walk into any supermarket or wine store armed with his book, you will come out with something good that suits your taste and your pocketbook. Parker grades wines on a scale from 50 to 100, and anything above an 80—the equivalent to a high school grade of B—will be excellent; i.e., you don't have to buy the usually more expensive wines in the 90-or-above range to get something good. Even a wine graded 79 will be pleasant; perhaps not very complex, but then, with many of my menus complex wines aren't necessarily the best wines to serve.

As Robert Parker repeatedly stresses, it's important to become acquainted with the names of good producers in any given region. You can know what type of wine you are looking for, but if you don't have any idea of whose wine to look for, you can come home with a bottle of something that is industrial-tasting and headache-producing.

SERVING WINE

You will appreciate your wines ever so much more if you serve them at the appropriate temperatures. White wine and rosé should never be ice-cold (as they are too often served). The temperature should be between 50 or 55 and 60 degrees. If it's lower than 50 degrees, you won't really be able to discern the flavors and nuances of the wine. Jon Winroth, a Paris-based wine writer, recommends serving champagne and sweet white wines at around 45 or 46 degrees. It takes only two hours in the refrigerator, or 15 to 30 minutes in an ice bucket, to chill wine properly. If you have kept your wine in a very cold refrigerator for some time, remove it a half hour before serving and keep cold in an ice bucket.

Red wine, on the other hand, is usually served too warm. A full-bodied red wine should be at 62 to 67 degrees. Light red wines, from the Loire and Beaujolais for example, should be slightly chilled and should be served, like white wines, at temperatures of 55 to 60 degrees. In summer, if the weather is very hot, all red wine should be put in an ice bucket or it will become too warm.

Should the wine breathe? White wine never needs to breathe, and according to Robert Parker, red wine may not need to breathe either but should be poured into a clean decanter within 15 to 30 minutes of being opened. That said, rarely do I decant my red wine. I find that, after about 15 minutes of being opened, sturdy red wines do seem to smooth out and open up a bit in the bottle.

It's important that your glasses be recently washed and properly rinsed and odor-free. Make sure there is no soapy residue on glasses, as the wine will be affected by its flavor.

ONE WINE OR TWO?

There is no hard-and-fast rule that says you must serve two different wines with your meal. For large dinners I usually serve only one wine that will work throughout the meal, with all the courses. It's most often a fairly light, fruity, drinkable red. The wines I choose are either from the Loire or, more often, from the south of France. Some of my most frequent choices are Coteaux du Tricastin or Côtes-du-Rhône or Côtes-du-Rhône Villages from the Rhône Valley, Bandol, Gamay de Touraine (my favorite producer is Henri Marionnet, Domaine de la Charmoise), a Vin du Pays Catalan from Mas Chichet and a Côtes du Roussillon from Sarda-Malet.

If I serve one white wine throughout the meal, it tends to be from Alsace. I find that good dry Rieslings and Tokay Pinot Gris d'Alsace can make very good drinking over the course of an evening. Dry rosé will also make a perfect wine from start to finish when I serve a lusty fish dinner.

If you are serving more than one wine, the progression should always be from light to dark or from simple to complicated. White wine should precede rosé should precede red; light, fruity reds should precede big, spicy, or complicated reds. Young wines should be drunk before older ones and simple wines before *grands crus*. As wine expert Jon Winroth says, "The wine you are drinking should never make you want to go back to the one you just finished."

The adage that you should drink local wine with local food when you travel also applies to serving wine at home. If you are serving Mediterranean food, then well-chosen wines from the Mediterranean—southern France, Italy, Spain—will make good matches, whereas wines from the Loire or Burgundy or Bordeaux might match dishes that originated in more northern climates.

The lists on the following pages are by no means complete. Burgundies, Bordeaux, cabernet sauvignons, merlots, and Pinot Noirs from the New World, many Italian wines, and wines from southwestern France are given short if any shrift. This is a personal chapter about wines I have bought and enjoyed, wines that will go with the dishes in this book. But by all means try your own favorite wines and work out your own personal style.

WHITE WINES

Three styles of white wine concern us here: light, dry, crisp white wines; medium-body white wines; and big, complex white wines. As with all matching of wine and food, simpler whites should accompany simpler foods.

Light, Dry, Crisp Whites

Here are some of the adjectives that have been used to describe light, crisp whites: flinty, herbaceous, delicate, refreshing, flowery, fruity, chalky, grassy, stony, pleasantly acidic, dry, austere, reminiscent of wet stones. This might confuse more than enlighten you, but as you get to know some of the wines mentioned below, you'll begin to recognize some of those flavors. This style of wine perfectly matches simple seafood dishes and shellfish, especially oysters. The wines also go well with goat cheeses, egg dishes, and vegetables, so they would be good accompaniments to quiches, creamy pasta dishes, and many soups. They also go well with uncomplicated chicken dishes, grains, and some bean dishes.

LIGHT, DRY, CRISP WHITES AT A GLANCE

France:

Muscadet (Loire) (the best Muscadets are Muscadet de
Sèvre et Maine, and of these the best wines are
Muscadets-sur-Lies; these wines have more character be-
cause they've been left on their sediment, or lees, during
the winter after the harvest)
Sauvignon Touraine (Loire)
Sancerre (Loire)
Reuilly (Loire)
Quincy (Loire)
Pouilly Fumé (Loire)
Entre-Deux-Mers (Bordeaux)
Pinot d'Alsace (Alsace)
Côtes de Provence (Provence)
Côtes du Luberon (Provence)
Côtes du Ventoux (Rhône)

Italy:

Müller-Thurgau (from the Alto Adige/Südtirol, Terlano, and
Valle Isarco, and Eisacktaler)
Sauvignon del Collio
Sauvignon dei Colli Orientali del Friuli
Sauvignon dei Colli Berici
Soave
Cortese di Gavi and Gavi di Gavi

Germany:

Kabinett

California:

Sauvignon Blanc or Fumé Blanc
Chenin Blanc
French Colombard
Pinot Blanc

Medium-Body White Wines

These wines aren't "big," but they are more complex than the wines in the first category. They go well with the same foods that the crisp, dry wines go with but can also stand up to spicier and richer dishes. Words used to describe some of these wines include spicy, fleshy, aromatic, nutty, zesty, fruity, applelike, lemony, mineral-scented, floral, and thirst quenching. One of the most versatile of French wines that falls into this bracket is Alsace Riesling. Alsace Rieslings, contrary to what you may think, are not at all sweet. They are balanced and dry but rounder than the wines in the "crisp, dry" category (and indeed, some of them would fall into the "bigger, richer" category). The reason you may think Rieslings are sweet is because many (but not all) German and California Rieslings are. But not those made in Alsace. They are terrific with seafood, with charcuterie, with curries, pork, and many chicken dishes. Another medium-body white I love is from Savennières, in the Loire Valley. This is a flinty, spicy white, a wine that perfectly matches subtly spiced fish dishes.

Some delicious white wines are made near the Mediterranean seaside town of Cassis; Cassis whites make natural partners for *bouillabaisse* and other Provençal fish dishes. Another very good medium-body white wine is a little-known and hard-to-find white wine from the Côte d'Azur near Nice, called Bellet. Some excellent medium-body white wines are made in the Mâconnais, in Burgundy. These are less expensive than the big Burgundies from the Côte de Beaune and can be very pleasant. One other light yet full-flavored, fruity wine from Italy is worth mentioning here, the Vernaccia di San Gimignano, which Robert Parker claims is Tuscany's best dry white table wine. In California, Sémillon grapes are often mixed with sauvignon blanc to make a smooth, medium- to full-bodied white wine.

MEDIUM-BODY WHITE WINES AT A GLANCE

Alsace Riesling
Savennières (Loire)
Cassis (Provence)
Bellet (Provence)
Mâcon and Mâcon-Villages (Burgundy)
Rully (Burgundy)
St.-Véran (Burgundy)
St.-Aubin (Burgundy)
Mercurey (Burgundy)
Auxey-Duresses (Burgundy)
St.-Romain (Burgundy)
Santenay (Burgundy)
Montagny (Burgundy)

Palette (Provence; especially Château Simone)
Spätlese (Germany)
Auslese (Germany)
Vernaccia di San Gimignano (Italy)
Sémillon from California

Bigger, Richer White Wines

This category includes a range of wines, which have been described variously as intriguing and spicy (Gewürztraminers), big, muscular, creamy, fleshy, buttery, rich, fruity, perfumed, unctuous, elegant, luxurious, aromatic, floral, oaky, reminiscent of ripe fruit, tropical fruit, pineapples, honeysuckle, acacia, apricots, pears, and almonds. These can be very sexy wines. They go well with savory chicken and rabbit dishes, such as the Rabbit Simmered in Chicken Stock with New Potatoes on page 149; with rich pasta dishes (those not containing tomatoes); with *risotti* such as those on pages 256, 258, 314, 328, and 330, and with rich-fleshed fish like salmon, trout, mackerel, swordfish, and tuna. They also go very well with egg and cheese dishes and with creamy dishes. Gewürztraminers and German Spätleses and Ausleses, which are fruity and floral as well as spicy, go well with curries, some Oriental dishes, with the *mole* on page 156, as well as with pork and game fowl.

BIGGER, RICHER WHITE WINES AT A GLANCE

France:

Gewürztraminer (Alsace)
Alsace Riesling Grands Crus
Tokay Pinot Gris d'Alsace
Vouvray (Loire)
Côte de Beaune (Burgundy)
Chablis (Burgundy)
Châteauneuf-du-Pape (Rhône)
Hermitage (Rhône)
Crozes-Hermitage (Rhône)
Condrieu (Rhône)
St.-Joseph (Rhône)
Côtes-du-Rhône (Rhône)
Côtes-du-Rhône-Villages (Rhône)
Graves (Bordeaux)

Italy:

Pinot Grigios from Alto Adige–Trentino, Friuli, and Lombardy

Pinot Biancos from the Alto Adige–Trentino, Friuli, and the Veneto

California, Australia, New Zealand:

Chardonnay

Sémillon

Viognier

Germany:

Spätlese

Auslese

ROSÉ

What I said about rosé in my discussion of aperitifs applies here. They can be marvelous, elegant wines. I discovered the best of rosés when I met the Peyraud family at Domaine Tempier in Bandol about 10 years ago. I brought a bottle to my landlady, who said, *"Il fallait que Martha vienne de Texas pour que je connaisse un très bon rosé"* ("Martha's had to come from Texas for me to discover a good rosé"). She ordered four cases the next day. At their best—from Bandol, from Château Simone in Appellation Palette, from Tavel, and Charles Joguet's rosé from Chinon—rosés are fragrant, fruity, full-bodied yet dry and crisp. They go well with garlicky dishes, Mediterranean fish soups, garlicky Niçoise omelets, and tapenade. They are perfect with light summer meals, with grilled fish, with vegetable dishes like *ratatouille,* and with pasta with tomato-based sauces. Rosé from Bandol or Provence makes a perfect match with other anchovy dishes.

ROSÉS AT A GLANCE

Bandol (Provence)

Tavel (Rhône)

Côtes de Provence

Coteaux d'Aix-en-Provence

Palette (Provence)

Chinon (Loire)

RED WINES

I serve red wine much more often than white, and I love the style of reds that I serve. They fall into two (very) broad categories: fruity, light- to medium-bodied reds and sturdy, medium- to full-bodied fruity and spicy reds. Although I love to drink them, I don't often serve big, complex red wines from Bordeaux, Burgundy, Italy, or California with my meals. They just don't go with my food.

Light to Medium Red Wines

These are some of the most drinkable of wines. At their lightest they have straightforward, uncomplicated fruit flavors. As they become a little more complex, other, more herbal, vegetal, and flowery flavors develop. Words that have been used in describing these wines include fruity, light, supple, delicate, soft, heady, seductive, compact, cherry, strawberry, berries, herbaceous, cedary, vegetal, herb-tinged, violets, curranty, drinkable, quaffable, refreshing, straightforward, thirst quenching. The wines, which should be served slightly chilled, go well with many fish, rabbit, and chicken dishes, with pasta, hearty salads (they are especially good with bean salads), and savory vegetable tarts like the mushroom tart on page 23. They can also be drunk with Mexican food and other spicy cuisines.

LIGHT TO MEDIUM RED WINES AT A GLANCE

France:

Beaujolais
Beaujolais-Villages
Beaujolais Crus (these are the best of the Beaujolais; they
    include Moulin-à-Vent, Brouilly and Côte de Brouilly,
    Chiroubles, Juliénas, St.-Amour, Morgon, Fleurie,
    Chénas, and Regnié)
Gamay de Touraine (Loire)
Bourgueil (Loire)
Saumur-Champigny (Loire)
Chinon (Loire)

Italy:

Bardolino Classico
Valpolicella
Dolcetto d'Alba
St. Magdalener
Cabernets (from Veneto, Friuli, Trentino, and Alto Adige/
  Südtirol)
Merlot

Sturdy, Medium- to Full-Bodied Fruity and Spicy Red Wines

These are the wines that go so well with my Mediterranean dishes, wines that have immediate fruit flavors but also spicy, earthy, herbal tastes. Some of them are relatively light and uncomplicated; others are truly complex and age-worthy. They are southern wines, made in sunny places. The French wines in this category are from the Rhône, Provence, and the Languedoc-Roussillon. Italian wines like Barberas and Chiantis also fall into this group, as do the mature, intense, full-bodied Spanish wines from the Rioja, Penedès, Ribera del Duero, Toro, and Navarra viticultural regions. The sturdy, friendly, fruity wines from the New World are zinfandels from California and Australian Shiraz (Shiraz is the same grape as the Syrah, which is widely used in the Rhône Valley and Provence). Words that have been used in reference to various wines from this group include vivid, fruity, gutsy, intense, jammy, silky, concentrated, black-berry fruit, black currants, wild thyme, complex, fresh, currants, tree bark, leather, peppery, tobacco, red and green peppers, lusty, heady, fleshy, full-bodied, noble, spicy, robust, generous, truffles, nutmeg, smoked meats, succulent, robust, rich, plums, oaky, licorice, full-throttle. Many of these words can also describe Bordeaux and Burgundies; but the wines I'm talking about here are more fun, more readily enjoyable and generous. They are wines that can be drunk with both red meats and light meats like rabbit and poultry. They also go with grilled and garlicky fish dishes.

STURDY, MEDIUM- TO FULL-BODIED FRUITY AND SPICY RED WINES AT A GLANCE

France:

Bandol (Provence)
Bellet (Provence)
Coteaux d'Aix-de-Provence (Provence)
Coteaux des Baux-en-Provence (Provence)
Palette (Provence)
Côtes de Provence (Provence)
Côtes du Luberon (Provence)
Cornas (Northern Rhône)
Côte Rôtie (Northern Rhône)
Crozes-Hermitage (Northern Rhône)
Hermitage (Northern Rhône)
St.-Joseph (Northern Rhône)
Gigondas (Southern Rhône)
Châteauneuf-du-Pape (Southern Rhône)
Lirac (Southern Rhône)
Côtes-du-Rhône-Villages (Cairanne, Rasteau, Sablet,
    Séguret, Valréas, Visan, Beaumes de Venise and
    Vacqueyras) (Southern Rhône)
Côtes-du-Rhône (Southern Rhône)
Coteaux du Tricastin (Southern Rhône)
Côtes du Ventoux (Southern Rhône)
Côtes du Roussillon (Languedoc-Roussillon)
Côtes du Roussillon-Villages (Languedoc-Roussillon)
Vin du Pays Catalan (Languedoc-Roussillon)
Collioure (Languedoc-Roussillon)
Corbières (Languedoc)
Hérault (Languedoc)
Vin de Corse

Italy:

Barbera
Pinot Nero
Chianti
Chianti Classico

California and Australia:

Zinfandel
Shiraz

Spain:

Rioja
Penedès
Ribera del Duero
Toro
Navarra

Good Values and Lighter Red Wines from Burgundy:

Savigny-Les-Beaune
Pernard-Vergelesses
Chassagne-Montrachet
Mercurey
St.-Aubin
Rully
Irancy

SWEET WINES

I find that most sweet wines do not make good accompaniments to desserts. Rather, they should *be* dessert. If they are served with anything, it should be fruit, cheese, or simple pastries like cookies. The often complex flavors in sweet wines will do battle with the sugar in most desserts, and you, the drinker, will lose out.

What many of these wines do go with beautifully are goat cheeses and intense, salty cheeses, such as Roquefort, Stilton, or other blue cheeses such as Fourme d'Ambert. On my 40th birthday my husband bought me a bottle of amber-colored Sauternes that was older than I was, and Eric, the sommelier at the Restaurant Arpège, where we drank it, served it with a fabulous Fourme d'Ambert. It was a perfect marriage.

The sweet wines mentioned in the chapter on aperitifs make equally good desserts and go well with cheese. They are high in alcohol and should be served in small wineglasses or sherry glasses. They age well. The white ones should be served cold.

SWEET WINES AT A GLANCE

Sauternes (Bordeaux)
Cadillac (Bordeaux)
Loupiac (Bordeaux)
Sainte-Croix-du-Mont (Bordeaux)
Cérons (Bordeaux)
Barsac (Bordeaux)
Coteaux du Layon (Loire)
Bonnezeaux (Loire)
Quarts de Chaume (Loire)
Vouvray Moelleux (Loire)
Gewürztraminer Vendanges Tardives (Alsace)
Sélection de Grains Nobles (Alsace)
Muscat de Beaumes de Venise (Rhône)
Muscat de Rivesaltes (Languedoc-Roussillon)
Muscat de Frontignan (Languedoc-Roussillon)
Banyuls (Languedoc-Roussillon)
Moscato d'Alba (Italy)
California and Australian Muscats
Late-Harvest Riesling (California)
Late-Harvest Scheurebe (California)
Délice du Sémillon (California)
Beerenauslese (Germany)
Trockenbeerenauslese (Germany)
Port (Portugal)

METRIC CONVERSION CHART

Conversions of Quarts to Liters

Quarts (qt)	Liters (L)
1 qt	1 L*
1½ qt	1½ L
2 qt	2 L
2½ qt	2½ L
3 qt	2¾ L
4 qt	3¾ L
5 qt	4¾ L
6 qt	5½ L
7 qt	6½ L
8 qt	7½ L
9 qt	8½ L
10 qt	9½ L

* Approximate. To convert quarts to liters, multiply number of quarts by 0.95.

Conversions of Ounces to Grams

Ounces (oz)	Grams (g)
1 oz	30 g*
2 oz	60 g
3 oz	85 g
4 oz	115 g
5 oz	140 g
6 oz	180 g
7 oz	200 g
8 oz	225 g
9 oz	250 g
10 oz	285 g
11 oz	300 g
12 oz	340 g
13 oz	370 g
14 oz	400 g
15 oz	425 g
16 oz	450 g
20 oz	570 g
24 oz	680 g
28 oz	790 g
32 oz	900 g

* Approximate. To convert ounces to grams, multiply number of ounces by 28.35.

Conversions of Pounds to Grams and Kilograms

Pounds (lb)	Grams (g); kilograms (kg)
1 lb	450 g*
1¼ lb	565 g
1½ lb	675 g
1¾ lb	800 g
2 lb	900 g
2½ lb	1,125 g; 1¼ kg
3 lb	1,350 g
3½ lb	1,500 g; 1½ kg
4 lb	1,800 g
4½ lb	2 kg
5 lb	2¼ kg
5½ lb	2½ kg
6 lb	2¾ kg
6½ lb	3 kg
7 lb	3¼ kg
7½ lb	3½ kg
8 lb	3¾ kg
9 lb	4 kg
10 lb	4½ kg

* Approximate. To convert pounds into kilograms, multiply number of pounds by 453.6.

Conversions of Fahrenheit to Celsius

Fahrenheit	Celsius
170°F	77°C
180°F	82°C
190°F	88°C
200°F	95°C
225°F	110°C
250°F	120°C
300°F	150°C
325°F	165°C
350°F	180°C
375°F	190°C
400°F	205°C
425°F	220°C
450°F	230°C
475°F	245°C
500°F	260°C
525°F	275°C
550°F	290°C

* Approximate. To convert Fahrenheit to Celsius, subtract 32, multiply by 5, then divide by 9.

Conversions of Inches to Centimeters

Inches (in)	Centimeters (cm)
$^1/_{16}$ in	$^1/_4$ cm*
$^1/_8$ in	$^1/_2$ cm
$^1/_2$ in	$1^1/_2$ cm
$^3/_4$ in	2 cm
1 in	$2^1/_2$ cm
$1^1/_2$ in	4 cm
2 in	5 cm
$2^1/_2$ in	$6^1/_2$ cm
3 in	8 cm
$3^1/_2$ in	9 cm
4 in	10 cm
$4^1/_4$ in	$11^1/_2$ cm
5 in	13 cm
$5^1/_2$ in	14 cm
6 in	15 cm
$6^1/_2$ in	$16^1/_2$ cm
7 in	18 cm
$7^1/_2$ in	19 cm
8 in	20 cm
$8^1/_2$ in	$21^1/_2$ cm
9 in	23 cm
$9^1/_2$ in	24 cm
10 in	25 cm
11 in	28 cm
12 in	30 cm
13 in	33 cm
14 in	35 cm
15 in	38 cm
16 in	41 cm
17 in	43 cm
18 in	46 cm
19 in	48 cm
20 in	51 cm
21 in	53 cm
22 in	56 cm
23 in	58 cm
24 in	61 cm
25 in	$63^1/_2$ cm
30 in	76 cm
35 in	89 cm
40 in	102 cm
45 in	114 cm
50 in	127 cm

* Approximate. To convert inches to centimeters, multiply number of inches by 2.54.

INDEX